A

NARRATIVE OF EVENTS,

SINCE THE FIRST OF AUGUST, 1834,

by JAMES WILLIAMS,

AN APPRENTICED LABOURER

IN JAMAICA

A JOHN HOPE FRANKLIN CENTER BOOK

A book in the series

LATIN AMERICA OTHERWISE:

LANGUAGES, EMPIRES, NATIONS

Series editors:

Walter D. Mignolo, *Duke University*

Irene Silverblatt, *Duke University*

Sonia Saldívar-Hull, *University*

of California at Los Angeles

A

NARRATIVE OF EVENTS,

SINCE THE FIRST OF AUGUST, 1834,

by JAMES WILLIAMS,

AN APPRENTICED LABOURER

IN JAMAICA

———

JAMES WILLIAMS

———

Edited and with an introduction by
DIANA PATON

DUKE UNIVERSITY PRESS

Durham & London

2001

© 2001 Duke University Press
All rights reserved Printed in the United
States of America on acid-free paper ∞   Designed
by Amy Ruth Buchanan and typeset in Monotype
Garamond by Tseng Information Systems, Inc.
Library of Congress Cataloging-in-Publication
Data appear on the last printed
page of this book.

The eight letters from Joseph Sturges
to John Clark in 1837 are included courtesy
of the Angus Library, Regents Park College,
University of Oxford, from their
Fenn collection (D/FEN).

ABOUT THE SERIES

Latin America Otherwise: Languages, Empires, Nations is a critical series. It aims to explore the emergence and consequences of concepts used to define "Latin America" while at the same time exploring the broad interplay of political, economic, and cultural practices that have shaped Latin American worlds. Latin America, at the crossroads of competing imperial designs and local responses, has been construed as a geocultural and geopolitical entity since the nineteenth century. This series provides a starting point to redefine Latin America as a configuration of political, linguistic, cultural, and economic intersections that demand a continuous reappraisal of the role of the Americas in history, and of the ongoing process of globalization and the relocation of people and cultures that have characterized Latin America's experience. *Latin America Otherwise: Languages, Empires, Nations* is a forum that confronts established geocultural constructions, that rethinks area studies and disciplinary boundaries, that assesses convictions of the academy and of public policy, and that, correspondingly, demands that the practices through which we produce knowledge and understanding about and from Latin America be subject to rigorous and critical scrutiny.

In 1837 James Williams related an extraordinary document, a searing indictment of apprenticeship, a modified form of slavery on the island of Jamaica. Williams's story, one of the few first-person accounts of that terrible institution in the Caribbean, stands as a singular contribution to the history of slavery and its abolition in the Americas. As the edition's editor, Diana Paton, ably reminds us, the *Narrative* also represents much more.

With critical insight, Paton explores the circumstances governing the *Narrative*'s creation. She makes painfully clear that Williams's account was significantly shaped by outside hands and could have only seen print under the tutelage of Joseph Sturge, a well-known figure in England's abolitionist movement. Paton, meticulously examining the ensemble of Williams's words and Sturge's stewardship, illuminates how life histories are never simply personal accounts. In her words, "the *Narrative* cannot speak for itself" and we must attend to the broader conditions of its production.

This book is a welcome addition to our series. We contend that the forces shaping Anglophone Jamaica's past are incomprehensible apart from those that also shaped the Caribbean and the Americas as a whole. The *Narrative* is a contribution to the historical record and is also the story of how certain accounts can be forgotten, shunted aside, ignored. Not reprinted in full for one hundred and sixty-three years, the work has until now been lost to a broader audience.

CONTENTS

LIST OF ILLUSTRATIONS

FIGURES

ILLUSTRATIONS

EDITOR'S ACKNOWLEDGMENTS

I would like to thank Melanie Newton, Kate Chedgzoy, Mary Turner, and the anonymous readers for Duke University Press for reading and commenting on the manuscript; David Eltis, Rebecca Flemming, Dominic Montserrat, Joanne Ichimura of SOAS special collections, and the Southwark Local History Library, for help with research questions; Neil McIntosh for drawing the maps; Maisie Miller and the Rev. Everald Allan at the Browns Town Baptist Church, Mr. Lawrence of Beverley, St. Ann, and Peggy Soltau for facilitating my visits to St. Ann; Valerie Millholland, my editor at Duke; and many archivists and librarians: in Jamaica at the Island Record Office, the National Library of Jamaica, the University of the West Indies Library, and the Jamaica Archives; and in Britain at Friends House Library, the Angus Library at Regents Park College, Oxford, the British Library, the Public Record Office, the Bodleian Library, and Rhodes House Library.

INTRODUCTION

In June 1837 a short pamphlet, twenty-four pages of densely printed prose, was published in London and Glasgow, to be sold for one penny. It was titled *A Narrative of Events, since the First of August, 1834, by James Williams, an Apprenticed Labourer in Jamaica.* The *Narrative*'s story of violence, abuse of women, and corruption of the law played a major role in the campaign to end the system known as apprenticeship that had replaced, but not fully abolished, slavery in Britain's colonies. Its shocking central allegation was that, far from improving the lives of former slaves, apprenticeship was in many ways worse than the system that preceded it. "Apprentices," claimed Williams, "get a great deal more punishment now than they did when they was slaves; the master take spite, and do all he can to hurt them before the free come."

James Williams's *Narrative* was sold throughout Britain and reprinted in newspapers in both Britain and Jamaica. In the months after publication Williams's name became iconic; public speakers and writers used it to conjure up scenes of the appalling circumstances experienced by apprentices throughout Britain's colonies. Using detailed narrative descriptions of the suffering of others to provoke an emotional, and through this a political, response was a key abolitionist rhetorical strategy. As well as its political importance, the text is significant because it is one of very few testimonial narratives by Caribbean former slaves. Its publication led to an investigation in which many other apprentices told their stories, creating probably the most substantial collection of first-person accounts of their experiences by Caribbean slaves or former slaves.

The antiapprenticeship campaign, in which the publication of the *Narrative* and the inquiry's evidence played a major part, was successful. In August 1838, two years earlier than had been envisaged by the abolition act of 1833, apprenticeship came to an end in Britain's colo-

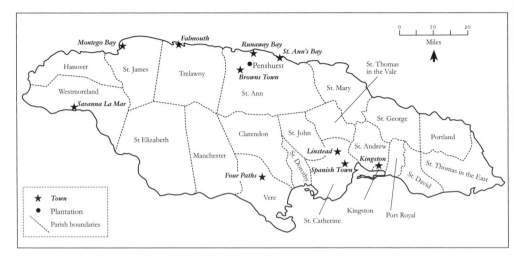

Fig. 1. Jamaica in the 1830s

nies in the Caribbean, the Cape Colony (South Africa), and Mauritius. The campaign, based as it was on the emotive recounting of the stories of Caribbean apprentices, including that of James Williams, relied on an alliance among the former slaves who provided the stories to be told, the missionaries who organized the transmission of information to Britain, and the British-based abolitionists who mobilized people there to the point where the colonial secretary wrote in early 1838 that "the force of [British] public opinion" required the early end of apprenticeship.[1] Despite this alliance, the apprentices who participated in the campaign have been almost entirely forgotten. Joseph Sturge, the leader of the antiapprenticeship campaign, is less well known today than less radical abolitionists such as William Wilberforce and Thomas Fowell Buxton. Even so, he is commemorated in several biographies, in the republication of his writings, in a statue in Birmingham, and in the name of Sturge Town in Jamaica.[2] In contrast, James Williams merits at most a few lines in histories of abolition, apprenticeship, and emancipation.[3] Until now, his *Narrative* had not been republished in full since 1838. Even in Williams's home parish of St. Ann, Jamaica, the public memory of Joseph Sturge and of John Clark, the Baptist missionary who lived there for forty years, is far more prominent than that of James Williams.[4]

The relative attention to Sturge and neglect of Williams is not surprising. It was foreshadowed in the circumstances under which the *Narrative* was produced. For if the antiapprenticeship campaign relied on an alliance among apprentices, missionaries, and British abolitionists, it was an alliance whose terms were always unequal. Sturge, a wealthy and influential businessman, provided the money with which Williams purchased his freedom, paid for Williams's passage to England, organized for Williams to work with an amanuensis to produce the *Narrative,* and then, only four months after Williams had arrived in England, sent him back to Jamaica. It was Sturge, not Williams, who spoke at abolitionist public meetings, where he described in great detail the conditions under which James Williams and other apprentices suffered. Joseph Sturge controlled the conditions under which James Williams could narrate the events of his life.

These circumstances of its production make the *Narrative* a complicated text. Like many slave narratives, it was told to a white writer and so cannot be treated as Williams's work alone. The *Narrative* cannot "speak for itself" as the unmediated voice of a former slave, as Thomas Price, who wrote its prefatory "Advertisement," hoped it would. We must read it not just for the information it provides about the experience of apprenticeship, but equally importantly as a call to action created through a complex collaborative process, in which the authors' perceptions of what would constitute a politically effective text was an important consideration. The point is not that the *Narrative* is likely to record events that never happened; the integrity of the narrator was of such political importance that Williams and his collaborators were careful to include only events whose occurrence could not be convincingly contradicted. In addition, the inquiry produced corroborative testimony from a large number of apprentices and free people. The *Narrative* has further significance, however: as well as documenting events in the lives of Jamaican apprentices, it is itself a document providing evidence about the strategies and assumptions of those involved in the transatlantic campaign against apprenticeship.

Apprenticeship and the Production of A Narrative of Events

James Williams's *Narrative* forms a part of the broad African diasporic tradition of slave narrative. The genre includes narratives produced by former slaves from the British Caribbean and Cuba, but by far the

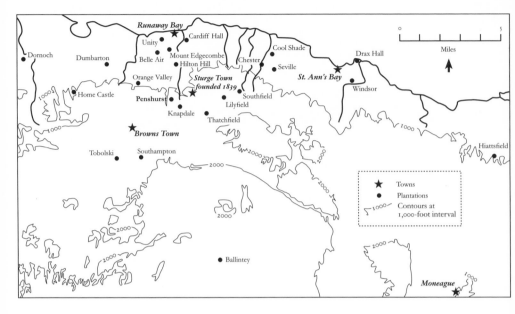

Fig. 2. St. Ann, Jamaica, 1830s

largest body of work is from the United States. Analyses of slave narratives often stress their formulaic quality, a result of the political purpose for which they were written. Slave narrators, claimed the literary
critic James Olney in an influential article published in 1985, faced a ten-
sion between the desire to demonstrate their individuality and the need
to be representative, to exemplify the oppression suffered by "every
slave" in order to convince a free and presumed-white audience that
slavery was both evil and possible to resist.[5] James Williams confronted
many of the problems of form and content that critics have emphasized
in the "standard" slave narrative, but the political context in which he
wrote required a structure different from that of the standard narrative.
Whereas most slave narratives recount the narrator's life from birth,
culminating in his or her escape from slavery and establishment as a
free person, Williams's *Narrative* limits itself to the events of less than
three years, those occurring, as the title notes, "since the first of August, 1834." The significance of that date must be understood to com-
prehend the context of the *Narrative*'s production and the influence of
those circumstances on its content and form.

The first of August 1834 marked the beginning of a new system of law and labor, known as "apprenticeship," in the British slave-based colonies.[6] The system was introduced as a measure that would ultimately lead to the complete abolition of slavery. It was a compromise between the immediate emancipation demanded by abolitionists and slave rebels, and the indefinite perpetuation of slavery that planters and the West India interest hoped to achieve. This compromise heavily compensated slave owners for their loss of human property, both directly—£20 million of public money was used to compensate planters—and indirectly, in the form of the continued unfree labor required of the apprentices. Apprentices were still forced to labor for those who had previously owned them. They were not to receive wages for the work that was legally required of them, nor could they choose the master or mistress to whom they were apprenticed. The system was to last for six years, until August 1840, although one group of apprentices, the "nonpraedials," a category that included James Williams, were to be freed on 1 August 1838.[7]

Lord Stanley, the British colonial secretary at the time of the abolition act's passage, argued that apprenticeship would allow slave owners and slaves to develop trust in one another and to appreciate their supposedly mutual interest in productivity and order.[8] Instead, the transition from slavery to apprenticeship was marked by increased conflict between apprentice holders and apprentices, as the former tried to sustain slavery-era levels of exploitation, while the latter pushed for the enforcement and expansion of their new legal rights. Because the new system made it illegal for planters to punish apprentices directly, instead requiring that they take their workers before a newly created set of state representatives known as stipendiary magistrates, the state became involved in enforcing plantation discipline to a far greater extent than previously.[9]

Williams's *Narrative* set out to demonstrate the increased conflict in Jamaica, and in particular to expose the deep involvement of officials representing the imperial government in maintaining an exploitative system. Focusing on apprenticeship rather than slavery, Williams's *Narrative* is not technically a slave narrative. Thus, in contrast to the emphasis on the master-slave relationship that is central to many slave narratives, Williams's *Narrative* returns time and again to the relationship between apprentices and state representatives. The text demonstrates that literary production by former slaves is more heterogeneous than is implied by the delineation of a "master outline" for slave narratives.[10] Whereas many slave narratives are structured by a story of transition from captivity to redemption, with roots in the traditions of the Indian captivity and Christian conversion narratives, Williams's text revolves around a different set of concerns.[11] Williams recounts the events leading up to his many experiences of punishment on the orders of magistrates—seven floggings and four periods of imprisonment—as well as the similar experiences of many of his fellow apprentices. In the course of arguing that apprenticeship has actually worsened the conditions of Jamaican slaves, Williams provides his reader with a wealth of detailed evidence about conflicts among planters, magistrates, and apprentices; about apprentices' efforts to combat their masters' domination; and about conditions and conflicts within the St. Ann's Bay House of Correction. Much of his discussion of the prison focuses on the sufferings inflicted on imprisoned apprentices by the treadmill, a punitive technology that, largely as a result of Williams's and Sturge's efforts, came to symbolize what was wrong with apprenticeship. Williams's most graphic descriptions invoked the anxiety about exposure of women's bodies that had for a long time been crucial to the abolitionist critique of punishment. For instance, in this passage describing two young women's efforts to "dance the mill," Williams moves between the two concerns: "them don't know how to dance the mill, and driver flog them very hard; they didn't tie up their clothes high enough so their foot catch upon the clothes when them tread the mill, and tear them;—and then between the Cat and the Mill—them flog them so severe,—they cut away most of their clothes, and left them in a manner naked; and the driver was bragging afterwards that he see all their nakedness." In this critique condemnation of the physical violence inflicted on women merged with condemnation of the sexual abuse believed to inhere in female nakedness.

Despite extensive conflicts, including strikes in several islands that were suppressed with military force, early reports in Britain of the progress of apprenticeship were optimistic. The national antislavery leadership wound down its mass mobilizations and its propaganda machine, limiting itself to asking the Colonial Office to investigate cases of "abuse" of apprentices. In 1836 a House of Commons select committee, including the prominent antislavery leader Thomas Fowell Buxton, concluded that, although there were some problems with the operation of apprenticeship, there was no need for major changes in the law.[12]

More radical abolitionists, including Joseph Sturge and many involved in the women's antislavery societies, opposed apprenticeship from the beginning, believing that its perpetuation of a system of unfree labor was a betrayal of antislavery principles. As Thomas Price's reference at the end of Williams's *Narrative* to the "monstrous sacrifice of British treasure" suggests, radical abolitionists were particularly angered by the payment of compensation money to slaveholders. The activists devoted themselves during 1834 and 1835 to publicizing the failures of apprenticeship. After the publication of the 1836 select committee report, Sturge decided to go to the Caribbean himself so that he would be able to report firsthand on the abuses and oppression he was sure he would find there. In November 1836 he set out for Barbados with three others, Thomas Harvey, William Lloyd, and John Scoble. Once in the Caribbean the four divided into two groups of two, each pair visiting a different set of colonies.[13]

Sturge and Harvey spent about half of their time in Jamaica, arriving there in January 1837 and leaving in early April. It was during their stay in the island that Sturge met James Williams, supplied the money with which Williams purchased his freedom, and arranged to bring him to Britain. Jamaica was Britain's most populous and most productive sugar colony, and in British debates about slavery it had often stood for the Caribbean as a whole. Sturge and Harvey knew that the island had experienced some of the most intense conflict between planters and apprentices during the first two years of apprenticeship. In gathering information they relied heavily on the extensive network of Baptist missionaries that had been developing in Jamaica since the early nineteenth century. The missionaries provided them with contacts and information. They also supplied translation, without which Sturge and Harvey would not have been able to understand the Creole speech of the Afro-Jamaican population.[14] According to one contemporary, in a comment that reveals cultural difference within Britain while it describes the linguistic difficulties of newly arrived Britons in Jamaica, the speech of Afro-Jamaicans "would be as totally unintelligible to you as the dialect of some parts of Lancashire."[15]

Sturge and Harvey began their Jamaican investigations in Kingston, then headed to the north coast of the island, where many of the largest sugar estates were located. On 23 February they arrived at Browns Town, an inland market town in the northern parish of St. Ann, where they stayed with the Baptist missionary John Clark and where they met James Williams, then an apprentice on Penshurst plantation. Although Clark had been in Jamaica only a year, he was the minister of a well-established congregation that had for several years been led by James Finlayson, an apprentice from the same plantation as Williams. Finlayson had converted to Christianity in the late 1820s after hearing a sermon given by a Baptist missionary in another parish. His evangelism to other slaves in his area resulted in the official founding of the Browns Town Baptist Church in 1830. Although no white missionary had been active in the area, the church had an initial membership of forty-four.[16]

Slaves from Penshurst and its neighboring plantations, Knapdale and Hilton Hill, formed the core of the church's membership. James Williams was on the fringes of the group, although he was not a member of the church. In the wake of the 1831 slave rebellion the Browns Town church members took their religion underground. Planters blamed the rebellion on the influence of missionaries. They violently attacked nonconformist missionaries and slaves who belonged to dissenting churches. Although the rebellion had centered in Jamaica's western parishes, extensive repression took place in St. Ann, where the planters' vigilante organization, the Colonial Church Union, was based. The CCU destroyed Baptist and Methodist chapels and attacked slaves who practiced Christianity.[17] According to stories still told in the area, the Browns Town church members met for services led by James Finlayson in a cave now known as "Finlayson's cave." Thus, when John Clark became the missionary in Browns Town in 1836, his congregation's experiences had already created a strong sense of solidarity among them. Such a situation, in which slaves rather than missionaries were the most significant evangelists, was common in Jamaica.[18]

Given the Browns Town church's history, it is significant that Williams emphasizes that James Finlayson, whom he describes as "a leader in the church," arranged both his first and second meetings with Sturge and Harvey. Finlayson had purchased his own freedom during the early period of apprenticeship and was now established as an artisan in Browns Town. We do not know when Sturge decided to purchase the freedom of an apprentice and bring him or her to Britain to tell his or her story, although the decision must have been made with the recent models of the narratives of Mary Prince and Ashton Warner in mind.[19] Sturge would also have been aware of the antislavery movement's use in the late 1820s and early 1830s of stories of the sufferings of individual slaves, usually transmitted to Britain via missionaries.[20] It is clear, however, that once this course of action was decided on, Finlayson was instrumental in selecting Williams as the appropriate person, in arranging that he meet with Sturge, and in persuading him to undertake the trip to England. Finlayson's action is a further example of the essential contribution of Caribbean former slaves to the antiapprenticeship campaign.

What characteristics led Finlayson to recommend Williams as the man whose story could stand (to quote Thomas Price again) for the "tale of near eight hundred thousands of our fellow-subjects"? Clearly, Williams's intelligence, articulateness, and prodigious memory—most of the incidents he recounts in the *Narrative* were verified by testimony at the inquiry—made him a suitable candidate. But the testimony given by several of the other Penshurst apprentices, Amelia Lawrence and William Dalling being the most prominent, demonstrates that these were not qualities possessed uniquely by Williams. Nor was his experience of multiple punishments, conflict with his master and mistress, and unfair treatment by stipendiary magistrates especially unusual. It may have been that, of the many people who could have played Williams's role, he was best placed to do so because of his lack of family commitments. Unlike Dalling and Lawrence, he had no spouse or children. His youth, which distinguishes him from many slave narrators, made him available for the task in a way that many others were not. Some time in March 1837 Williams purchased his freedom with money given to him by John Clark, then went to meet Sturge, who was by now in Spanish Town.[21] The two of them, and probably Harvey as well, traveled to Britain via New York, arriving at the port of Liverpool on 15 May 1837.

Penshurst Plantation, St. Ann

Williams's *Narrative* tells us nothing about his life prior to the beginning of apprenticeship, but other sources allow us to reconstruct some of the circumstances in which he lived, if not the specific events of his life. Penshurst, St. Ann, was a pimento plantation of about two hundred acres, belonging to a brother and sister, Gilbert William and Sarah Jane Keith Senior. At least fifty-seven slaves lived there in 1832. Barry Higman has calculated that almost 50 percent of Jamaican slaves in 1832 lived in units of more than 150 slaves, and only 25 percent lived in units of fewer than 50, largely in urban areas. In Jamaican terms Penshurst was thus a small plantation, although it was large compared to those in the United States, where, in 1860, 75 percent of slaves lived in units of fewer than 50 slaves.[22] Penshurst's small size was not uncommon, however, for a non-sugar-growing establishment. The Seniors and their enslaved workers operated a cattle pen and raised pimento (known outside Jamaica as allspice), a minor export crop that represented 3 percent of the value of Jamaican exports in the 1820s and 1830s.[23] Unlike sugar, which dominated the island's economy, pimento could be grown on mountainous terrain such as the inland part of St. Ann's parish, where Penshurst was situated. The crop is still grown in the area today. Cattle pens supplied the livestock required by sugar estates and other agricultural businesses. Both operations required much less capital than was needed to run a successful sugar estate.[24]

Jamaican slave owners had been required since 1817 to submit lists of the slaves they owned every three years. The measure had been introduced with the aim of preventing the importation of slaves, banned in the British colonies since 1807. The returns created as a result, indicating the names of the mothers but not the fathers of slaves who belonged to the same owner, allow for a partial reconstruction of the kin networks of Caribbean slaves in the late period of slavery. The family trees below provide such a reconstruction for the Seniors' slaves registered as living on Penshurst.[25] The Seniors' slave registration returns appear to be incomplete: many of the people referred to by Williams and/or who gave evidence to the inquiry are not listed.[26] Nevertheless there is significant overlap between the names given by the Seniors and the people mentioned in the *Narrative*. James himself appears on Sarah Senior's return of June 1820 as "James, Negro, 2 years 4 months, Creole, son of Mira no 11." James's mother, the woman brusquely labeled in the return as "Mira no 11," was African and had been brought to Jamaica as a slave when she was a child. Still only thirty herself in 1817, she had a fifteen-year-old Jamaican-born daughter, Doll, which means she must have been in Jamaica by 1802, when she was fifteen. We have no evidence about where in Africa Mira came from. We do know that her childhood experience of the middle passage was increasingly common in the late eighteenth century. In the last quarter of the eighteenth century more than 23 percent of those crossing the Atlantic as slaves were less than fifteen years old.[27]

James never refers to his mother in his *Narrative,* nor do any of the Penshurst apprentices mention a woman named Mira. She may have been dead by the time the events described in the *Narrative* and at the inquiry took place. James does refer on two occasions to his father: in the *Narrative* he mentions an occasion when his father lent him money, and from England he sent his love via Sturge to his "father, sister, and two brothers." These references to his father emphasize that the slave registration returns served the administrative purposes of imperial management but did not include all the significant relationships in enslaved people's lives. Although we have no way of knowing from the returns who James's father was, it is clear that the relationship was important.

Despite the limitations of the sources, even the partial reconstruction of the relationships among Penshurst slaves demonstrates kin connections among most of the people resident there. Between 1817 and 1832, when the last returns were made, the Seniors listed a total of sixty-two people as their slaves, of whom fifty-seven were alive in 1832. Of the sixty-two, thirteen were part of a four-generation family headed by a Jamaican-born woman named Mary (see figure 3). Many of the members of this family, including William Dalling and his children, Nanny, Ellen, and Adam, are mentioned in the *Narrative* and/or played key roles at the inquiry. Twenty-five others belonged to one of four three-generation family groups, headed by three women: James's mother Mira, a woman named Mary, and one named Myrtilla (figures 4–6). Another seven were members of two-generation families, headed by women named Judy and Cuba (figures 7 and 8). From the slave registration returns, seventeen slaves appear to have been kinless. However, twelve of these were men, many of whom were probably integrated into family groups through relationships with women that were not recorded by the slave registration system. For instance, Peter William Atkinson, listed in Gilbert Senior's 1817 return as "Peter, Negro, 20 [years old], Creole," appears from these sources to have been kinless. We know from other sources, including testimony given to the inquiry, that Atkinson's mother was called June but was no longer present at

The family trees on the following pages are based on information in Gilbert and Sarah Senior's slave registration returns (P.R.O. T 71/43–46, 48, and 50), with the exception of the marriage of Maria and William Dalling, which is evidenced by plentiful information in the *Narrative* and inquiry. Unless marked as "African," "mulatto," or "sambo," the individuals are all designated in the records as "Negro" and "Creole." Names in bold indicate that the person is probably the same individual as someone mentioned in the *Narrative* or *Report of Evidence;* where I am less confident about the identification, this is indicated with a question mark (?) after the name. Names in square brackets are those established from evidence external to the registration returns, for example, **James [Williams]**.

In addition, the following people are mentioned in the *Narrative* or *Report of Evidence* as Penshurst apprentices, but there is no correspondingly named person in the Penshurst slave registration returns:

Abis
Thomas Brown Lawrence
Richard Brown
Margaret Ellis
William Graham
Edward Lawrence
Richard Lawrence
Amelia Lawrence
Eliza Finlayson
Thomas Mills
Alexander Mills
Phillis
Jane Shaw Pennock
Lavinia Trowers

The following people, all listed on Gilbert or Sarah Senior's slave registration documents, had no kin identifiable from the Penshurst returns:

Jane	African	b. 1793	d. 1827
Rose	African	b. 1787	
Lucy	African	b. 1787	
Ann [Campbell]	African	b. 1789	
Matilda	African	b. 1782	

Henry [James]	African	b. 1787	
Ben [Benjamin Higgins]		b. 1789	
William [Mills?]	African	b. 1787	
William Grant	Mulatto	b. 1781	
[Charles] Trueman	African	b. 1767	
John	African	b. 1787	d. 1825
Ormond		b. 1769	
Robert	African	b. 1787	
Thomas	African	b. 1787	
Peter [William Atkinson]		b. 1797	
Quashie		b. 1787	d. 1820

Fig. 3. Mary's family

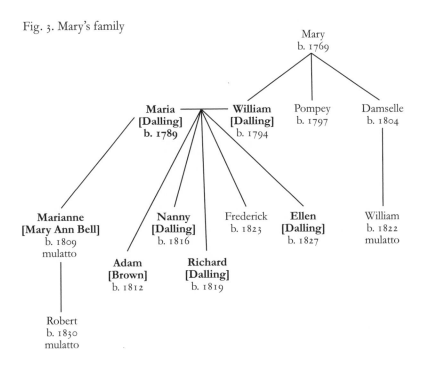

Fig. 4. Mira's family

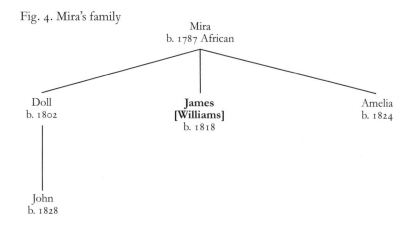

Mira
b. 1787 African

Doll
b. 1802

James
[Williams]
b. 1818

Amelia
b. 1824

John
b. 1828

Fig. 5. Mary's family

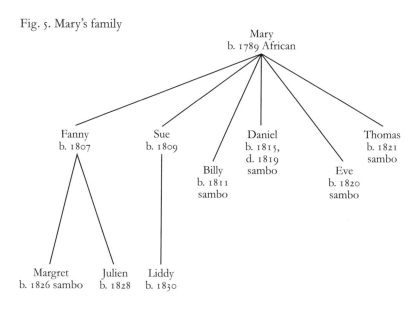

Mary
b. 1789 African

Fanny
b. 1807

Sue
b. 1809

Billy
b. 1811
sambo

Daniel
b. 1815,
d. 1819
sambo

Eve
b. 1820
sambo

Thomas
b. 1821
sambo

Margret
b. 1826 sambo

Julien
b. 1828

Liddy
b. 1830

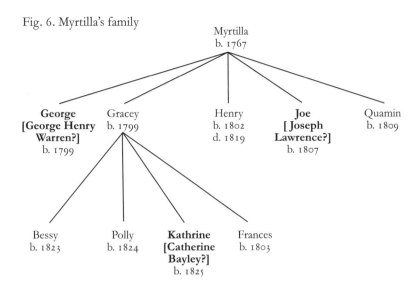

Fig. 6. Myrtilla's family

Myrtilla
b. 1767

**George
[George Henry
Warren?]**
b. 1799

Gracey
b. 1799

Henry
b. 1802
d. 1819

**Joe
[Joseph
Lawrence?]**
b. 1807

Quamin
b. 1809

Bessy
b. 1823

Polly
b. 1824

**Kathrine
[Catherine
Bayley?]**
b. 1825

Frances
b. 1803

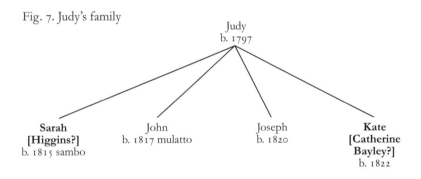

Fig. 7. Judy's family

Judy
b. 1797

**Sarah
[Higgins?]**
b. 1815 sambo

John
b. 1817 mulatto

Joseph
b. 1820

**Kate
[Catherine
Bayley?]**
b. 1822

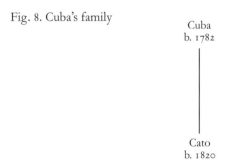

Fig. 8. Cuba's family

Cuba
b. 1782

Cato
b. 1820

Fig. 9. The Lawrence and Senior families

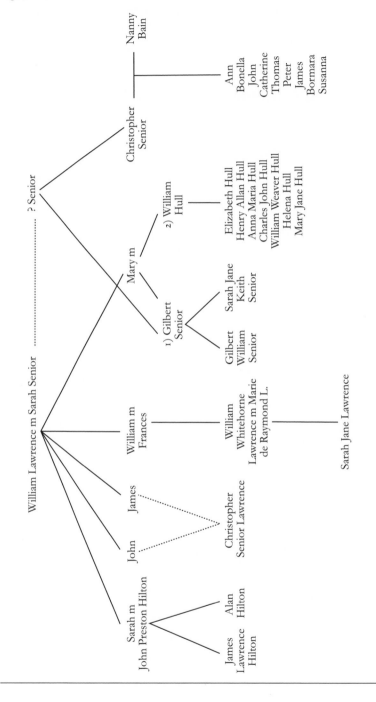

Penshurst by 1817, that he had a brother, Thomas, who was also a Penshurst slave, and that he was married to a woman on the neighboring Knapdale estate, with whom he had two children.[28] It is likely that many of the other apparently kinless men were in fact part of families on Penshurst and elsewhere, and also that the families that can be reconstructed from the Penshurst slave returns were significantly more complex than the figures reveal. James Williams's father may have been one of these apparently kinless men.

Like their slaves, Penshurst's owners, Gilbert and Sarah Senior, were connected through kinship to many of their neighbors (see figure 9). By the 1830s both were in their fifties or older; neither was married or had any legitimate children. Their mother, Mary, was the daughter of major landholders, William and Sarah Lawrence. William Lawrence had received six hundred acres of land in St. Ann from the Crown between 1740 and 1755.[29] In his will he referred specifically to more than seven hundred acres of land, leaving the "residue"—presumably the major share—to his eldest son, John. John was one of five Lawrence children who between them owned a great deal of land in the area, although by the nineteenth century the family's fortunes were declining. Mary Lawrence (later Mary Senior, and then, after her second marriage, Mary Hull) inherited relatively little from her parents; the bulk of their estate went to her eldest brother. Because she was a woman, she received only slaves in property.[30]

Many of the Penshurst slaves recorded in the slave registration returns came into Sarah Jane Keith Senior's possession through her grandmother Sarah Lawrence's will. On her death Lawrence divided her sixty-eight slaves among fourteen children and grandchildren. Although she kept children with their mothers in this distribution, Sarah Lawrence's efforts to provide for her family must have torn apart many relationships of family and friendship among those she used as the means of provision. Of the sixty-two slaves who appear in the Seniors' registration list, twenty-four were either bequeathed to them by Sarah Lawrence or were the children or grandchildren of slaves so bequeathed.[31]

Gilbert and Sarah Senior's father, also called Gilbert Senior, was from a less prosperous branch of Mary's family, based in the parish of Westmoreland.[32] Marriage between distant members of the same family was common among the British middle class and aristocracy in the eighteenth and nineteenth centuries, and was probably practiced even more frequently among creole whites in the Caribbean, where racial exclusiveness meant there were few "suitable" marital partners.[33] The Seniors seem to have inherited Penshurst from an unmarried uncle on their father's side of the family, Christopher Senior.[34] Although he never married, Christopher had a long relationship and nine children with Nanny Bain. Bain was free and, according to Senior's will, "a quadroon woman," that is, she probably had one black and three white grandparents. Despite Christopher's acknowledging paternity of their children in his will, on his death his property passed to his white, legitimate relatives, including Gilbert and Sarah Senior, whereas his children received only a lump sum when they reached the age of twenty-five, and rights of residence on, but not ownership of, ten acres of land.[35] The Seniors' familial relationships demonstrate the Jamaican planter class's techniques of self-perpetuation, reinforcing racial and gender hierarchy as it transmitted its property. Race and gender considerations—the refusal to marry anyone not deemed white, the inheritance by legitimate eldest sons of the major share of family property—were intertwined with those of class in ways that are impossible to disentangle.

James Williams's Narrative *and the Politics of Authenticity*

This was the background James Williams left behind when he set out to meet Joseph Sturge in Spanish Town. Nearly two months passed between Williams's arrival in Spanish Town and his and Sturge's disembarkation in Liverpool, a period during which, according to Sturge, James put on "nearly ⅓ in weight." Sturge was already feeling somewhat uneasy about his new protégé: he wrote to John Clark that Williams "excites so much notice that I fear he will be injured by it." The theme of attention leading to injury was one to which Sturge would return. In the same letter he noted that "Dr Palmer has been writing his [James's] history & observations since the 1st of August 1834 and we are getting it through the press as fast as we can."[36] Dr. Palmer was Archibald Leighton Palmer, a Scottish medical doctor who had been in Jamaica since the 1810s. He had returned to Britain in late 1836, to protest against his recent dismissal from his position as a stipendiary magistrate.[37] While agitating against his own dismissal he became a leader in the campaign against apprenticeship. As well as writing the *Narrative* with James Williams he spoke at antiapprenticeship rallies and became the secretary of the Central Negro Emancipation Committee, an organization formed in November 1837 to coordinate opposition to apprenticeship. He presumably was chosen as amanuensis because of his familiarity with Jamaican speech as well as his experience in St. Ann, where he had briefly served as a stipendiary magistrate. According to the *Narrative,* Williams and Palmer had met during that period.

William L. Andrews points out that narratives by former slaves composed with amanuenses were necessarily written "in the context of a power relationship that gave the supposed passive amanuensis ultimate control over the fate of the manuscript and considerable influence over the immediate future of the narrator." [38] James Williams's experience certainly confirms Andrews's point, and his *Narrative* cannot be understood without awareness of the circumstances of its production. This does not, however, preclude analysis of it as both a literary and a historical text. Indeed, unless we are prepared to discard the few texts that Caribbean slaves were involved in producing, we have to attend to amanuensis-written texts such as those of Williams and Mary Prince, considering the interaction within them of the voice of the narrator with that of the amanuensis. [39] With only the partial exceptions of Olaudah Equiano and Robert Wedderburn, no Caribbean narratives exist that can claim to be "written by [the former slave] him/herself." [40] In addition, we should recognize that no "authentic" slave narrative, uncontaminated by white concerns, exists. As much recent criticism shows, literate slave writers, as well as narrators who dictated their stories, had to contend with their presumed white audiences; the words available to them necessarily "belong to the other." [41] Frederick Douglass and Harriet Jacobs had to confront the requirements and limitations of the slave narrative genre, as did James Williams. [42] The problems entailed in reading an "as told to" narrative like Williams's are thus of the same order as, although not identical to, those that arise in reading a text that can authentically claim to be "written by him/herself." Although in reading Williams's *Narrative* we cannot extricate Williams's own efforts to mold his memories into a piece of political prose from the efforts of Archibald Palmer, we should not assume that all of the molding was done by the amanuensis, none by Wil-

liams. Recent work on Latin American *testimonio,* a genre of life-writing
that is almost always produced in collaboration between a narrator and
an amanuensis, has demonstrated the narrator's ability to exert control over the writing process despite inequalities of power.[43] Most important, we should recognize Williams's involvement in the production of the *Narrative* as a political act on his part, without which the
transatlantic movement that succeeded in bringing apprenticeship to
an early end would have been considerably weaker.

While Palmer served as Williams's unacknowledged amanuensis,
Thomas Price was the named framer of the *Narrative,* writing a pre-
liminary "Advertisement" and a final call to arms. Sturge could have
written equivalent pieces, but probably asked Price, the minister of the
Devonshire Square Baptist Church in east London and an active abolitionist, to write these pre- and postscripts so as to provide an additional
layer of authentication. In this way the *Narrative*'s authors hoped to
avoid the accusation that Sturge's word alone provided the guarantee of
the *Narrative*'s truth. As was true of all slave narratives, the strength of
the narrator's claim to truthfulness was central to the *Narrative*'s effec-
tiveness.

The addition to a slave narrative of documents that both interpret
and guarantee the truth of the former slave's words was by the 1830s already standard practice. The most immediate and important British/
Caribbean predecessor to Williams's *Narrative* was the 1831 narrative *The
History of Mary Prince, a West Indian Slave, Related by Herself,* which contained a preface by the white abolitionist Thomas Pringle. Such authenticating texts, which range from a couple of paragraphs by an editor
to the letters and reports signed by nineteen different individuals that
preface the *Narrative of the Life and Adventures of Henry Bibb,* testify to
the problem faced by slave narrators: their existence and truthfulness
would not be assumed.[44] Slave narrators had to contend with a tradition
of Euro-American letters and philosophy that assumed the ignorance,
ineducability, and mendacity of Africans and their descendants. The
black narrator had to prove that he or she was, in William L. Andrews's
words, "despite all prejudice and propaganda, a truth-teller, a reliable
transcriber of the experience and character of black folk."[45]

How could the existence of the author and the truthfulness of his
or her words be established? The most common technique was for
white male abolitionists to declare both that they knew the narrator

and that they had received some other form of corroboration of his or her claims.[46] For instance, in Thomas Pringle's preface to Mary Prince's narrative he tells us that after the narrative was written he "carefully examin[ed]" Prince on "every fact and circumstance detailed" and also consulted Mr. Joseph Phillips, a white man who had known Prince in Antigua.[47] This process assumes the self-evident truthfulness of Pringle and Phillips, making Prince's claims dependent on them. Thomas Price's "Advertisement," which appears in Williams's *Narrative* between the title page and the text, is similarly concerned to establish Williams's existence and his truthfulness. Price's "Advertisement," though, differs subtly but importantly from Pringle's preface in the manner by which it makes its claim. Although Price signs and dates the "Advertisement," the claim to authentication within it turns out to rest on the word of black people, not whites. "I have now before me," writes Price, "a document, signed by two free negroes and six apprentices, all members of a Christian church in Jamaica, in which they affirm, that they have known the narrator from his infancy, and that he '*is steady, sober, industrious, of good moral character, and that his word may be relied upon.*'" To give the names of these witnesses would put them in danger, so readers are asked to trust Price's word that he has seen the document he claims to have seen and that it says what he claims it does. Readers are thus required to trust not only Price but also eight "negroes." It is, of course, their status as "members of a Christian church" that makes them trustworthy, suggesting that black people who were not Christians would not be extended the same trust. Nevertheless, for a slave narrative to be authenticated by black knowledge and truthfulness is, as far as I am aware, unique.[48] By relying on black authenticators the *Narrative* goes some way to subvert the paternalist relationship between Williams and his white patrons that was otherwise established in the structure of the *Narrative* and in the actual relationship between Williams and Sturge.

It is not only Price and the unnamed black Christians who establish Williams's claim to truth-telling. Additionally, the very language of the text is said to proclaim its status as truth. The *Narrative* has been "taken down from his [Williams's] own lips," Price asserts. Like the use of external authenticators, this claim directly echoes one made in the preface to Mary Prince's *History,* where Thomas Pringle stated that the narrative "was taken down from Mary's own lips by a lady who happened to be at the time residing in my family as a visitor." However, there is again a difference: Pringle goes on to undermine Prince's claims to intelligence and intelligibility by referring to the "narrator's repetitions and prolixities" and noting the need for alterations "to exclude redundances and gross grammatical errors, so as to render it clearly intelligible."[49] Prince's *History* is written almost throughout in standard English. Of Williams, Price instead writes, "It was deemed better to preserve his own peculiar style, rather than by any attempt at revision, to endanger the self-evident proof of fidelity, which his account bears."[50] Williams's *Narrative* is written in an anglicized version of Jamaican Creole.

Williams's is the only slave narrative that I am aware of to employ dialect or Creole as the dominant narrative language. Indeed, many other slave narratives seem to shy away from nonstandard English or reserve it for representing the speech of slaves other than the author.[51] Slave narrators who wrote their own texts frequently employed a high-register literary English to demonstrate their own intelligence and distance from slavery, and thus to represent their race's humanity and intelligence. They did so, in addition, because they were aware of the extended history of derisive white representations of the speech of black people in both the Caribbean and the United States. Edward Long, in his influential *History of Jamaica* (1774), referred to the language of creole slaves as "bad English" and "gibberish" and claimed that "they confound all the moods, tenses, cases, and conjugations, without mercy."[52] Given this context, any attempt to represent black speech sympathetically was bound to be fraught. Frederick Douglass expressed resentment of abolitionist "friends" who suggested that he adopt Southern black dialect when he spoke in public, telling him that he had "better have a *little* of the plantation manner of speech . . . 'tis not best that you seem too learned."[53] For some readers, the *Narrative*'s attempt to use Creole must have lent Williams "the plantation manner," making him appear simple and stressing his lack of formal education. The context in which readers came across the *Narrative*'s creolized English, sandwiched between Price's exaggeratedly high-flown standard English prose, would have added to this effect. Nevertheless, such a reading would not have been straightforwardly disparaging. Rather, it would have drawn on romantic assumptions that elevated the supposedly simple and natural on the grounds that those who were closer to the "primitive" had greater access to truth.[54]

We should not assume, however, that readers necessarily read the *Narrative*'s language as indicative of simplicity. After all, its use of Creole also demonstrated the power of Williams's language, its ability to evoke a scene and to convey both analysis and a range of emotions. As Pringle's comments about Mary Prince's use of language suggest, it was not possible for a speaker of an African-Caribbean Creole to produce a text that did not in some way confront the greater prestige and power of standard English. If Palmer were to have represented Williams's language as conforming to standard English, his decision to do so would have suggested that Creole and its speakers were inferior to standard English and its speakers. As many Caribbean artists and intellectuals have argued and others have demonstrated in their work, to write only in standard English (or the dominant forms of other European languages) implicitly accepts the dominant language's claim to be *the* marker of intellectual capacity. Palmer, of course, was not influenced by this consideration in his decisions. Ironically, though, in its unusual use of Creole Williams's *Narrative* could be seen as a problematic but real part of a powerful tradition in Jamaican writing and performance that includes the poetry of Claude McKay, Jean Binta Breeze, and Louise Bennett; the Sistren collective's autobiographical narratives; and the experimental academic prose of Carolyn Cooper.[55]

Nevertheless, the use of Creole in Williams's *Narrative* is limited. Many common features of Jamaican Creole are hardly used. For instance, where Jamaican almost always uses the first-person subject pronoun "me" (or "mi" in F. G. Cassidy's Jamaican orthography), the *Narrative* usually uses "I."[56] Where the *Narrative* employs Jamaican rather than English grammatical structures it sometimes does so in ways that suggest that Jamaican is merely an ungrammatical version of English. Articles are—from the point of view of standard English—left out, verbs lack their standard English endings, plural nouns appear in the singular. But the ways in which native Jamaican speakers indicate difference in time, speaker, and number are never used. For example, the suffix "dem," used in Jamaican Creole to indicate a plural (thus in Jamaican, "di pikni" means "the child"; "di pikni dem" means "the children"), never appears in the *Narrative*. This may be because Williams modified his language to talk to Palmer, a white man—a process referred to by linguists as "code-switching." Barbara Lalla and Jean D'Costa comment that Williams used a "formal and mesolectal" (middle-level) version of Jamaican Creole.[57] However, the limited use of Jamaican grammatical features may also result from Palmer's careful management of the *Narrative*'s language to give an impression of difference, of nonstandard speech, while remaining close enough to standard English to be easily comprehensible to British readers. Thus even as the *Narrative* demonstrated the descriptive, emotional, and analytic possibilities of the Jamaican language, this potential was limited by the sense that communication had to be on the terms of the British audience.

The use of Creole did more than just attempt to represent Williams's language; it also supplied the *Narrative*'s "self-evident proof of fidelity," allegedly demonstrating that no white editor had rearranged, rewritten, or invented the events Williams recounts. Ironically, for at least some of its audience the *Narrative*'s use of Creole had the opposite effect. In passing on the *Narrative* to a colleague, Henry Taylor, the influential undersecretary at the Colonial Office, cautioned: "I think it would have looked better if it had not been put into the negro dialect which seeems to have been done for purposes of affect [*sic*], and has something false about it since it is out of the question that the method and whole getting up of this thing could be the work of an uneducated negro, and indeed it does not profess to be so, and therefore the more simple and straightforward way would have been for those who wrote the narrative to have sworn it in their own language."[58] Taylor thus transformed the *Narrative*'s use of language to assert fidelity into a sign of its falsehood. Despite Taylor's refusal to read the *Narrative* as its producers intended, his comments confirm that choices about how to represent the speech of Caribbean people were necessarily politically freighted.

The attempt to represent Williams's speech provoked anxiety among those involved in reproducing the *Narrative*. All the various new editions published in 1837 and 1838 made many minor changes to the original edition, usually altering the grammar in some way. For instance, in the version produced in Jamaica, the *Narrative*'s use of the word "woman" as a plural is almost always changed to "women." However, not all of the changes made in later editions "correct" Williams's language. Some of the changes move the *Narrative*'s language away from standard English, toward what the editors or typesetters assume to be authentic Jamaican speech. For instance, in one edition the phrase "Massa say he did not make the people take in the pimento crop clean" is altered by the removal of "the" before "pimento." Whoever made this alteration presumably did so because it seemed a more "Jamaican" usage, although the attempt at authenticity did not extend, as it might have, to a change along the lines of "Massa say him no make the people take in pimento crop clean." None of the editions made consistent changes, suggesting that, although all wanted to make the text both "authentic" and comprehensible, there was no consensus about how to achieve this.

Williams's *Narrative* contains a catalogue of horrific abuses taking place under apprenticeship, exemplifying the abolitionist critique of the system. There are, however, tensions within the text, especially between the narrative itself and the introductory material, that suggest that the *Narrative* is not structured only by the abolitionist need for an exemplar of apprentices' suffering. The *Narrative* itself is less conventional than the abolitionist introduction suggests. Price claims that the "revolting picture" drawn by the text is made bearable only by Williams's Christ-like "enduring patience," conjuring up a long-standing image of the nobly suffering slave-victim. But this image is not borne out by the events described. Williams suffers all kinds of abuses, but he is not characterized merely by patience. Rather, he narrates his involvement in a variety of strategies of resistance, including running away, appealing to state authorities to intervene on his behalf, verbally confronting his master, stealing from him, and challenging unfair magistrates to "do justice" by him. He also describes a community made up of many interconnected people who act in solidarity with one another. In doing so, he creates a narrative whose subject at points seems to be a collective one—the apprentices of Penshurst, the inmates of the St. Ann's Bay House of Correction—rather than the singular "I" traditionally taken to be the hallmark of autobiographical writing.

Responses to the Narrative *in Britain and Jamaica*

A Narrative of Events since the First of August, 1834 was on sale in Britain by June 1837. A slightly different edition was produced in Glasgow at the same time, and by 1838 there were seven editions in circulation. Produced at around the same time as the first edition of the *Narrative* was an engraving entitled "A Treadmill Scene in Jamaica" that illustrated many of the *Narrative*'s points about prisons, and a short pamphlet entitled *A Statement of Facts illustrating the Administration of the Abolition Law and the Sufferings of the Negro Apprentices in the Island of Jamaica*. All seem to have sold well. "The people here seem alive to this dreadful suffering," wrote a bookseller from Reading, England, to the Anti-Slavery Society. "I should be glad if you could spare me 100 *Narratives* and 50 *Statements of Facts* and 200 treadmill pictures." Others ordered the various pamphlets in even larger quantities.[59] The *Narrative* was widely circulated and gained substantial attention. The *Patriot,* a London-based newspaper aimed at members of the nonconformist churches, published extracts from it and in the same issue "entreat[ed] our readers to procure the pamphlet."[60] The *British Emancipator,* a newspaper established to campaign for the immediate end of apprenticeship, referred to the *Narrative* repeatedly in its issues of early 1838, assuming that readers would be familiar with its contents. For instance, in an article on a shocking case in which a woman died while on the treadmill, the *Emancipator* interjected, "Refused to step the wheel, and was in consequence tied by the arms to the hand-rail! Those who have read James Williams' Narrative will understand what this refusing to step the wheel means."[61]

Immediately on publication Sturge sent a copy of the *Narrative* to the Colonial Office, which forwarded it to Sir Lionel Smith, the governor of Jamaica. The accompanying letter demonstrated considerable skepticism. "I feel it my duty," wrote Lord Glenelg, the colonial secretary, "to express considerable distrust of a statement of this nature put into public circulation at a distance from the spot where the facts are alleged to have occurred, and with respect to which no opportunity has been afforded for enquiry or investigation."[62] The producers of the *Narrative* had been right to expect that its claims to truth would come under intense and immediate scrutiny. Nevertheless, Glenelg asked Smith to arrange for the *Narrative*'s claims to be investigated. Smith duly appointed two magistrates, John Daughtrey and George Gordon, to conduct the investigation.[63]

Meanwhile, the Jamaican pro-planter press launched a vigorous attack on both Sturge and Williams. The extent of the Jamaican reaction suggests that planters considered the *Narrative*'s accusations to constitute a serious political blow. Referring scornfully to "the *boy James,*" the

Kingston-based *Jamaica Despatch* solicited attacks on Williams. "He is said," the newspaper continued, "to have told his ARTLESS TALE, and of course the poor fellow caused the Saints to sigh, and clasp their hands in mute amazement; the old women too, no doubt, groaned and shed tears." The paper contrasted the credulity of the abolitionist "Saints" and "old women" to its own knowing understanding of the supposed reality of black people's lies, exclaiming, "What a farce— a negro boy's '*artless tale!*'"[64] This comment demonstrates the difficulties faced by slave narrators: "truth" is equated with "artlessness"; any sense that a piece of writing requires creativity also implies that it is necessarily untruthful. In the next few weeks the *Despatch* published articles about Sturge, Williams, and the *Narrative* every few days. The *St. Jago de la Vega Gazette* declared the *Narrative* to be a "tissue . . . of falsehoods" and challenged Sturge to name the six black Christians who had vouched for Williams's character.[65] Meanwhile both the *Despatch* and the *Falmouth Post* published the *Narrative*. The plantocratic *Despatch* disparaged the *Narrative* editorially, while the antiapprenticeship *Falmouth Post* used it to demonstrate the abuses taking place under apprenticeship.

Gilbert Senior responded immediately to the *Despatch*'s request for information about Williams. He published several letters in Jamaican newspapers and organized some of his apprentices to make affidavits disputing the *Narrative*'s claims.[66] Senior's main approach was to attack Williams's integrity, describing him repeatedly as "insolent" and alleging that he had on many occasions committed theft. James, said the former master, was a "great villain"; his "evil propensities" had displayed themselves early in his life, despite the "kind treatment" he had received. Senior inverted the meaning of the incidents described in the *Narrative*, acknowledging that James had been punished on multiple occasions, but arguing that, far from indicating the oppressiveness and abusiveness inherent in the apprenticeship system, his repeated punishments were proof of his moral weakness. As a result, he was not to be trusted. From the abolitionist point of view, such claims carried little weight. Sturge responded that Senior's letters in fact corroborated rather than undermined Williams's claims. As he pointed out, Senior did not deny that Williams was flogged and imprisoned. Indeed, Senior even supplied the dates for many of the incidents recorded in the *Narrative*.

The Inquiry and Its Evidence

Amid this public discussion, Daughtrey and Gordon opened their Commission of Inquiry in Browns Town on 20 September 1837. Over three weeks the inquiry heard evidence from a large number of people, including more than 120 apprentices. The only record of the evidence was kept by John Castello, a free man of color and the editor of the liberal newspaper the *Falmouth Post*.[67] Castello published the evidence in a 119-page pamphlet, which he sold for 6s 8d. The evidence, as recorded by Castello, was also reprinted more cheaply by the recently formed Central Negro Emancipation Committee in Britain under the title *James Williams's Narrative fully confirmed in the report of a Special Commission issued from the Colonial Office*. A new version of the engraving of the treadmill was produced and bound with the evidence. For reasons of space, only about one-fifth of the testimony is reprinted here; the testimony selected has been chosen to demonstrate the variety of issues raised without too much repetition.

The evidence given at the inquiry vindicated Williams's claims: Daughtrey and Gordon reported in late October 1837 that "every material fact has been supported and corroborated by an almost unbroken chain of convincing testimony." For readers now, the testimony is equally interesting for the multivocal account of apprenticeship it creates. In contrast to slave narratives, which necessarily focus on the story of one individual, this evidence opens up a sense of a broader community. The network of apprentices around Penshurst and Knapdale becomes, through this evidence, a group of people with a particular shared history. Rather than revealing a simple binary divide between free and apprentice, white and black, this testimony depicts the emergence of complex relationships within the apprentice community and between apprentices and freed people. In James Finlayson's evidence, for instance, we gain a sense of the processes by which former slaves were able to establish themselves as smallholders. Finlayson had bought his freedom in 1835 and since then had been able to obtain "a little land." He had also managed to acquire enough cash to enable him to lend money to at least two other apprentices, Peter Atkinson and Francis Johnson, so that they could also buy their freedom. Finlayson was clearly emerging as a significant broker in the area. Yet despite his relative success, his family was not self-sufficient: positioning himself as a respectable, responsible head of household, he noted that he was "still obliged to buy ground provisions, as I have so many mouths to feed" (p. 70). Finlayson's story suggests both possibilities and constraints in the process of moving out of slavery.

Like the *Narrative* itself, the inquiry's evidence must be approached with an understanding of the circumstances of its production. All the witnesses were participating in a political event. As in any legal procedure, witnesses told their stories for a purpose. The evidence apprentices gave was determined not only by their memories of the events they had experienced but also by their desire to highlight specific points and the fear that they probably felt of the potential consequences of giving evidence against their masters and other powerful people. Participating in such a public and controversial event involved risk and required solidarity. It is clear from the Seniors' letters and affidavits in response to the *Narrative* and inquiry that they felt angry toward and betrayed by their apprentices. They particularly blamed William Dalling, a formerly "faithful and attached servant," for, as they understood it, turning against them, and responded by treating him with great severity. He and the other Penshurst apprentices were almost certainly aware that by testifying as they did they ran the risk of antagonizing the Seniors. It is unlikely that they gave their evidence without discussing the purpose of doing so and what they aimed to convey. At the same time, the witnesses were not in control of the situation. Although Gordon and Daughtrey were relatively favorable toward the apprentices, they did not share their experience or perspective. They treated the apprentices primarily as sources of information rather than as interpreters of events. The testimony that we have is thus the result of a complex process in which both interrogator and witness were involved in creating what was said.

As well as considering the influence of the courtroom setting and the process of questioning, we need to bear in mind that the evidence that we have is not a direct transcript of what was said at the Commission of Inquiry. John Castello presents each witness's testimony as a first-person monologue, although it is clear that in fact witnesses responded to questions from Gordon and Daughtrey. We can assume that the apprentices, and quite likely many of the free witnesses as well, did not use the frequently euphemistic standard English in which their words are presented in Castello's pamphlet. It is at the very least improbable that Jane Gordon, an apprentice and a prisoner in the house of correction, employed precisely the words she is reported as speaking when she described how a prison guard "asked me to have an improper intimacy with him" (p. 82). Castello's decision was the reverse of that of the authors of the *Narrative:* where the *Narrative* stresses its linguistic verisimilitude, the *Report of Evidence* contains no discussion of the process by which it was produced, but silently alters the language of the speakers. However, though all processes of translation necessarily alter nuances of meaning, no accusations were made that Castello deliberately distorted the sense of the witnesses' words.[68]

The multiple accounts by women apprentices of the sexual exploitation they were commonly subjected to, and their strategies in resisting such abuse, provide some of the most interesting, and also the most problematic, testimony taken at the inquiry. This evidence was elicited by questions from Gordon and Daughtrey in response to the statement in Williams's *Narrative* that the workhouse drivers "constantly try to get after the young women that put into the workhouse, — even them that married, no matter" (p. 17). The evidence confirms Williams's claim that the prison drivers, despite being apprentices themselves, tried to use their relatively powerful positions to coerce or bribe women prisoners into sex.[69] Some witnesses testified that some women cooperated with the suggestions of the drivers. By doing so they might succeed in reducing the harshness of their experience of imprisonment. According to Joseph Lawrence, "the young women whom the drivers took a fancy to, were put by them to light work" (p. 60). Julian Morison described how fear of punishment led her to go three times at night to the field driver's room where she "consent[ed] to his wishes" (p. 74). As a result, she said, her work in the field was lessened. Similarly, according to rumors reported to the inquiry, Maria Henderson was able to escape being put on the treadmill due to what her master described as the "very improper intimacy which existed between her and the drivers" (p. 65).

The way apprentices discussed this issue suggests that they subscribed to an implicit set of values in which certain responses to sexual aggression were considered appropriate and others were condemned. Leanty Thomas reported seeing Bella Richards, who was from the same estate as she, "in the field crying" on release from the workhouse. According to Thomas, Richards was crying because "the rest of the people carried her name to her husband, saying that one of the drivers, Charles Rose, had had improper intercourse with her" (p. 81). It is notable that the "rest of the people" believed that they should report the event to Richards's husband, and that Thomas thought that this provided a convincing explanation for Richards's crying. The implication is that Richards was held responsible among apprentices in general for submitting to Rose's sexual demands.

Perhaps those women who had sex with prison drivers were criticized in part because they were compared to other women who found ways of refusing the drivers' demands. Sometimes these women came up with ingenious methods of protecting one another. Amelia Lawrence reported resisting the pressure to have sex put on her by a driver, James Thomas. She also observed another driver, Jenkins, propositioning a girl of fifteen or sixteen, named Catherine Bayley. According to Lawrence, "I was obliged to say that Catherine Bayley was my daughter, in order to protect her from Jenkins" (p. 61). This was apparently successful, indicating, at least in this case, an interesting degree of respect on the part of the drivers for a mother's authority, or perhaps the drivers' awareness of the significance and power of the wider network of kin relations within which Lawrence's claim located Bayley. In a similarly successful case of subterfuge, Susan White reported that when Thomas White put "bad questions" to her she borrowed a ring from her sister, and used it to "prove" that she was a married woman, although in fact she was not. As a result, White did not bother her again (p. 65).

The *Report of Evidence* thus provides rich material for analysis of sexual politics during apprenticeship. Much of the evidence speaks to issues discussed by recent historians of slavery, in particular relating to slave (or apprentice) resistance and the negotiation of conflict between unfree people and their masters and within communities of slaves. Thus Peter Atkinson gives a detailed account of his conflict with Gilbert Senior over the use of his house on Penshurst for prayer meetings (pp. 57–58), and William Dalling reports that when ordered to flog James Williams he "laid the flogging on lightly, as lightly as I could," because he was aware that Williams had not yet recovered from a previous flogging (p. 52). This evidence gives us rare apprentice testimony on topics that can usually only be approached through the descriptions of planters or missionaries.

Joseph Sturge and James Williams after the Narrative

Back in Britain, Sturge was finding his relationship with Williams increasingly difficult. We have only Sturge's letters to John Clark to recount the relationship between Sturge and Williams. These letters document Sturge's growing sense that Williams was "indolent" and was in danger of being "ruined," but do not detail any behavior that led to this conclusion. What seems most likely, though, is that Sturge's fantasy of his relationship with Williams as one defined by the older man's generosity and the younger's gratitude was disrupted by Williams's autonomous existence and in particular by his relationships with others. Williams's interests in England probably extended beyond his usefulness to "the cause"; his own imagined future was not identical to the one Sturge envisaged for him. Sturge's repeated complaints of the effect on Williams of the "attention" he was receiving suggest a jealous desire to keep Williams to himself.

By August 1837, Sturge had concluded that the "kindest thing" was for Williams to return to Jamaica. "I think the only means of bringing him to a proper sense of situation is for him to be compelled to labour for his bread," he wrote.[70] This conclusion echoed—rather eerily, considering Sturge's hostility to apprenticeship—the arguments of the supporters of gradual emancipation. In Sturge's discourse, as in that of advocates of apprenticeship, former slaves, here represented by Williams, needed a period of enforced labor that would lead them to submit to regular wage labor and work discipline. We do not know if Williams wanted to return to Jamaica or would have preferred to stay in England. We do know that, after spending four months in England, Williams left for Jamaica in September 1837. Sturge intended that he be apprenticed to a trade in Kingston, and wrote to a missionary friend there asking him to ensure that this was accomplished.

Williams arrived back in Jamaica in early November, soon after Daughtrey and Gordon submitted their report. By the time the ship docked in Kingston Williams and some of the other passengers had contracted smallpox. Although Sturge continued to correspond with John Clark until the 1850s, after 1838 his letters contain no further references to James Williams. However, we know that Williams recovered from his illness and renewed his relationships with people from Penshurst. In February 1838 Williams, along with the Penshurst apprentices Amelia Lawrence, Eliza Finlayson, William Dalling, Thomas Brown Lawrence, and William Mills, gave evidence to the Grand Jury for Middlesex, the Jamaican county that included St. Ann. They charged Gilbert Senior with false imprisonment of James Williams, with providing insufficient food for Henry James, and with assault of Eliza Finlayson. However, the jury, made up of white male property owners and apprentice holders, decided that there was insufficient evidence to pursue the prosecution.[71]

Apart from this fleeting snippet, there is little evidence of what happened to the other apprentices who gave evidence at the inquiry. The Seniors, having decided that William Dalling was the root cause of the problems among their apprentices, made his life extremely difficult: in early 1838 John Clark wrote to Sturge asking for assistance in raising the money so that Dalling could purchase his freedom and thus escape the "persecution" he was suffering.[72] William and Maria Dalling's son, Richard, trained as a minister at the recently established Baptist Calabar College.[73] It is likely that some former Penshurst apprentices moved to Sturge Town, a new village established in 1839 with the financial assistance of Joseph Sturge and the political and organizational support of John Clark. Sturge Town, less than three miles from Penshurst, was part of the "free village movement" supported by missionaries in the 1830s and 1840s, in which former slaves established themselves as a peasantry by purchasing land. Many of these villages were named after prominent British men who had been active abolitionists: as well as Sturge Town, settlements were named after Thomas Buxton, William Wilberforce, and Thomas Clarkson. The movement allowed many former slaves to own their own homes, and many of the missionaries involved supported ex-slaves' struggles for improved wages and working conditions. Nevertheless, the missionaries did not want freed people to become completely independent of their former masters. Rather, they expected that the male residents of free villages would work for wages on nearby estates while maintaining Victorian standards of patriarchy and domesticity in their new homes.[74] Several Sturge Town graves bear the name Lawrence, and people of that name still lived there in 1998. This family may—but may not—descend from Amelia, Joseph, or Edward Lawrence.

Meanwhile, the *Narrative* was one of several pieces of propaganda that together succeeded in mobilizing the British public against the apprenticeship system. The battle for truth was won by the antiapprenticeship forces. In particular, the *Narrative* focused attention on the Jamaican prison system. As a result of this and of the continued resistance of imprisoned apprentices to punishment on the treadmill and other aspects of the prisons' regimes, Jamaican prisons became a central focus of the antiapprenticeship campaign, and a political scandal. More than 130 antiapprenticeship public meetings took place in England, Scotland, Wales, and Ireland from December 1837 to March 1838.[75] Meetings of thousands took place regularly in Exeter Hall, London, calling for an immediate end to apprenticeship. The British government took very moderate steps in response, passing legislation that was supposed to restrain some of the worst abuses. Despite its moderation, apprentices and their masters and mistresses throughout the Caribbean knew of the passage of the Act to Amend the Emancipation Act, and most interpreted it as a sign that the British government would not allow planters to get away with abusing their apprentices. Although it did not succeed directly in dismantling apprenticeship, the British campaign gave Caribbean apprentices greater confidence with which to resist the system's iniquities. In this way it reciprocated the earlier function of resistance by slaves and apprentices, which had throughout the abolition campaign provided campaigners in Britain with arguments and stories with which to make their case. This combination of factors led the Jamaican assembly along with the other colonial legislatures to abolish apprenticeship early. The system ended at midnight on 31 July 1838.[76]

Scholars have rightly emphasized the continued inequality, racism, and marginality faced by Caribbean freed people after the advent of supposed "full freedom."[77] Nevertheless, the early abolition of apprenticeship was a real victory for the apprentices. It was an achievement to which the contribution of Caribbean people, including James Williams, has been insufficiently acknowledged. After 1838 self-congratulatory narratives about the abolition of slavery became foundational to British national identity. Until very recently such stories excluded any mention of the participation of enslaved and apprenticed people in the movement for emancipation. In its sustained challenge to this view of history we find a lasting significance in James Williams's *Narrative of Events since the First of August, 1834.*

INTRODUCTION

NOTES

1. Glenelg to Colonial Governors, 2 April 1838, quoted in Alex Tyrrell, *Joseph Sturge and the Moral Radical Party in Early Victorian Britain* (London: Christopher Helm, 1987), 81.

2. Henry Richard, *Memoirs of Joseph Sturge* (London: S. W. Partridge, 1864); Stephen Hobhouse, *Joseph Sturge: His Life and Work* (London, 1919); Tyrrell, *Joseph Sturge.* Tyrrell describes the Birmingham statue on 243. Joseph Sturge and Thomas Harvey's *The West Indies in 1837,* originally published in 1838, was republished twice in 1968, by Frank Cass and Wm. Dawson, respectively.

3. W. L. Burn, *Emancipation and Apprenticeship in the British West Indies* (London: Jonathan Cape, 1937), 342–43; Thomas C. Holt, *The Problem of Freedom: Race, Labor, and Politics in Jamaica and Britain, 1832–1938* (Baltimore: Johns Hopkins University Press, 1992), 426; Robin Blackburn, *The Overthrow of Colonial Slavery, 1776–1848* (London: Verso, 1988), 460; William Law Mathiesen, *British Slave Emancipation 1838–1849* (London: Longmans, Green, 1932), 15. The most extensive discussion of Williams's *Narrative* in a history of antislavery is in William Law Mathiesen, *British Slavery and Its Abolition, 1823–1838* (London: Longmans, Green, 1926), which discusses the book and the ensuing controversy on 282–90.

4. For instance, a commemorative plaque was erected in 1997 at Sturge Town, St. Ann, with text specifically mentioning Joseph Sturge and John Clark.

5. James Olney, "'I Was Born': Slave Narratives, Their Status as Autobiography and as Literature," in *The Slave's Narrative,* ed. Charles Davis and Henry Louis Gates (Oxford: Oxford University Press, 1985), 148–75.

6. As well as Jamaica the colonies that adopted the apprenticeship system were the Bahamas, Barbados, Belize (British Honduras), the British Virgin Islands, British Guiana, Dominica, Grenada, Montserrat, Nevis, St. Kitts, St. Lucia, St. Vincent, Trinidad, Tobago, the Cape Colony, and Mauritius. Antigua and Bermuda did not undergo an apprenticeship period; the legislatures in those colonies decided instead to abolish slavery immediately.

7. Apprentices were categorized as either "praedial" (agricultural workers) or "nonpraedial" (nonagricultural workers). The latter group included domestics and craftspeople. The hours of forced labor required from praedial apprentices were limited, whereas those of nonpraedials were not; for this reason nonpraedials were to be released from apprenticeship two years prior to praedials. In practice, the early end of apprenticeship meant that all apprentices became free at the same time, in August 1838.

8. Hansard *Parliamentary Debates,* Commons, 14 May 1833, 1192–231.

9. For discussions of the conflicts generated by apprenticeship, see Holt, *Problem of Freedom,* 61–71; Swithin Wilmot, "Not 'Full Free': The Ex-Slaves and the Apprenticeship System in Jamaica, 1834–1838," *Jamaica Journal* 17 (1984): 2–10; W. K. Marshall, "Apprenticeship and Labour Relations in Four Windward Islands," in *Abolition and Its Aftermath: The Historical Context, 1790–1916,* ed. David Richardson

INTRODUCTION

(London: Frank Cass, 1985), 203–24; Robert S. Shelton, "A Modified Crime: The Apprenticeship System in St. Kitts," *Slavery and Abolition* 16, no. 3 (1995): 331–45; Diana Paton, "No Bond but the Law: Punishment and Justice in Jamaica's Age of Emancipation, 1780–1870" (Ph.D. diss., Yale University, 1999), chs. 3–4.

10. Olney, "I Was Born," 152.

11. On the influence of the Indian captivity and spiritual conversion narratives on early slave narratives, see John Sekora, "Black Message/White Envelope: Genre, Authenticity, and Authority in the Antebellum Slave Narrative," *Callaloo* 34 (1987): 482–515; William L. Andrews, *To Tell a Free Story: The First Century of Afro-American Autobiography, 1760–1865* (Urbana: University of Illinois Press, 1986), 39–47.

12. Burn, *Emancipation and Apprenticeship*, 336–38.

13. Tyrrell, *Joseph Sturge*, 76–78.

14. I use the terms "Creole," "Jamaican," or "Jamaican Creole" to describe the language, derived primarily from English and a variety of West African languages, spoken by African Jamaicans. The term "creole" is also sometimes used to refer to nonindigenous people of all races born in Jamaica (or in other colonial or post-colonial settings) rather than in Africa or Europe. Except when quoting, I use the term in that way only as an adjective and always in lowercase. For discussion of issues related to Jamaican and other Caribbean Creoles, see Barbara Lalla and Jean D'Costa, eds., *Language in Exile: Three Hundred Years of Jamaican Creole* (Tuscaloosa: University of Alabama Press, 1990); Frederic G. Cassidy, *Jamaica Talk: Three Hundred Years of the English Language in Jamaica* (London: Macmillan, 1960); Mervyn Alleyne, *Roots of Jamaican Culture* (London: Pluto Press, 1988); Carolyn Cooper, *Noises in the Blood: Orality, Gender and the "Vulgar" Body of Jamaican Popular Culture* (London: Macmillan Caribbean, 1993).

15. Report from the Select Committee appointed to inquire into the working of the Apprenticeship System in the Colonies, *British Parliamentary Papers* 1836 (560) xv, Evidence of Augustus Hardin Beaumont, 353.

16. George E. Henderson, *Goodness and Mercy: A Tale of a Hundred Years* (Kingston, Jamaica: The Gleaner Co., 1931).

17. On the 1831 rebellion and the Colonial Church Union, see Mary Turner, *Slaves and Missionaries: The Disintegration of Jamaican Slave Society, 1787–1834* (Urbana: University of Illinois Press, 1982), chs. 6 and 7.

18. These circumstances dated back to the establishment of the Baptist Church in Jamaica, which was initially undertaken by former slaves from the United States. The black Baptists subsequently invited the Baptist Missionary Society in Britain to help develop the Jamaican Baptist Church. Although many white Britons became missionaries to bring "light" to people they believed were "ignorant heathens," the first challenge facing new missionaries was often the need to gain the respect of congregations with established ideas about appropriate forms of worship and the meaning of Christianity. We do not have any letters from Clark describing his arrival in Browns Town, but if his experience was similar to that of other missionaries, he would have been surprised at his congregation's degree of organization and religious autonomy. For instance, a missionary of the London

Missionary Society reported the following conversation with Afro-Christian apprentices soon after his arrival in St. Ann in 1835: "A deputation of these men waited on me only yesterday, telling me in fact that I should not be able to do without them. They said, that they were glad that minister was come, and that he had much company (large congregations) but, that he would not be able to find members; that leaders were ministers right hand—that they could bring plenty." Letter of William Alloway, 19 May 1835, London Missionary Society Papers, Box 1, Folder 1, Jacket C, School of Oriental and African Studies, University of London. See also Turner, *Slaves and Missionaries;* Clement Gayle, *George Liele: Pioneer Missionary to Jamaica* (Kingston, Jamaica: Jamaica Baptist Union, 1982); Shirley C. Gordon, *God Almighty Make Me Free: Christianity in Preemancipation Jamaica* (Bloomington: Indiana University Press, 1996); Emilia Viotti da Costa, *Crowns of Glory, Tears of Blood: The Demerara Slave Rebellion of 1823* (New York: Oxford University Press, 1994).

19. Mary Prince, *The History of Mary Prince, A West Indian Slave, Related by Herself,* ed. Moira Ferguson (London: Pandora Press, 1987); S. Strickland, *Negro Slavery Described by a Negro: being the narrative of Ashton Warner, a native of St. Vincents. With an Appendix, containing the Testimony of Four Christian Ministers, Recently Returned from the Colonies, on the System of Slavery as it now Exists* (London, 1831). The slave narrative tradition dated back to the eighteenth century. Many of the earlier narratives are collected in Henry Louis Gates Jr. and William L. Andrews, *Pioneers of the Black Atlantic: Five Slave Narratives from the Enlightenment, 1772–1815* (Washington, DC: Civitas, 1998).

20. For discussion of these controversies, see Turner, *Slaves and Missionaries,* chs. 4 and 5.

21. Joseph Sturge later repaid John Clark the money he gave to Williams for the purchase of his freedom.

22. Barry Higman, *Slave Population and Economy in Jamaica, 1807–1834* (Kingston, Jamaica: The Press of the University of the West Indies, 1995 [1976]), 69. Higman designated each group of slaves listed under the same owner as a "unit." He would therefore have counted Penshurst twice, once as a unit of seven slaves (those registered by Gilbert Senior) and once as a unit of fifty (those registered by Sarah). It was not uncommon for two or more individuals to own slaves on the same property. As a result, Higman probably overestimates the proportion of Jamaican slaves who lived on small properties. In comparative terms, then, Penshurst's small size was more marked than Higman's figures suggest.

23. William A. Green, *British Slave Emancipation: The Sugar Colonies and the Great Experiment, 1830–1865* (Oxford: Clarendon Press, 1976), 44.

24. On livestock pens, see Verene Shepherd, "Alternative Husbandry: Slaves and Free Labourers on Livestock Farms in Jamaica in the Eighteenth and Nineteenth Centuries," *Slavery and Abolition* 14, no. 1 (1993): 41–66.

25. The Seniors' slave registration returns are in P.R.O. T 71/43–46, 48, and 50.

26. This may be because the slaves are listed in the registration returns under names different from those by which they were usually known, because other people owned slaves on Penshurst, or because the Seniors did not report all the

slaves they owned. If the last reason is the case, and if this practice of underreporting was common, parts of Higman's demographic analysis of Jamaican slave society may be inaccurate. Higman discusses this issue in *Slave Population and Economy in Jamaica,* 46–49, concluding that "the degree of under-registration is very unlikely to have been more than 1 per cent of the total slave population" (47).

27. Personal communication from David Eltis, 27 October 1999, based on David Eltis, David Richardson, Herbert S. Klein, and Stephen D. Behrendt, *The Transatlantic Slave Trade: A Database on CD-Rom* (Cambridge: Cambridge University Press, 2000). See also David Eltis and Stanley L. Engerman, "Fluctuations in Sex and Age Ratios in the Transatlantic Slave Trade, 1663–1864," *Economic History Review* 46, no. 2 (1993): 308–23, table 1, which shows an increasing proportion of enslaved children over time: in 1663–1700, 12.2 percent of the enslaved were under fifteen, increasing to 22.7 percent from 1701–1809 and 46.1 percent in 1810–1867.

28. Will of Sarah Lawrence, proved 5 July 1805, Jamaica Island Record Office (hereafter IRO) Wills, l 74 f 208. Slave registration returns of Gilbert and Sarah Senior. See also Atkinson's evidence to the inquiry, 55–59.

29. Upon colonization, all the land in Jamaica, as in other Caribbean colonies, was declared to belong to the Crown. It was then distributed in exchange for a small fee to settlers, who received thirty acres each plus thirty acres for each family member, servant, or slave they imported. Thus, purchasing slaves became a means to acquire land. Generous land patents to white settlers in the seventeenth and early eighteenth centuries meant that Jamaican plantations tended to be very large. See Richard S. Dunn, *Sugar and Slaves: The Rise of the Planter Class in the English West Indies, 1624–1713* (New York: Norton, 1973), 154–56, 166–67. William Lawrence's land patents are recorded in Index to Jamaica Land Patents, 1B/11, Jamaica Archives, Spanish Town.

30. Will of William Lawrence, proved 2 Febuary 1779, IRO, Wills, l 43, f 137; Will of Sarah Lawrence. Content, an estate owned in the late eighteenth century by William Lawrence, was sold by his sons to John Blagrove in 1805 (Christopher Senior Lawrence to John Blagrove, IRO Deeds, 1805, l 535 f 183). By the mid-nineteenth century the Blagroves were the major landowning family in St. Ann. See Trevor Burnard, "Family Continuity and Female Independence in Jamaica, 1655–1734," *Continuity and Change* 7, no. 2 (1992): 181–98, for an analysis of white inheritance patterns in one Jamaican parish in the late seventeenth and early eighteenth centuries. Burnard shows that daughters very rarely inherited land, and that it was even unusual for them to inherit slaves.

31. Will of Sarah Lawrence. Five others were either bequeathed by or purchased from other family members, or were the children of people so bequeathed or purchased. Will of Christopher Senior, proved 24 October 1806, IRO Wills l 76 f 187; Deborah Senior to Gilbert William Senior and Sarah Jane Keith Senior, IRO Deeds, 1808, l 575 f 200. I have found no records of how the other slaves came into the Seniors' possession.

32. Mary's mother Sarah's unmarried name was Senior; Mary and Gilbert were probably first or second cousins.

33. Randolph Trumbach, *The Rise of the Egalitarian Family: Aristocratic Kinship and Domestic Relations in Eighteenth-Century England* (New York: Academic Press, 1978), 18–22; Leonore Davidoff and Catherine Hall, *Family Fortunes: Men and Women of the English Middle Class, 1780–1850* (Chicago: University of Chicago Press, 1987), 219–21. Amanda Vickery, *The Gentleman's Daughter: Women's Lives in Georgian England* (New Haven: Yale University Press, 1998), centers on the life of a Lancashire gentry woman whose first marriage, in 1751, was to her second cousin. With the exception of some articles by Trevor Burnard, there is little research on the marriages of white people in Jamaica. See Burnard, "Inheritance and Independence: Women's Status in Early Colonial Jamaica," *William and Mary Quarterly* 3d series, 48, no. 1 (1991): 93–114; Burnard, "A Failed Settler Society: Marriage and Demographic Failure in Early Jamaica," *Journal of Social History* 28, no. 1 (1994): 63–82; Burnard, "Family Continuity and Female Independence." On white marriage strategies in other colonial societies, see Bridget Brereton, "The White Elite of Trinidad, 1838–1950," in *The White Minority in the Caribbean,* ed. Howard Johnson and Karl Watson (Kingston, Jamaica: Ian Randle Publishers, 1998), 32–70; Verena Martinez-Alier, *Marriage, Class, and Colour in Nineteenth-Century Cuba: A Study of Racial Attitudes and Sexual Values in a Slave Society* (Ann Arbor: University of Michigan Press, 1989 [1974]); Ann Stoler, "Carnal Knowledge and Imperial Power: Gender, Race, and Morality in Colonial Asia," in *Gender at the Crossroads of Knowledge: Feminist Anthropology in the Postmodern Era,* ed. Micaela di Leonardo (Berkeley: University of California Press, 1991), 51–101.

34. An 1812 map shows the area later described as Penshurst as "land of Christopher Senior." National Library of Jamaica map collection, St. Ann 190.

35. Will of Christopher Senior.

36. Sturge to Clark, 30 May 1837, D/FEN 1/2, Angus Library, Regent's Park College, University of Oxford, reprinted this volume, 95–96.

37. Palmer had a long record of conflict with Jamaican planters. In 1831 he used his position as a magistrate to intervene in support of two enslaved women who were severely flogged and otherwise abused by their owners, the custos (chief magistrate) of the parish of Port Royal and his wife, over a period of several months. The resulting Council of Protection decided not to prosecute, but the case was widely publicized by abolitionists. In August 1834 Palmer was made a stipendiary magistrate, a decision that was almost immediately attacked by planters, who, with reason, believed him to be hostile to their interests. During his time as a stipendiary he regularly wrote to the British Anti-Slavery Society, sending reports of Jamaican events that the Society then used in its propaganda. He repeatedly came into conflict with planters and the colonial authorities because he usually took the side of apprentices in conflicts between them and planters, rather than "neutrally" enforcing the law—that is, ensuring the continued subordination and coerced labor of the apprentices—as was required of someone in his position. Married to a black or colored Jamaican, and with six children, he returned to Jamaica after his trip to Britain and continued to correspond with Joseph Sturge and the Anti-Slavery Society. In 1844 he was elected to the Jamaican House

of Assembly, where he was associated with the liberal Town Party. For a detailed, if unsympathetic, discussion of Palmer's career as a stipendiary magistrate, see Burn, *Emancipation and Apprenticeship*, 240–52. For a brief discussion of his later career, see Gad Heuman, *Between Black and White: Race, Politics, and the Free Coloreds in Jamaica, 1792–1865* (Westport, CT: Greenwood Press, 1981), 140.

38. Andrews, *To Tell a Free Story*, 21.

39. For an example of such an approach, see Sandra Pouchet Paquet, "The Heartbeat of a West Indian Slave: *The History of Mary Prince*," *African American Review* 26, no. 1 (1992): 131–46.

40. Equiano, although born in Africa, spent considerable time as a slave in the Caribbean. Robert Wedderburn, the revolutionary author of "The Horrors of Slavery," was born free to an enslaved Jamaican woman. Olaudah Equiano, *The Interesting Narrative and Other Writings*, ed. Vincent Caretta (New York: Penguin, 1995 [1789]); Robert Wedderburn, *The Horrors of Slavery and Other Writings by Robert Wedderburn*, ed. Iain McCalman (Princeton, NJ: Markus Wiener Publishers, 1991).

41. Andrews, *To Tell a Free Story*, 273. Andrews is drawing here on the work of Mikhail Bakhtin. For useful introductions to recent theoretical work on autobiography, see Sidonie Smith and Julia Watson, "Introduction: Situating Subjectivity in Women's Autobiographical Practices," in *Women, Autobiography, Theory: A Reader*, ed. Smith and Watson (Madison: University of Wisconsin Press, 1998), 3–52; Laura Marcus, *Auto/biographical Discourses: Criticism, Theory, Practice* (Manchester, England: Manchester University Press, 1994).

42. Eric J. Sundquist, ed., *Frederick Douglass: New Literary and Historical Essays* (Cambridge, England: Cambridge University Press, 1990); Jean Fagan Yellin, introduction to *Incidents in the Life of a Slave Girl, Written by Herself*, by Harriet A. Jacobs (Cambridge, MA: Harvard University Press, 1987), xiii–xxxiv; Deborah M. Garfield and Rafia Zafar, eds., *Harriet Jacobs and Incidents in the Life of a Slave Girl* (Cambridge, England: Cambridge University Press, 1996); Valerie Smith, *Self-Discovery and Authority in Afro-American Narrative* (Cambridge, MA: Harvard University Press, 1987), ch. 1; Alice A. Deck, "Whose Book Is This? Authorial versus Editorial Control of Harriet Brent Jacobs' *Incidents in the Life of a Slave Girl: Written by Herself*," *Women's Studies International Forum* 10, no. 1 (1987): 33–40.

43. See especially Doris Sommer's work on Rigoberta Menchú: "No Secrets," in *The Real Thing: Testimonial Discourse and Latin America*, ed. George Gugelberger (Durham, NC: Duke University Press, 1996), 130–57; and "Resisting the Heat: Menchú, Morrison, and Incompetent Readers," in *Cultures of United States Imperialism*, ed. Donald Pease and Amy Kaplan (Durham, NC: Duke University Press, 1994), 407–32. For a similar argument in relation to North American edited life-writing, see Anne E. Goldman, *Take My Word: Autobiographical Innovations of Ethnic American Working Women* (Berkeley: University of California Press, 1996), esp. chs. 3 and 4. Goldman argues that an "editorial agenda can mask but not obliterate the imperatives of the speakers" (68).

44. Bibb's narrative is reprinted in Yuval Taylor, ed., *I Was Born a Slave: An Anthology of Classic Slave Narratives* (Chicago: Lawrence Hill Books, 1999).

45. Andrews, *To Tell a Free Story,* 1.

46. The significance of this type of "authenticating document" has been much stressed by literary critics, in particular Robert Stepto. See his "Narration, Authentication, and Authorial Control in Frederick Douglass' Narrative of 1845," in *Afro-American Literature: The Reconstruction of Instruction,* ed. Dexter Fisher and Robert B. Stepto (New York: Modern Language Association, 1979), 178–211; and *From Behind the Veil: A Study of Afro-American Literary History* (Urbana: University of Illinois Press, 1979), ch. 1. See also Sekora, "Black Message/White Envelope"; Olney, "I Was Born."

47. Prince, *History,* 45–46. For fine discussions of this narrative, see Moira Ferguson, *Subject to Others: British Women Writers and Colonial Slavery, 1670–1834* (New York: Routledge, 1992), 281–98, and Paquet, "Heartbeat of a West Indian Slave."

48. The partial exception is Frederick Douglass's *My Bondage and My Freedom,* which was published without authenticating documents, effectively suggesting that Douglass's word did not need to be authenticated by others. The book was published with an introduction by James McCune Smith, an African American. Thanks to an anonymous reader for this point.

49. Prince, *History,* 45.

50. By "peculiar," Price means specific or individual, rather than odd.

51. Andrew Levy, "Dialect and Convention: Harriet A. Jacobs's *Incidents in the Life of a Slave Girl,*" *Nineteenth-Century Literature* 45, no. 2 (1990): 206–19, argues that this is how Harriet Jacobs uses dialect.

52. Edward Long, *The History of Jamaica, or General Survey of the Antient and Modern State of that Island: With reflections on its situations, settlements, inhabitants, climate, products, commerce, laws, and government* (London: Frank Cass, 1970 [1774]), 2:426–27.

53. Douglass, *My Bondage and My Freedom,* 362.

54. The popularity of Sir Walter Scott's novels, which incorporated regional dialects, suggests the interest in European folk language in this period. This was also the period in which the Grimm brothers made their collection of folk tales. See Lalla and D'Costa, *Language in Exile,* 29, for discussion of the relevance of these movements to contemporary representations of Jamaican language use.

55. Poetry by McKay, Bennett, and Breeze (along with that of many other writers working in both Creole and standard English) is in Alison Donnell and Sarah Lawson Welsh, eds., *The Routledge Reader in Caribbean Literature* (London: Routledge, 1996), 64–68, 145–50, 456–60; Sistren, with Honor Ford Smith, *Lionheart Gal: Life Stories of Jamaican Women* (London: Women's Press, 1986); Cooper, *Noises in the Blood,* esp. 91–95. The use of (and discussion of the use of) African-Caribbean Creoles or patois of course stretches far beyond Jamaica; it has, for instance, been a major concern of Francophone Caribbean intellectuals. See especially Edouard Glissant, *Caribbean Discourse: Selected Essays,* trans. J. Michael Dash (Charlottesville: University Press of Virginia, 1989).

56. F. G. Cassidy and R. B. LePage, *Dictionary of Jamaican English* (Cambridge, England: Cambridge University Press, 1980 [1967]).

57. Lalla and D'Costa, *Language in Exile,* 165.

58. Taylor to Spedding, 3 June 1837, P.R.O. CO 137/224.

59. Burn, *Emancipation and Apprenticeship*, 343, quoting Anti-Slavery Society Papers.

60. *The Patriot*, 8 June 1837.

61. *British Emancipator*, 25 April 1838.

62. Glenelg to Smith 28 June 1837, British *Parliamentary Papers* 1837–1838 (154) XLIX. The *British Emancipator* of 23 May 1838 responded to the suggestion that Sturge should have immediately revealed the problems he discovered in Jamaica by arguing that Smith could not have been relied on to resolve them without the kind of publicity generated by the publication of the *Narrative* in Britain.

63. Smith to Glenelg 25 August 1837, British *Parliamentary Papers* 1837–1838 (154) XLIX, p. 140.

64. *Jamaica Despatch and New Courant*, 29 July 1837.

65. *St. Jago de la Vega Gazette*, 15–22 July 1837.

66. Some of his letters and supporting affidavits are published in this volume.

67. On Castello, see Heuman, *Between Black and White*, 62.

68. Pro-planter forces did attack the inquiry's integrity in other ways, arguing that Daughtrey and Gordon were too close to Baptist missionaries to be unbiased, that they allowed missionaries to coach the witnesses, and that the witnesses were able to hear previous witnesses' evidence (*Jamaica Despatch*, 6 October 1837).

69. The prison drivers played supervisory roles within the prisons, analogous to the role of a slave driver on a plantation. They were mostly apprentices who were serving life sentences in the workhouses for offenses committed during slavery. Jamaican prisons in this period relied heavily on the use of long-term prisoners for low-level supervisory purposes.

70. Joseph Sturge to Rev. John Clark, Browns Town, 15 August 1837, D/FEN 1/4, Angus Library, Regents Park College, Oxford; reprinted this volume, pp. 97–99.

71. Middlesex Grand Jury, February 1838, reported in *British Emancipator*, 28 July 1838. In addition to the cases against Senior, John Clarke of Knapdale was charged with false imprisonment of Eliza Osborn, and Malcolm Dow was charged with assault of Eliza Christie. Both cases involved evidence given to Daughtrey and Gordon's inquiry. Neither was pursued.

72. Sturge to Glenelg, 8 and 11 February 1838, P.R.O. CO 137/236. Dalling had earlier attempted to purchase his freedom; a list of valuation records from 1834 and 1835 shows that he had been valued at £70 but did not pay the price, presumably because he was unable to afford it (Abstract of Valuations of Apprentices in Jamaica, from 1 August 1834 to 1 June 1835, enc. in Sligo to Glenelg, 22 June 1835 No. 149, British Parliamentary Papers 1836 (166) XLVIII, 20–27).

73. Henderson, *Goodness and Mercy*, 151.

74. Catherine Hall, "White Visions, Black Lives: The Free Villages of Jamaica," *History Workshop Journal* 36 (1993): 100–132; Swithin Wilmot, "Sugar and the Gospel: Baptist Perspectives on the Plantation in the Early Period of Free-

dom," *Jamaican Historical Society Bulletin* 8 (1983): 211–15; Sidney W. Mintz, *Caribbean Transformations* (Baltimore: Johns Hopkins University Press, 1974), 160–79.

75. *British Emancipator*, 14 March 1838.

76. Burn, *Emancipation and Apprenticeship*, 351–58; Holt, *Problem of Freedom*, 105; Green, *British Slave Emancipation*, 156–60.

77. Among others, see Holt, *Problem of Freedom;* O. Nigel Bolland, "The Politics of Freedom in the British Caribbean," in *The Meaning of Freedom: Economics, Politics, and Culture after Slavery,* ed. Frank McGlynn and Seymour Drescher (Pittsburgh: University of Pittsburgh Press, 1992), 113–46; Douglas Hall, *Free Jamaica 1838–1865: An Economic History* (New Haven: Yale University Press, 1959); Richard D. E. Burton, *Afro-Creole: Power, Opposition, and Play in the Caribbean* (Ithaca, NY: Cornell University Press, 1997); Karen Fog Olwig, ed. *Small Islands, Large Questions: Society, Culture and Resistance in the Post-Emancipation Caribbean* (London: Frank Cass, 1995).

A NOTE ON THE TEXT

Several editions of James Williams's *Narrative* were published during 1837 and 1838. The *Narrative* is basically the same in each version, but the title page and, in some, the advertisement and final text are different. In addition to the copy text, published by John Haddon and held in the British Library (call number 1389.c.22), I have located the following editions. Their prefaces and afterwords present the text of the *Narrative* in slightly different ways, which I indicate here.

1. An edition identical to the copy text, except that it includes the following text at the very end:

ADDRESS.

As this publication is intended to diffuse a knowledge of the actual condition of the negro apprentices in our colonies, with a view to the mitigation or removal of their sufferings, it is urgently entreated of the reader to turn the feelings of horror and disgust with which he must rise from the disclosure of this Narrative, into some practical efforts for the attainment of so desirable an object.

AUXILIARY SOCIETIES, MINISTERS OF THE GOSPEL, or *philanthropic individuals,* may procure this tract wholesale, at the cost of paper and print by applying to the Printer, J. Haddon, *Castle Street, Finsbury Square.*

Price 6s. per 100, or 50s. per 1000.

ALSO,

Just published, in 8vo, price 6d, and a Cheap Edition, in 12mo. price 2d.

A STATEMENT OF FACTS, Illustrating the Administration of the Abolition Law, and the Sufferings of the Negro Apprentices, in the Island of Jamaica.

Auxiliary Societies, &c. may also be supplied with the 12mo Edition of this Tract, by applying as above.

Price 10s per 100, or 41 per 1000.

J. Haddon, Castle Street, Finsbury.

2. *A Narrative of Events, since the first of August, 1834, by James Williams, an apprenticed labourer in Jamaica.* 3rd ed. London: William Ball, Aldine Chambers, Paternoster Row, 1837. Price six pence. Includes the same "Advertisement" and final exhortation as the copy text. The advertisement for *Slavery in America* is replaced by two pages of "New Works published by William Ball," including *Montgomery's Christian Correspondent, The Philanthropist; or Selfishness and Benevolence Illustrated,* by A Lady, and *The History of Protestant Noncomformity in England,* vol. 1, by Thomas Price, D.D.

3. *Narrative of the Cruel Treatment of James Williams, A Negro Apprentice in Jamaica, from 1st August 1834, till the purchase of his freedom in 1837, by Joseph Sturge, Esq., of Birmingham, by whom he was brought to England.* Glasgow: Printed by Aird & Russell, 75, Argyll Street; And sold by G. Gallie, Buchanan Street; J. McLeod, Argyll Street; D. Robertson, Trongate; and William Smeal, Gallowgate, 1837.

This edition does not include Price's "Advertisement" or closing exhortation. It replaces Price's final words with the following text:

The foregoing narrative has been carefully taken down from the lips of the narrator—his own peculiar style being faithfully adhered to.

Joseph Sturge has in his possession a document, signed by six members of a Christian church, who had all known James Williams for several years, and in that document they bear testimony to his character for veracity.

Horrible and afflicting as is this picture of negro-suffering, since the *pretended* Abolition of Slavery; it bears the strong impress of self-evident truth and fidelity; additional and corroborative evidence, however, will not be wanting in proper season, shewing that this is but a sample of the general system; that cruelties and atrocities in various forms and modifications are now being perpetrated throughout several of our larger colonies.

Then, as copy text from "Let it not be forgotten" until "the struggle is over." The final sentence is slightly different:

Imediately re-organize your Anti-Slavery Societies; let the country be aroused; and let the people, with one voice, instruct their representative peremptorily to demand the *instant,* the *unconditional,* and the *everlasting* annihilation of the accursed system!

June 1st, 1837

4. *A Narrative of Events, since the first of August, 1834, by James Williams, an apprenticed labourer in Jamaica.* London: Printed by J. Rider, 14, Bartholomew Close.

This version is identical, save a few minor differences in punctuation, to version 3.

5. *A Narrative of Events, since the First of August, 1834, By James Williams. An Apprenticed Labourer in Jamaica.* London: Printed by John Haddon, Castle Street, Finsbury. Sold by William Ball, Aldine Chambers, Paternoster Row; and All Other Booksellers. Price One Penny.

This version is the same as the copy text, except that the final exhortation is replaced with the following:

Official Confirmation of this Narrative. Dec 27 1837.

When the foregoing tract was first put into circulation, a copy was transmitted to the Colonial Office; and it was there deemed of such importance as to require a solemn investigation. It was, accordingly, sent out to the Governor of Jamaica, who appointed a Commission of Inquiry, consisting of a Special Magistrate and a Local Justice, who both appear to have most faithfully and efficiently performed the duty assigned to them.

At the close of their labours, they handed in to the Governor the following Report:

[Reprints Daughtrey and Gordon's report.]

With reference to the foregoing, it appears that the Editor of the Jamaica Falmouth Post was about to publish a pamphlet, containing the whole of the evidence taken on this occasion. We have no doubt it will prove a highly interesting document; and so soon as it arrives in this country, the whole case, with all its enormities, shall be laid before the public in a separate pamphlet, published cheap, for universal circulation.

AUXILIARY SOCIETIES, MINISTERS OF THE GOSPEL, or *phil-anthropic individuals,* may procure this tract wholesale, at the cost of paper and print by applying to the printer, J. Haddon, Castle Street, Finsbury Square.

Price 6s. per 100, or 50. per 1000.

6. *A Report Of Evidence Taken at Brown's-Town and St. Ann's Bay, In the Parish of St. Ann's, under a Commission from His Excellency Sir Lionel Smith Governor of Jamaica directed to George Gordon, Esquire, Justice of the Peace for the Parish of St. James, and John Daughtrey, Esquire, Special Magistrate, St. Eliza-beth. To which is prefixed, A Narrative of Events Since the 1st of August, 1834 by James Williams, Late an Apprenticed Labourer to G. W. Senior, Esquire.* Jamaica: Printed and Published by John Castello, Proprietor of "The Falmouth Post," Trelawny, 1837.

This version does not include Thomas Price's "Advertisement."

Instead of "Narrative &c" after the Advertisement, this edition heads the text with its title: "A Narrative of Events, Since the 1st of August, 1834. By James Williams, an Apprenticed Labourer in Jamaica," and adds the note *"The numbers, in James Williams's Narrative, in Parenthe-ses, are placed for the purpose of giving the Reader an idea of the questions proposed to Mr. Senior and the other witnesses, by the Commissioners of Inquiry."*

This edition replaces the closing exhortation (from "The tale of Williams is the tale of near eight hundred thousands of our fellow-subjects") with the text of Daughtrey and Gordon's report on the in-quiry. This text is reprinted here after the extracts from the inquiry text.

It then continues with the evidence from the inquiry itself. The ex-tracts from the inquiry reprinted here are copied from this edition.

7. [Outer title page:] *James Williams's Narrative fully confirmed in the re-port of a special commission issued from the Colonial Office.* With a Steel En-graving of the Treadmill, Price One Shilling.

The next page has an engraving showing a treadmill and various other scenes taking place inside a prison, entitled "An Interior View of a Jamaican House of Correction."[1] This engraving is reproduced in this volume on p. 44.

[Inner title page:] *A Narrative of Events Since the 1st Of August, 1834 By James Williams, together with the Evidence Taken under a Com-*

mission appointed by the Colonial Office to ascertain the Truth of the Narrative; And the Report of the Commissioners thereon: The Whole Exhibiting a Correct Picture of a Large Proportion of West Indian Society; And the Atrocious Cruelties Perpetrated under the Apprenticeship System. London: Printed for the Central Emancipation Committee, Token-House Yard. Sold By G. Wightman, 24, Paternoster Row. *Price Six Pence.* 1838.

This edition replaces Price's "Advertisement" with the following text:

ADVERTISEMENT. When the NARRATIVE by JAMES WIL-LIAMS first appeared, great doubts were entertained as to the possibility of its truth; these doubts having been suggested to the Members of Her Majesty's Government, at their instigation a Commission of Inquiry was issued by His Excellency, Sir Lionel Smith, Governor of Jamaica, directed to the Justice of the Peace of the parish of St. James, and the Special Magistrate of St. Elizabeth, to ascertain whether facts so disgraceful to human nature, and so flagrantly opposed to the Act of Emancipation, could possibly be true. As soon as the Commission had concluded their investigation, their Report was published in Jamaica; and a private copy having found its way into this country, it was determined that no time should be lost in laying it before the public. The Government has acknowledged the Report; but where is the EVIDENCE? Why is it not produced? Has it been read at the Colonial Office? If so, why is there a moment's delay in placing before the nation a document so important and interesting?

That the evidence may more correctly be understood, the Narrative of James Williams is prefaced to it; and such references given as may identify the Narrative with the Examination.

J. Haddon, Castle Street, Finsbury

Like the *Falmouth Post* edition, this version heads the *Narrative* with its full title and notes that numbers are placed in parentheses to identify questions posed by commissioners.

Also like the *Falmouth Post* edition (no. 6), this one replaces the closing exhortation with the text of Daughtrey and Gordon's report on the inquiry, and then goes on to reprint the inquiry's evidence, copying it from the *Falmouth Post* edition. It does not include the twenty-two additional cases investigated by Daughtrey and Gordon after the close of the official inquiry.

In addition to these versions, the *Narrative* and the minutes of the inquiry were published in the British Parliamentary Papers of 1837–1838, vol. 49, paper 154, pp. 140–269. The full text of the *Narrative* was also published in several newspapers, including the *Jamaica Despatch,* 11 August 1837, and the *Falmouth Post,* 23–30 August 1837. Extracts were published in the *Patriot,* 8 June 1837 and the *Christian Advocate,* 26 June 1837. The *British Emancipator* published extracts from the minutes of the inquiry on several occasions.

More recently, extracts from the *Narrative* have been published in Jean D'Costa and Barbara Lalla, eds., *Voices in Exile: Jamaican Texts of the 18th and 19th Centuries* (Tuscaloosa: University of Alabama Press, 1989), 75–84, and Barbara Lalla and Jean D'Costa, eds., *Language in Exile: Three Hundred Years of Jamaican Creole* (Tuscaloosa: University of Alabama Press, 1990), 165–68.

The various editions made multiple minor changes to the original text, which I have not indicated in the notes to avoid cluttering the text. Many of the changes followed patterns suggesting that editors were attempting to correct the English of the original or to bring it into line with the editor's expectations of Jamaican speech.

These patterned changes include:

1. Shifts in pluralization, especially the substitution of "women" for "woman": e.g., "The boatswain flog the people as hard as he can lay it on—man and woman all alike" is changed to "men and women all alike" in the *Falmouth Post* and Central Emancipation Committee editions.

2. Altering of verb tenses: e.g., "After the flogging, he got quite sick, and began coughing blood" is altered in the *Falmouth Post* and Central Emancipation Committee editions to "After the flogging, he got quite sick, and begin coughing blood."

3. The addition and removal of articles ("the" and "a"): e.g., "Massa say he did not make the people take in the pimento crop clean" is altered in Rider's edition to: "Massa say he did not make the people take in pimento crop clean."

4. The addition of subject pronouns that are not in the original ("they" etc.).

5. Altering subject pronouns ("they" for "them" and vice versa; "them" for "their" and vice versa): e.g., "if the people not able to catch the step, then hang by the two wrist" is altered in one edition to "then they hang by the two wrist," in another to "then them hang by the two wrist."

6. The inclusion of "to" before verbs: e.g., "we sent in say we come" is altered in two editions to "we sent in to say we come."

7. The addition or removal of prepositions and conjunctions: e.g., "Capt. Dillon say that him don't think Henry James was sick" is changed in Rider's edition to "Capt. Dillon say that him don't think that Henry James was sick." Similarly, "they would rather work the four hours" is changed in two editions to "they would rather work for the four hours."

There are also minor differences among the texts that are not related to the question of the use of Creole. These include the use of commas, dashes, capitalization, minor differences in punctuation (e.g., greater use of exclamation points), numbers spelled out or given in numerals, words joined together or not.

I have silently corrected obvious errors in the copy text such as clearly missing punctuation and "did'nt" for "didn't." These were usually corrected in other versions.

Information in the notes to the *Narrative,* the *Report of Evidence,* and additional documents is drawn from a wide range of primary and secondary sources. The notes do not indicate directly the source of general information; all sources consulted except for standard reference works such as dictionaries are listed in the bibliography.

In the *Narrative,* footnotes indicated * are from the original text; editorial notes are numbered.

NOTE

1. Of the three copies of this edition I have seen, at the British Library, the Elsa Goveia Room of the University of the West Indies Library, Mona, Jamaica, and the Friends House Library, London, only the last includes this engraving.

A NARRATIVE OF EVENTS,
SINCE THE FIRST OF AUGUST, 1834,
BY JAMES WILLIAMS,
AN APPRENTICED LABOURER
IN JAMAICA[1]

ADVERTISEMENT

The following narrative of James Williams has been carefully taken down from his lips. It was deemed better to preserve his own peculiar style, rather than by any attempt at revision, to endanger the self-evident proof of fidelity, which his account bears. I have now before me a document, signed by two free negroes and six apprentices, all members of a Christian church in Jamaica,[2] in which they affirm, that they have known the narrator from his infancy, and that he *"is steady, sober, industrious, of good moral character, and that his word may be relied upon."* Their names and the estates to which they belong, should be given, did I not know the consequences which would probably follow to themselves from the disclosure. The negro apprentice unhappily is not in a situation to give evidence against his master with impunity. He cannot tell his tale of woe without subjecting himself to the brutal wrath of his oppressor. James Williams, however, is in the land of freedom, and his narrative will speak for itself. It is a revolting picture which he draws — a dark assemblage of human crimes, unrelieved by a single virtue, save the enduring patience of the sufferer. That heart must be callous and brutal, the deepest feelings of which are not stirred by his narrative, and that man must possess a very partial acquaintance with the Christian law of duty, who does not rise from its perusal determined to exert all his powers for the extinction of the system under which our African brethren groan and bleed. In the course of the investigations instituted on the spot by Mr. Sturge and his associate,[3] confirmatory evidence of some of the most revolting of Williams's statements was obtained. The minutes of these examinations are before me; and were it consistent with a due regard to the interests of the witnesses, they should be presented to the reader. But I must content myself with affirming that they leave no doubt in my mind, and could leave no doubt in the mind of any impartial man, that, horrible as is the account which Williams gives, it is entitled to the full confidence of the British public.

Thomas Price, D.D.,[4]

Hackney, London.

June 20, 1837.

NARRATIVE, &c.

I am about eighteen years old. I was a slave belonging to Mr. Senior and his sister, and was brought up at the place where they live, called Penshurst, in Saint Ann's parish, in Jamaica.[5]

I have been very ill treated by Mr. Senior and the magistrates since the new law come in.[6] Apprentices get a great deal more punishment now than they did when they was slaves; the master take spite, and do all he can to hurt them before the free come;—I have heard my master say, "Those English devils say we to be free, but if we is to free, he will pretty well weaken we, before the six and the four years done; we shall be no use to ourselves afterwards."[7]

Apprentices a great deal worse off for provision than beforetime; magistrate take away their day, and give to the property;[8] massa give we no salt allowance, and no allowance at Christmas; since the new law begin, he only give them two mackerel,—that was one time when them going out to job.[9]

When I was a slave I never flogged,—I sometimes was switched, but not badly; but since the new law begin, I have been flogged seven times, and put in the house of correction four times.

Soon after 1st August, massa tried to get me and many others punished; he brought us up before Dr. Palmer, but none of us been doing nothing wrong, and magistrate give we right.[10]

After that, Mr. Senior sent me with letter to Captain Connor,[11] to get punished, but magistrate send me back—he would not punish me, till he try me; when I carry letter back to massa, he surprise to see me come back, he been expect Captain Connor would put me in workhouse. Capt. Connor did not come to Penshurst; he left the parish. Massa didn't tell me what charge he have against me.

When Dr. Thompson[12] come to the parish, him call one Thursday, and said he would come back next Thursday, and hold court Friday

morning.[13] He come Thursday afternoon, and get dinner, and sleep at
Penshurst, and after breakfast, all we apprentices called up. Massa try
eight of we, and Dr. Thompson flog every one; there was five man,
and three boys: them flog the boys with switches, but the men flog
with the cat.[14] One of the men was the old driver, Edward Lawrence;
Massa say he did not make the people take in the pimento crop clean;
he is quite old—head quite white—haven't got one black hair in it, but
Dr. Thompson ordered him to be flogged; not one of the people been
doing any thing wrong; all flog for trifling, foolish thing, just to please
the massa.[15]

When them try me, massa said, that one Friday I was going all round
the house with big stone in my hand, looking for him and his sister,
to knock them down. I was mending stone wall round the house by
massa's order; I was only a half-grown boy that time.[16] I told magistrate, I never do such thing, and offer to bring evidence about it; he
refuse to hear me or my witness; would not let me speak; he sentence
me to get 39 lashes; eight policemen was present, but magistrate make
constable flog at first;[17] them flog the old driver first, and me next; my
back all cut up and cover with blood,—could not put on my shirt—
but massa say, constable not flogging half hard enough, that my back
not cut at all;—then the magistrate make one of the police take the
cat to flog the other three men, and him flog most unmerciful. It was
Henry James, Thomas Brown, and Adam Brown that the police flog.[18]
Henry James was an old African; he had been put to watch large corn-
piece—no fence round it—so the cattle got in and eat some of the
corn—he couldn't help it, but the magistrate flog him for it.[19] After
the flogging, he got quite sick, and began coughing blood; he went
to the hot-house,* but got no attention, them say him not sick. He go
to Capt. Dillon [20] to complain about it; magistrate give him paper to
carry to massa, to warn him to court on Thursday;[21] that day them go
to Brown's Town, Capt. Dillon and a new magistrate, Mr. Rawlinson,
was there.[22] Capt. Dillon say that him don't think Henry James was sick;
he told him to go back, and come next Thursday, and he would have
doctor to examine him; the old man said he did not know whether he
should live till Thursday. He walk away, but before he get out of the
town, he drop down dead—all the place cover with blood that he puke

* Hospital

– 6 –

up. He was quite well before the flogging, and always said it was the flogging bring on the sickness.

Same day Henry James dead, Massa carry me and Adam Brown before magistrate; he said I did not turn out sheep till nine o'clock on Wednesday morning; I told magistrate the sheep was kept in to be dressed, and I was eating my breakfast before dressing them; but Capt. Dillon sentence me and Adam Brown to lock up in the dungeon at Knapdale for ten days and nights;[23] place was cold and damp, and quite dark—a little bit of a cell, hardly big enough for me to lie full length; them give me a pint of water[24] and two little cocoa or plantain a day;[25]—hardly able to stand up when we come out, we was so weak; massa and misses said we no punish half enough; massa order we straight to our work, and refuse to let we go get something to eat.

The week after we let out of dungeon, Mr. Rawlinson come to Penshurst, and tell some of the people he not done with me yet about the sheep;[26] we only put in dungeon for warning, and he would come back next Thursday, and try we again for it; he did come Thursday about four o'clock, and send call us; when we come, him and massa and misses was at dinner—we sent in say we come—them said, Never mind till morning. We know this magistrate come to punish we for nothing, so we go over to Capt. Dillon at Southampton to complain; he write paper next morning to police-station, and policeman take us home. Mr. Rawlinson gone already, and Misses said he left order that we to lock up every night, and keep at work in day-time, till he come back—but police say no, Capt. Dillon order that we not to punish till he try we himself on Thursday, at Brown's Town;—Them took us there, but Capt. Dillon did not come, but send paper for the other magistrate to try it, and said them couldn't try us for the same thing again. Mr. Rawlinson said it was not the same thing; Mr. Senior said, No, we had been insolent to him; we call constable to give evidence, and he said we not insolent; Then magistrate say to Mr. Senior, "you mean insolence by manner." Massa answer, "Yes, that is what I mean, insolence by manner." It was magistrate self that put massa up to say this;—Then the magistrate sentence us to get twenty lashes apiece, which was given in front of court-house by police; the punishment was very severe— both of us fainted after it—we lie down on the ground for an hour after it, not able to move; A free man in the place sent some rum and camphor to bring we round. We went home that night, and went into hospital—them would hardly receive us, we stop there that night and Friday, lock up all day and night, and no feeding; Saturday morning massa turned both of us out—we back all sore, quite raw, and we not able to stoop.

Ten days after the flogging at Brown's Town, Mr. Rawlinson come again to Penshurst on the Monday, and slept there. Next morning massa brought me up, and said that after the last punishment, when we got home, I did not turn out the horses and cows that night. I told magistrate I was sick with the flogging, and went to the hot-house, but Mr. Rawlinson order me twenty-five lashes for it; Mr. Senior said, Let it be done on the place—magistrate said yes, and ordered constable, William Dalling, to do it.[27] I begged magistrate not to flog me again, as the other flogging not well yet, but no use, he wouldn't hear me, but rode away from the place. Massa said he have no Cat, but he would find some switches to do it with; I was flogged with lancewood switches[28] upon the old flogging—it tear off all the old scabs, and I not able to lie down on my back for two or three weeks after—was made to work with my back all sore.

About a month after the last flogging, massa said to me one day, that he would send for magistrate, and oblige him to do his duty, that all the gates in the pasture was down, and I never told him, and that I took up too much time to get in two turn of food for the horses; I said I couldn't do more than I was doing, I had too many things to do—first thing in the morning I had to blow shell,[29] then to go to pasture and get in milking cow, and to milk them—then had to look over the sheep and cows, and all the stock, and to dress them that have sores—then to get them altogether, and give to one little boy to take them to pasture; at nine o'clock go to breakfast for half an hour, then have to go mend gaps in the stone wall, after that have to take two asses and a bill, to cut bread-nut fruit for the horses[30]—had to climb the high trees to cut the bread-nut—then to chop it up, and load the two asses and take it home, and to come back for another load:—This finish between four and five, and by that time the little boy bring in all the cattle. I have to look over them and to turn them into different pastures, then have to go and get a bundle of wood for a watch-fire, and after that to supper the horses in the stable at night; they don't allow me to go to negro-houses—obliged to keep watch all night, sleeping in the kitchen, and to answer to all call; Massa said I was only four years apprentice, and don't entitle to any time—that only one day in a fortnight due to me to work my ground and feed myself.

Massa never give me food; he allow me every other Sunday to work my ground, and sometimes he let me change it for another day.[31] Magistrate say that was all the time the law allow.

As to the gates being down, massa go through them every day himself and see it, but he say I ought to have told him, and he will make magistrate punish me for it, him swear vengeance against me.

Mr. Rawlinson come on a Friday evening, and I was to have take next day for my day; but massa send me word that me not take the day, as he want to bring me before the magistrate; I was frightened and didn't go next morning: Then I heard that magistrate said as I take the day against orders, when him and me meet he would settle it: I was quite frightened when I heard this, and I go away to Spanish Town to see the governor—but didn't see him, as he was up in the mountain: I go back to St. Ann's, and hide in the woods about Penshurst and Knapsdale;[32] I stop about seven weeks, and then go back to Spanish Town; I went to Mr. Ramsay, and he gave me paper to Mr. Emery, the captain of police, at St. Ann's[33]—I met him on the road—he took me and put me in dungeon at Carlton—was kept there from Wednesday till Friday morning, then policemen came and took me to Brown's Town, and put me in cage till next day; then Mr. Rawlinson had me handcuffed and sent me to Penshurst, and put me in dungeon ten days before he try me.

On the eleventh day Mr. Rawlinson came and slept there that night; next morning he had me brought out, and asked me about the running away, and I told him I go away because I was frightened when I hear how him and massa threaten me; then he sentence me to St. Ann's Bay workhouse, for nine days, to get fifteen lashes in going in—to dance the treadmill morning and evening, and work in the penal gang: and after I come back from the punishment, I must lock up every night in dungeon till he visit the property again, and I have to pay fifty days out of my own time for the time I been runaway.

Then they handcuff me to a woman belonging to Little-field,[34] to send to the workhouse; she have a little child carrying on her back and basket on her head, and when she want to give pickaniny suck,[35] she obliged to rest it on one hand to keep it to the breast, and keep walking on; police don't stop to make her suckle the child. When we get to the workhouse, that same evening they give me the fifteen lashes; the flogging was quite severe, and cut my back badly; Then they put collar and chain upon my neck, and chain me to another man. Next morning they put me on the treadmill along with the others:[36] At first, not knowing how to dance it, I cut all my shin with the steps; they did not flog me then—the driver show me how to step, and I catch the step by next day; But them flog all the rest that could not step the mill, flogged them most dreadful. There was one old woman with grey head, belonging to Mr. Wallace, of Farm,[37] and she could not dance the mill at all: she hang by the two wrists which was strapped to the bar, and the driver kept on flogging her;—she get more than all the rest, her clothes cut off with the Cat—the shoulder strap cut with it, and her shift hang down over that side—then they flog upon that shoulder and cut it up very bad; but all the flogging couldn't make she dance the mill, and when she come down all her back covered with blood. They keep on putting her on the mill for a week, and flog her every time, but when they see she could not dance it, they stop putting her on; if they no been stop, they would have kill her.

There was about thirty people in the workhouse that time, mostly men; nearly all have to dance the tread-mill morning and evening; six or eight on the tread-mill one time, and when them done, another spell go on, till them all done; every one strap to bar over head, by the two wrists, quite tight; and if the people not able to catch the step, then hang by the two wrist, and the mill-steps keep on batter their legs and knees, and the driver with the cat keep on flog them all the time till them catch the step. The women was obliged to tie up their clothes, to keep them from tread upon them, while they dance the mill; them have to tie them up so as only to reach down to the knee, and half ex-pose themself; and the man have to roll up their trowsers above the knee, then the driver can flog their legs with the cat, if them don't dance good; and when they flog the legs till they all cut up, them turn to the back and flog away; but if the person not able to dance yet, them stop the mill, and make him drop his shirt from one shoulder, so as to get at his bare back with the cat. The boatswain[38] flog the people as hard as he can lay it on—man and woman all alike.

One day, while I was in, two young women was sent in from Mo-neague side, to dance the mill, and put in dungeon, but not to work in penal gang; them don't know how to dance the mill, and driver flog them very hard; they didn't tie up their clothes high enough, so that their foot catch upon the clothes when them tread the mill, and tear them;—and then between the Cat and the Mill—them flog them so severe,—they cut away most of their clothes, and left them in a manner naked; and the driver was bragging afterwards that he see all their nakedness.

Dancing tread-mill is very hard work, it knock the people up—the sweat all run down from them—the steps all wash up with the sweat that drop from the people, just the same as if you throw water on the steps.

One boatswain have to regulate the pole* of the mill, and make it go fast or slow, as him like; sometimes them make it go very fast, and then the people can't catch the step at all—then the other boatswain flogging away and cutting the people's legs and backs without mercy. The people bawl and cry so dreadful, you could hear them a mile off; the same going on every time the mill is about; driver keep the Cat always going while the people can't step.

When they come off the mill, you see all their foot cut up behind with the Cat, and all the skin bruise off the shin with the mill-steps, and them have to go down to the sea-side to wash away the blood.

After all done dance the mill, them put chain and collar on again, and chain two, three, and sometime four together, and turn we out to work penal gang—send us to different estate to work—to dig cane-hole, make fence, clean pasture, and dig up heavy roots, and sometimes to drag cart to bring big stone from mountain side, about two or three miles from the bay; have to drag cart up steep hill. About ten o'clock they give we breakfast—one quart of corn boiled up with a little salt; sometime they give we a shad between two or three of we.[39]

They keep us at work till between four and five o'clock, then take us back to the workhouse—take the chains off we all, and make us go upon the mill again, same fashion as in the morning. After that them put us into the bar-room—put the chain and collar on again, and our foot in the shackle-bar, to sleep so till morning. All the woman put into one room, and all the man in another;—them that have any of the breakfast left from morning, them eat it after lock up, but them that eat all the allowance at breakfast, must starve till morning.

*The lever

We keep on so every day till Sunday. Sunday the women sent to Mr. Drake's yard,*[40] to clean it—and half the man go cut grass for his horses, and the other half carry water for the workhouse.[41] After that they have to grind all the hoes, and the bills, and the axes, ready for Monday. Them work we all with chains on, on Sunday, but they don't put us on tread-mill that day.

When the nine days done, them send me home; I so weak I hardly able to reach home; when I get there, Mr. Senior put me in the dungeon, and keep me there for four days and nights; he give me four little bananas and a piece of pumpkin with a little dry salt, and a pint of water. Magistrate didn't order me to be locked up in the day, only at night, but massa do it of his own will.[42]

Then I begg'd massa to let me out, and I would do whatever I can to please him, and he do so, and order me to get bundle of wood and keep watch every night, instead of going to the dungeon.

After coming out of workhouse I never feel well, and about three weeks after I got quite sick with fever and head-ache, and pain in the stomach; almost dead with the sickness. Massa told me one day, another punishment like that, and it will just do for me—it would kill me quite. Dr. Tucker[43] pay good attention to me, and at last I get over it.

After this, it was long time before they punish me again, but they make me pay off the fifty days; them give me no Sunday at all; every Wednesday they give me half a day to work my grounds, the other half them take to pay off the fifty days;—For one year and three months, them keep on take the half day from me every week, and never give me any feeding.[44]

In November, about five or six weeks before this last Christmas,[45] one Friday, massa blow shell at nine o'clock for the gang to go to breakfast; it was the time them begin to get half Friday;—Them say no, they would rather work the four hours and a half one time, and then get the rest of the day.[46] Joseph Lawrence,[47] the constable, go to massa, and said the people would not go to breakfast, they wanted to work out the time at once. Massa said no, he would make them go to breakfast, and then work them till one o'clock. He ordered Lawrence to go away from the gang, and sent head constable, William Dalling, to order the people to breakfast; they said no, they would not; then massa go and

---

*Mr. Drake is supervisor of the house of correction at St. Ann's Bay.

order them himself, but they refused to go—then there was a great row and noise, and massa make them take up Joseph Lawrence the constable, and Thomas Brown; he say it must be them advise the people not to go to breakfast, and he put them in the dungeon—and he take William Mills and put in, because he don't go to breakfast, and Miss Senior call out for them to put in Benjamin Higgins, the old mason, for the same thing.[48]

While Massa was putting the people in the dungeon, I was passing from the pantry to the kitchen; Miss Senior was cursing at me, but I did not give any hearing to what she saying. Massa was standing near the kitchen—he ask me what I got to say about it; I say, Sir, I have nothing to do with it, I don't interfere; he say, You do interfere; I tell him no—he raise up his stick three times to lick me down. I said, you can't lick me down, Sir, the law does not allow that, and I will go complain to magistrate if you strike me. He answer, he don't care for magistrate, he will lick the five pounds out of me that the magistrate will fine him:—Then he order me to be lock up along with the rest.[49]

While they was putting me in, I said, "*It wasn't a man made this world, and man can't command it: the one that make the world will come again to receive it, and that is Jesus Christ!*" Massa called to William Dalling, the constable, to bear witness to what I was saying; he said he heard it, then they lock me up, and keep us there for twenty-four hours.

That same time massa sent for Mr. Rawlinson, he come Monday morning: four of us was tried, but he let off one and punish the other three. Massa tell the magistrates about the words I use—him tell the very words; magistrate ask me if I use them words? I tell him yes, but I wasn't mean any thing harm. Then him put constable on his oath, and he repeat the words I said; then Mr. Rawlinson told me I had no business to say so, and sentence me to get twenty lashes in the workhouse, and to dance the treadmill morning and evening, and work in penal gang for seven days.

At same time him try Joseph Lawrence and his sister Amelia Lawrence.[50] Massa said that on the Friday morning when he ordered Joseph Lawrence to go away from the gang, he disobeyed his order, and stopped at the gate. Mr. Rawlinson sentence him to get twenty lashes, and seven days in the workhouse, treadmill, and penal gang same as me, and he broke him from being constable, though he only swear him in for constable the Wednesday before.[51]

When Amelia Lawrence was tried, massa said that every time he go to the field, he always find she at the first row, and he want to know what let she always take the first row—being her brother was the driver, seem as if she want to take the lead. Amelia said massa ought to glad to see apprentice working at the first row, and doing good work. This was all the word that massa have to say against Amelia Lawrence, and Mr. Rawlinson sentence her to seven days in the workhouse, penal gang, and treadmill.

Amelia have four pickninys, two free and two apprentice,[52] she left them with her family to take care of while she in the workhouse. Them put us all three together into dungeon after the court done, and send for police to carry we to workhouse. We kept in dungeon till next morning. Them don't give we a morsel to eat, and not a so so drop of water;[53] but one of our friends, unknowing to massa, put a little victuals through a small hole.

In the morning three police take us out, and carry us down to the workhouse; them handcuff me and Joseph Lawrence together, and when we get there them take the handcuff off, and tie we up one after the other, and give we twenty lashes apiece: both of we very much cut up with the flogging. When the penal gang come back in the evening, them put us all on treadmill—after my back cut up that fashion, all over blood, it hurt me dreadful to dance the mill.

The workhouse was quite full this time, they hardly have enough collar and chain to put on all the people, they obliged to take off the collar and chain from some of the life people,* to put on the apprentice; and at night there wasn't enough shackle to fasten all the people, and hardly room enough for us all to lie down. There was a great many woman in the workhouse, and several have sucking child; and there was one woman quite big with child, and them make her dance the mill too morning and evening; she not able to dance good, and them flog her; she complain about her stomach hurt her, and I see her several time go and beg the overseer not to work her on the mill, but him say, not him send her there, and he must do his duty.

All the woman that not able to dance was flog most dreadful, in particular all the woman from Hiattsfield.[54] There was twenty-one woman from Hiattsfield, and one man—several of them have young children;

* *Convicts* for life.

I think they was in for fourteen days. I found them in when I got there, and they was let out on Saturday night; I was present when they let out, and I hear the list call, and counted the people, and it was twenty-one woman from Hiattsfield.

When I go to the workhouse on the Tuesday, there was only three of these woman able to work in the field, all the rest was in the hospital, from being cut up with the mill and the flogging; them all look quite shocking when them let out, some hardly able to walk to go home, the most lively among them was all mashed up with the mill,[55] all the skin bruised off her shin; she had a young child too: she tell me that she was put in workhouse three weeks before, and now them send her back again.

There was more than a hundred people in the workhouse this time — I reckon the life people and all; there was about seventeen or eighteen of them, and when penal gang turn out, them send ten or twelve of the life people along with apprentice, and all have to work together. The life people better treated more than apprentice; them get better feeding, them have quart of flour every second day instead of corn, and always get shad or salt fish every day: they don't put life people on treadmill, and I never see them put a lick upon one of the life people.[56]

Almost every apprentice that sent to workhouse by magistrate, have to dance treadmill, except the sick in the hospital. It was miserable to see when the mill going, the people bawling and crying most dreadful — so they can't dance, so the driver keep on flogging; them holla out, "massa me no able! my 'tomach, oh! me da dead, oh!"[57] — but no use, the driver never stop — the bawling make it rather worse, them make the mill go faster — the more you holla the more the mill go, and the driver keep on flogging away at all them not able to keep up; them flog the people as if them was flogging Cow.

One day one of the woman from Hiattsfield fainted on the mill; they been flogging at her, and the mill bruise all her shins; when she faint she drop off the mill, and look as if she dead; all her fellow apprentice set up crying, and ask if she going to dead left them;[58] she not able to speak — two men carry her out into the yard, and lay her out upon the ground, and throw water upon her to bring her to; but for a long time them think she dead already; she didn't come to till next morning.

There was one old woman, name Sally, from Mr. Cohen's at Cool Shade,[59] was in workhouse when I go there, and she stop in there long time; she was in shocking condition—they had been putting her on the mill, and she don't able to dance at all, and them been flog her most terrible, but still she not able to dance, and at last them obliged to leave off putting her on the mill: but them keep on make her go out to work in penal gang, and chain her to one of the strong woman; She was badly treated more than any body I ever see in the workhouse; every day them flog her, she hardly able to stand. Two of the drivers, James Thomas, and Robert Lyne,[60] make constant practice to flog this old woman, and Mr. Drake sometimes beat her himself with supple jack.[61]

One day we was working at Bank's negro-houses, cutting Penguin to plant at Springfield[62]—old Sally was chained to a young girl name Mary Murray; it was heavy rain time; driver was pushing the people on to run fast—was flogging them on,[63] the young girl was trying to get on, and was hauling and dragging the chain that was on him and Sally neck, as Sally don't able to keep up;[64] at last the old woman fall down, right in a place where a stream of water was running through a negro-house street, and she don't able to get up again, then the driver stand over her with the cat, and flog her, but she not able to get up with the chain on, so he take off the chain and make the young girl tie it round her body, and go along with the rest; then he stand over the old woman, and flog her with the cat till he make her get up, and keep on flogging at her till she get to the cook's fireside; the old creature stand there trembling, all wet up—for two or three hours she not able to move away, she look quite stupid; all the other people in the work-house quite pity this poor old woman, it would make any body heart grieve to see her. The under-driver tell the head-driver one day, that if him keep on beat her so, some of these days she will dead under it, and then he will get into trouble; every day I was in the workhouse, except to Sunday, I see them beat this old woman, and I left her still in.

All the drivers and boatswains in the yard, is people that sentence to the workhouse for life, two of them was very bad, them don't care how much them punish the apprentice.

Them woman that have young sucking child, have to tie them on their back, and go to the field chain two together; when it rain ever so hard they have to keep on work with the children tied on their backs, but when the weather dry, them put down the child at the fireside; when Mr. Drake there, he don't allow them to suckle the child at all, if it cry ever so much; him say the children free, and the law don't allow no time to take care of them; it is only the good will of the driver that ever let woman suckle the children.[65]

The drivers constant try to get after the young women that put into the workhouse, — even them that married, no matter; before day in the morning, when the driver open the door to take the people out of the shackles, he call for any one he want, to come to his room, and many of them worthless ones do it; Amelia Lawrence complain to her brother and me, that never one morning pass without the driver after her — she don't know what to do, she quite hurt and disheartened about it — but she did not give way; I heard him myself one morning calling her to come.

One day, Mr. Hilton,[66] who is clerk in the Court-House,* come to the workhouse soon in the morning, while the treadmill was going. I been on already, but another spell was on, and Mr. Hilton take off one of the weights from the pole, and make the mill go faster; after him gone, some of the people tell me that in the afternoon he often come half-drunk, while the mill is going, then him take off the weight, and take off the man from the pole, and let the mill go flying round: When the pole let loose so, no person can step the mill — them all throw off, and hang by them two wrist, then him take the Cat in his own hand, and flog all the people with all his strength.

Them say that sometimes he drive out with his wife, and come round by the workhouse, and if the mill going, he will leave his wife in the gig, and go in to punish the people, and all the call his wife can call him to leave off, no use.

On the Wednesday next week, they let us out, — we been sent for seven days, but they don't reckon the Sunday for one day; we reach home Thursday — I was quite weak with the flogging and the tread-mill, and the hard work in the penal gang; had a terrible pain in my stomach — hardly able to walk up hill; all the people that been flogged always complain of pain in the stomach.

The day after I come out of the workhouse, massa order me to go get bread-nut fruit for the horse. I said I was not able to climb tree; I was sick, and my shoulders was quite sore, and I could hardly use it, and I tell massa that this make six time that they flog me. He answer, he will make it ten times too, and if I sick, I must die. Every day he keep on order me to go for the bread-nut, but I was not able, and massa

---

*Deputy Clerk of the Peace, perhaps.

threaten me sorely—him tell me, that if I don't make an end of him, he will make an end of me.

On the Thursday next week, he told me he would take me to magistrate next day, and he swear very vengeance against me. I get frightened, and on Friday morning I go away to complain to the governor. When I get to Byndloss[67] late at night, the overseer, Mr. Allen, meet me, and take me up, and put me in confinement till next morning, then he put me in charge of two constables, who carry me to police station, and the captain, Mr. Mackaw, put handcuffs on me, and sent me to the special magistrate at Linstead,[68] and he put me in the workhouse, till massa should send for me; them chain me to another man, and make me work with the penal gang.[69]

On Thursday, William Dalling, the constable, came for me, and them deliver me up to him. We set out, and walk most of the night—get to Walton school, and slept there; in the morning we start again, and reach home about twelve o'clock at night. On Saturday morning, William Dalling take me down to massa, and he send me on to Brown's Town; when the magistrate come, he shook his head at me, and said, Are you here again? Then they hold court. Massa said he ordered me to cut bread-nut, and I would not do it: me disobeyed his order, and on Friday went away, and he did not see me again till this morning. I told magistrate that I did not cut bread-nut, because I was quite sick with my stomach, and massa threaten my life so hard, that make me go away to complain to the governor. Then the magistrate called the sergeant of police, and tell him, Lay hold of that fellow, and give him five-and-twenty good lashes—and after the flogging I must be sent to workhouse again for *seven* days, and after I come out of the workhouse, I might go to the governor or whoever I like to complain. I told him the old flogging is not well yet, but he would not listen to me; They take me into the market-place, and tie me up to a tree, and give me the twenty-five lashes; all the people surprise to see them flogging me again, when the old one not well. The flogging was very severe; after it was done, I lay down before the door of the court-house, rain came on, and the police came and told me to go inside. I went in to where the court was sitting, and I said to Mr. Rawlinson; You don't do justice betwixt I and master. He tell me, that constable swear that I run away without a cause. I ask the constable, and he declare he never say any further than he took me out of Rodney Hall workhouse. Then Mr. Rawlinson say I have been before him eight or nine times already; I say, if I have been twenty times before you, you ought to do justice 'twixt I and massa. He said, He do justice. I told him, You don't do justice. Then he said, If you say another word, I will put you out in the rain; then he made police take and handcuff me, to carry to workhouse. While I was standing outside the door, I hear massa say to Mr. Rawlinson, he had better let me stop in the workhouse for fourteen days; magistrate answer, That will make it till after new-year's-day; and then he said Yes.

The policeman carry me to St. Ann's Bay, but night catch me in the pass, and police take me into Cardiff Hall,[70] and we sleep there that night; next morning, Sunday, he take me on to workhouse, and I had to dance tread-mill and work penal gang like before.

The workhouse was nearly full like the last time, but most of them was different people—some that I left in I find still there; there was plenty of woman there, but only one have young child, that was Elizabeth Mason, from Mount Campbell,[71] she was in for seven days to dance the tread-mill; she not able to dance good; after she been on little time, she miss step and drop, and hang by her two wrists, then the boatswain flog her with the Cat, as hard as he could put it,—then she try to fetch up and catch the step, but fall again, and them keep on flog, and when they tire of flogging then they let her alone, and let the mill go on mashing her legs; all the skin was bruise of her shins, and her legs cut up with the Cat.

There was one young mulatto girl in for about ten days; she was name Margaret, and belong to Mr. Chrystie, the saddler, on the Bay;[72] she complain of her stomach, and not able to dance the mill well; they flog her severe, and all her leg bruise with the mill; one evening her master come to the workhouse, when she was on the mill—he beg the boatswain to let the mill go fast, and flog Margaret well, and make her feel it so that she will keep away from it after.

There was another woman from Drax Hall[73] on the mill—she didn't dance good, and they flog her very much, and when she find the flogging come too hard, she call out, "Massa, me no one flesh, me two flesh;" she was in family way, but the overseer said he didn't care, it wasn't him give her her belly,[74] and after that they was harder upon her.

On Christmas day them make me and five other men go cut grass for Mr. Drake's horses, and some of the woman go clean his yard and carry water.

As magistrate been sentence me only for seven day, I ask the over-seer on the Sunday if my time no up? He look at the book and say it was put down for fourteen day, so them keep me in till Tuesday night after New Year's day, that makes two weeks and a half, for they don't count the Sunday.

There was one girl, named Mary Murray,[75] in the workhouse same time as me, from Seville;[76] she tell me not the magistrate write the paper for she to come to the workhouse—the busha write it,[77] and show it to magistrate, and him say it was all right; she tell we all, that what make them send her to workhouse was, that busha say the gang didn't turn out soon in the morning, and when the magistrate, Major Light,[78] come, he send for the gang from the field, but them all frighten and run and hide—only she Mary Murray didn't run, and them take she be-fore the magistrate, and send her straight off to the workhouse. All the people that speak to me, complain very bad about Major Light; them say him always drunk;—I see him drunk myself many times, going about the properties,—sometimes I see his servant obliged to hold him in the chaise, he was so drunk; him name is quite common for drunk-ard through the parish; them tell me that where him sleep, him put the room in such condition that they were obliged to clean it all out next morning.

When he go upon the estate he call to the overseer, Have you got any thing for me to do,—any person to flog? and if they tell him yes, then him stop, and if they give him rum to drink, he will do whatever thing them want him.

One day when I was working in penal gang, I saw six or seven of the Windsor apprentices, was going to the workhouse to be flogged—it was Major Light sent them.

Another day I meet Major Light and the New Ground[79] book-keeper coming down to the bay, and six men, handcuffed, and tied with rope, was following after, with two constable in charge of them; they was carried down to workhouse and flogged, and then sent back. Every body say them never see crueller man than Major Light—him in a man-ner begging the overseer to let him punish the people. Mr. Sowley[80] was a king to Major Light.

The tread-mill at St. Ann's bay, mash the people up quite dreadful; I see two woman at Knapdale, one named Nancy, married to Jarvis

Webb, the other name Bessy, married to Philip Osborne;[81] them been sent to dance treadmill, and when them come back, all their legs bruise up, and make bad sore. I see them with bandage round their legs, and obliged to walk with stick; but the overseer and master no care for the work, or the time them lose, if them can only get the people well punish. Massa tell me to my face that he could do without me very well, if he could get me in the workhouse for six months.

One day Miss Senior say to me and some other apprentices, that Mr. Clarke, the busha at Knapdale,[82] tell her that him send two woman to the tread-mill,[83] and then come back so well hackled,[84] that them not able to do nothing for three or four months, and she don't know what the devil in we, that we not well mashed up, when we come back from the tread-mill.

Mary Ann Bell,[85] a mulatto girl, one of Miss Senior's house servants, was quite large in the family way; Mr. Rawlinson sent her to dance the tread-mill, and when she come back she quite sick, and them strap her hand so tight upon the mill that she partly lose the use of her right hand ever since; she can't hold nothing heavy in that hand.

One day when I was at home in the pastures, close the public road, I see policeman carrying down an old man and a woman handcuffed together; the man was very old, he look more than sixty years old—he was all trembling, and hardly able to walk. I beg the police to stop and let me give them some orange; he do so, and the woman tell me that them sending her to the workhouse about her not delivering her free child to the overseer to let it work.[86] I hear that many people begin to talk that the free child no have no right to stop on the property, and that they will turn them off if the mothers don't consent to let them work; this woman come from Orange Valley, but I don't know any thing more about her story.[87]

The old man tell me that Mr. Rawlinson send him down to gaol, but him don't say what for; but about two months after I see him coming back from St. Ann's Bay. It was between Penshurst and Hinton Hill:[88] him hardly able to crawl, his legs and back hackle most dreadful, and all his shirt and trowsers soak up with blood; I look at his right shoulder, and it was all in one sore, in a manner rotten up, with the flogging; I don't think him could live to reach home; he tell me he was two weeks coming from St. Ann's Bay (16 miles), obliged to beg victuals and shelter any place he come to. It was Mr. Rawlinson send him to gaol, and after been there for a little time, them take him out and carry him before Mr. Sowley, and him put the old man in the workhouse.[89]

Some of them magistrate don't care what them do to apprentice, as long as them can get good eating and drinking with the massa, and busha, and sometimes them set the massa on to do worse than them want. All the apprentice say that Major Light make it constant rule to do so, and myself see Mr. Rawlinson do so one time—it was the very morning them flog me with the lancewood switches; after the court over, Mr. Rawlinson order his mule ready to go away, and him and massa and Miss Senior was standing at the door; Misses was wanting something, and she called Nanny Dalling,[90] when Nanny come, her face "tie up" (*i.e. looked sour or displeased*)—I believe she been have some dispute with her fellow servant outside; Mr. Rawlinson say she look sulky and insolent, and him lay hold of her with him own hand, and haul her along to the dungeon, and push her in and lock the door; he left her child, a sucking baby, outside.

I was standing by the gate and see it all, and when Mr. Rawlinson mount his mule to go to Hinton Hill, I hear him say to massa, You must try to get up some good charge against that woman, and let me send her to the workhouse for about a fortnight; but massa answer that she have young child. The magistrate answer; That's no consequence, but massa didn't like to send her there. Mr. Rawlinson call again at Penshurst same day, as he coming back from Hinton Hill, and he make them bring Nanny Dalling out of the dungeon, and then he sentence her to be locked up in the dungeon for fourteen nights; and them did lock her up every night along with her young pickniny.

As I tell about other things, I want to tell about one time I do something bad; it was when massa get up a barrel of pork last year, in April; John Lawrence[91] tell me he know where the pork was put, and he would help them with a part of it; two or three nights after they open the barrel, John Lawrence get a long stick and tie a fork at the end of it, and then he go to the store window and stick the fork into the pork barrel, and get a piece of the meat and draw it to the window, but it couldn't come through the bars, so he come to the kitchen where I was sleeping, and he call me to come and help him; I go with him, and I hold the piece of pork while him cut it in two, and take and boil one half and give me some, and I eat it.

Misses and massa found out that the pork gone, and make noise about it, and accuse all the house servant about it; I can't bear to hear them accuse for wrongful, and I know who did it, so I tell William Dalling the constable that I know all about the pork. Then him tell massa, and they call me up and I tell the truth, that John Lawrence tief[92] the pork and I help him to cut it, and I eat some of it; them carry we before a magistrate about it, and I tell Mr. Rawlinson the same thing, and John Lawrence confess it, and magistrate sentence John Lawrence and me to pay ten shillings a piece to massa for the pork;[93] I borrow the money from my father[94] and another man, and pay it to misses. This is one bad action I do, them don't punish me for it.

It was the Tuesday evening after new year's day that they let me out of the workhouse, and I reach home next day. Miss Senior say them been looking out for me since last week, as I only sentence for seven days, and she think say, that I run away and go back to Rodney Hall again. She make pretence she don't know that magistrate alter it to fourteen days, and massa pretend the same, for him send William Dalling the constable to the magistrate the week before to say I don't come home yet, and him suppose me run away, but massa know very well that I was in the workhouse all the time.

Mr. Rawlinson self pretend him don't know I was in the workhouse so long, him say so to make William Dalling fool, because him was present when Mr. Rawlinson try me, and hear him sentence me to no more than seven days in the workhouse. Them don't know that I hear them make the bargain to keep me in all Christmas week.

Next time Mr. Rawlinson come to Penshurst massa try to get me punish again. Him say me didn't come home same day them let me out of the workhouse — he would have it me no come home till Thursday, but it was Wednesday, and I offer to call constable to prove it, and, at last, magistrate put an ending to it, and told massa he must accuse me wrongfully.

This was the last time they carry me before Mr. Rawlinson, and that was last January.[95]

One Saturday afternoon, about the end of February, Philip Osborn of Knapdale came to me, and say that James Finlayson want to see me at Brown's Town that night. James Finlayson was my fellow apprentice before that time, but been buy himself free, and he was a leader in the church.[96] He send tell me that two gentlemen was there that want to ask how apprentice treated, and him know me been treated very badly, so him send for me.

At night I go to the chapel, and see Mr. Sturge and Mr. Harvey, and I tell them all about my bad living; Mr. Sturge tell me, me mustn't discourage, that it only to last seventeen months; I tell him, I don't know if I can live to see the seventeen months out; I was quite maugre[97] and hungry that time, quite different to what I stand now,[98] I hardly able to get anything to eat then, my ground all gone to pieces, the time them put in workhouse, and if my father and other people no been give me something, I would have starve. Mr. Sturge give me a shilling, and then I go back home.

On Monday night, Finlayson send for me again, I go Tuesday night, and he send me to Mr. Clarke, the minister.[99] Him ask me if me would like to be free, I tell him, Yes, and him ask if I would pay him back when me free? I said, Yes, I would do all in my power, and try my best endeavour[100] to work hard and pay him back. Then Mr. Clarke tell him I must go to magistrate, to give warning to have me valued: I was quite happy and joyful, when I hear this; and on Saturday, I go to Mr. Rawlinson, at Brown's Town, and ask him to value me, but him say massa entitle to fourteen days' warning; he give me paper to serve massa, about it, and said he would be very glad if I could buy myself, as he have more trouble with me and massa than any body else. I give the paper to misses, as massa was in Spanish Town, and second Saturday after, I go to Brown's Town, to be valued; but when I get there, Mr. Rawlinson tell me, as massa don't come, he couldn't value me, and all I can say no use, he keep on refuse to value me; then I go to Mr. Clarke, the minister, and he come to the Court House, and speak to Mr. Rawlinson, and at last he agree to go on with the valuation.

Him and Mr. Abraham Isaacs and Mr. Fairweather value me;[101] Mr. Joseph Isaacs, that keep a store at Brown's Town, give evidence.[102] He say he want a boy like me, to mind his horse, and follow him to town, and when me free, he would be willing to give me two dollars a week, and feeding and clothes besides; so them fix the price upon me for eight doubloons, ten dollars and a half, and two bitts.* [103]

*That is £46. 4s 7d Jamaica currency, for one year and five months' service. The ordinary wage of a good *house* domestic in Jamaica, is a dollar and a half per week, out of which the servant is allowed half a dollar for his own support. A

After it done, Mr. Clarke take me to his house, and give me the money, and I carry it strait to Mr. Rawlinson, and then he give me my free paper, and when I come out of the Court House, I call out quite loud, "Bless God Almighty—thank the Lord, I get out of devil's hands." Mr. Clarke, the Busha at Knapdale, was present—he look quite black at me, but him don't speak.

Then I go straight to Mr. Joseph Isaacs' store, and I tell him, I going to come to him on Monday, as he say him would give me two dollars a week, and feeding, and clothes; he tell me he get a boy already, but he don't get any—he only take swear he would give that, to make them put high value upon me.

Then Mr. Clarke, the minister, told me, it was Mr. Sturge that pay the money for me, and I must go to him at Spanish Town, as he want to carry me to England.

I feel so happy, I don't know what to do with myself hardly; I bless the Lord; and I bless Mr. Sturge for him goodness. If he no been take me away, I couldn't have live long.

On Tuesday I start off, and get to Spanish Town next day, after that we go to Kingston; and two weeks after, Mr. Sturge take me with him on board the ship, and we go to New York, and then sail to Liverpool, and so here I am in England.

The tale of Williams is the tale of near eight hundred thousands of our fellow-subjects, many of them professors of the Christian faith, and heirs of eternal life. He speaks but the language of his class, and details atrocities which would be multiplied a thousand-fold, if his brethren were in like circumstances with himself. British Christians!—for to you we make the appeal—it is with your connivance, and will henceforth be with your sanction, that these outrages are perpetrated. Shall they be continued, or shall they cease for ever? We wait in confidence, but with thrilling interest for your reply. By your love of freedom, by your sympathy with suffering and dying humanity, by your fidelity to God, by your earnest longing for the salvation of men, by all, in a word, which

---

valuation according to this standard, together with the usual deduction of one-third for contingencies, would have brought the true value of James Williams's services to about the sum of £15 for the unexpired term of the apprenticeship!

can move to the discharge of duty or to the mitigation of suffering, we beseech you to be faithful to your high vocation. The friends of the negro race are about to muster on their behalf. Let them be borne onward in their righteous course, by your hearty co-operation and fervent prayers. The blessing of them who are ready to perish will then come upon you, and your name shall be had in everlasting remembrance.

Let it not be forgotten, that the people of England have paid twenty millions for the abolition of slavery, and that a large amount is still being annually drawn from the public revenue, for the support of more than one hundred stipendiary magistrates!

Yet, notwithstanding this costly—this monstrous sacrifice of British treasure, the object for which that sacrifice was made, has never been attained—*slavery has not been abolished*—it exists with unmitigated rigour, in its most ferocious, revolting, and loathsome aspect.

Cruelties unheard of—unthought of in the worst days of slavery, are now being "heaped like burning coals" on the heads of the long suffering and patiently enduring sons and daughters of Africa.

And will the people of England look tamely on, and accede to this as the fruition of their benevolent desires? Will they calmly brook the glaring insult offered—the treacherous fraud practiced, by the open and flagitious violation of a solemn compact? And will the people of England permit the deeply injured, the helpless, the unoffending negro, still to remain the victim of such accumulated misery and brutal outrage?

No! It must not be—the voice of justice, humanity, and religion, sternly demands that effectual steps be taken to secure full an immediate retribution;—we ask not the disgorgement of the misapplied twenty millions, but we demand the fulfilment of the bond—the ransom has been paid, but the captive is still retained in his galling fetters!

There is but one remedy—half measures are worse than useless—it requires but a single, brief, simultaneous, and energetic movement, and the struggle is over. Let our Anti-Slavery Societies be immediately re-organized—let the country be aroused—let the people, with one voice, instruct their representatives peremptorily to demand the instant, the unconditional, and the everlasting annihilation of the accursed system.

June 20, 1837.

Published in Monthly Numbers, Price 4d.

SLAVERY IN AMERICA[104]

A PERIODICAL

CONDUCTED BY THE REV. THOMAS PRICE, D.D.[105]

———————

The object of this work is to advocate the cause of UNIVERSAL EMAN-
CIPATION. Its title bears a special reference to America; because in that
great nation the system of Slavery wears such an aspect of inconsis-
tency and wickedness; because it prevails to so frightful an extent, and
has laid so strong a hold on the public mind, that it demands the first attention of all who are devoted to the interests of humanity and religion.
The deteriorating and paralising [*sic*] influence of this system upon the
Christian churches in that country, has excited the deepest concern
among their brethren in England. At the same time, considerable ignorance prevails respecting the mode and degree in which this influence
has insinuated itself throughout the entire structure of their religious
society. This ignorance, it will be the object of this publication to dis-
pel, and to combine the energies of Christians at home with those of
the Abolitionists in America. Its design, however, will not have reference solely to Slavery in the United States. It will supply intelligence respecting Anti-slavery operations throughout the world. It will afford its
best assistance to all efforts for the universal equality of civil rights and
privileges. It will also contain critical notices of works of this tendency;
and will omit no opportunity of enforcing upon the Christian world, at
home and abroad, by every argument derived from religious principles
and political expediency, the sacred duty of IMMEDIATE AND TOTAL
EMANCIPATION.

———————

PUBLISHED BY

GEORGE WIGHTMAN, 24, PATERNOSTER ROW.

NOTES

1. From the 1837 edition published by John Haddon in London. Haddon published many other abolitionist and Baptist publications in the 1830s. The missionary John Clark worked for him prior to going to Jamaica. See Ernest A. Payne, *Freedom in Jamaica: Some Chapters in the Story of the Baptist Missionary Society* (London: Carey Press, 1933), 50.

2. Two free negroes: probably James Finlayson and Peter William Atkinson, both of whom gave testimony at the inquiry. A Christian church in Jamaica: John Clark's Baptist congregation, based at Browns Town.

3. Sturge's associate was Thomas Harvey, his coauthor of *The West Indies in 1837*.

4. D.D.: Doctor of Divinity. The Rev. Thomas Price was the minister of the Devonshire Square Baptist Church at Bishopsgate, London, from 1827 to 1837. He was a founding member of the short-lived British and Foreign Society for the Universal Abolition of Negro Slavery and the Slave Trade (founded 1834) and the much longer lasting British and Foreign Anti-Slavery Society (founded 1839). In 1836 and 1837 he edited the monthly periodical *Slavery in America,* for which an advertisement appears at the end of Williams's *Narrative.* Price also edited *A Narrative of the Adventures and Escape of Moses Roper, from American Slavery,* also published in 1837. John Clark, the missionary at Browns Town, was connected to Price's church before going to Jamaica as a missionary. See Ernest A. Payne, *The Baptist Union: A Short History* (London: Carey Kingsgate Press, 1959), 55; Payne, *Freedom in Jamaica,* 51.

5. According to the slave registration returns, James Williams belonged to Sarah Jane Keith Senior, not Gilbert William Senior (the "Mr. Senior" referred to here).

6. The new law: apprenticeship.

7. The six and the four years: Apprenticeship divided former slaves into "praedial" apprentices, those who worked in agricultural and manufacturing tasks, and "nonpraedial" apprentices, primarily domestics. The apprenticeship of praedials was to last six years, that of nonpraedials four years. James Williams was designated a nonpraedial apprentice.

8. Jamaican slaves throughout slavery had produced most of the food for their own consumption on provision grounds, land that belonged to the estates but that the slaves worked in their "own" time, when they were not required to work in labor that directly benefited the estate. By the nineteenth century, slaves grew crops on provision grounds not only for their own needs but also to sell in the island's markets. Stipendiary magistrates could punish apprentices by ordering that they work additional time for the apprentice holders to whom they were bound. This punishment reduced the time in which apprentices could work in their provision grounds, thus making them "worse off for provision." There has been an extended debate among historians about the significance of the provision ground system in Jamaica and elsewhere, with some emphasizing the development of a "proto-peasant" tradition grounded in provision-ground cultivation, and others stressing that slaves who had to grow their own food suffered an

additional level of exploitation. See Sidney W. Mintz, "The Origins of the Jamaican Market System," in *Caribbean Transformations* (New York: Columbia University Press, 1974), 180–213; Roderick A. McDonald, *The Economy and Material Culture of Slaves: Goods and Chattels on the Sugar Plantations of Jamaica and Louisiana* (Baton Rouge: Louisiana State University Press, 1993); Ira Berlin and Philip D. Morgan, eds., *The Slaves' Economy: Independent Production by Slaves in the Americas* (London: Frank Cass, 1991); Ira Berlin and Philip D. Morgan, eds., *Cultivation and Culture: Labor and the Shaping of Slave Life in the Americas* (Charlottesville: University Press of Virginia, 1993); Ciro Flamarion S. Cardoso, "The Peasant Breach in the Slave System: New Developments in Brazil," *Luso-Brazilian Review* 25 (1988): 49–57.

9. During slavery, slaveholders usually provided regular allowances of imported salted fish or meat to slaves, as well as annual supplies of clothing and regular rations of rum. The supplies of protein were not required by law but were strongly enforced by custom and by the slaveholders' need to keep the slaves more or less capable of working.

10. Dr. Archibald Leighton Palmer was the amanuensis for the *Narrative*, although this fact is nowhere mentioned in the text.

11. Captain Nenon A. Connor, a former army captain, was appointed a stipendiary magistrate in February 1834. He died in February 1836.

12. Dr. Robert Thompson was appointed a stipendiary in November 1834. Still active in July 1836, he was dead by August 1837.

13. Stipendiary magistrates were required by apprenticeship law to visit all estates with forty or more apprentices every two weeks, to hear complaints by apprentices against apprentice holders and vice versa, and by apprentices against each other.

14. Cat: cat o' nine tails, a whip with nine separate knotted cords, usually made of leather.

15. Edward Lawrence was not listed by Sarah or Gilbert Senior in their slave registration returns. He later gave evidence at the inquiry, where he was described as being about sixty-five years old. Slaves' alleged failure to pick a pimento or coffee crop clean was a common cause of conflict between planters and slaves during slavery.

16. In 1834 Williams would have been fifteen or sixteen. By contemporary standards in both Britain and Jamaica he was thus more than a "half-grown boy," although not fully adult.

17. Section 39 of the Jamaican abolition act required that one or more apprentices on each property be sworn as "constables" who were responsible for implementing the punishments decided on by stipendiary magistrates. These constables retained all the duties of apprentices. They had often been headmen or drivers during slavery.

18. The Seniors' slave registration returns include two people named Henry, but one of them died in 1819. The other, who must be Henry James, is listed in 1817 as African and thirty years old, making him in his mid-forties when this incident took place, although he is later described as "an old African." The returns include

two Thomases, either of whom may have been Thomas Brown. One was an African in his late forties by the beginning of apprenticeship, the other was born in 1821, the son of Mary, and listed as "sambo." (The term "sambo" was used to designate an individual with one black and one mulatto parent.) The documents include one Adam, born in 1812, the son of Maria, who was almost certainly Adam Brown. Adam Brown later made an affidavit hostile to the other Penshurst apprentices, in which he identified William Dalling as his father (see pp. 114–15). Thomas and Adam Brown both gave evidence to the inquiry (p. 55). Thomas Brown is referred to in the *Minutes* as Thomas Brown Lawrence. According to the affidavit of Richard Inglis (p. 116), the incident described here took place on 19 December 1834.

19. Watching crops to protect them against livestock and theft was a task commonly given to old and disabled slaves and, later, apprentices. During apprenticeship watchmen were frequently prosecuted in similar circumstances to that described here; the cases were usually listed as "neglect of duty."

20. Captain T. Andrew Dillon, a retired military officer, was appointed a stipendiary magistrate in 1834, having previously been a magistrate in Ireland. He arrived in April 1835 and was assigned to duty in St. Ann. As a result of the inquiry into the *Narrative* he was briefly suspended in late 1837, but was back in post by mid-1838. He continued as a stipendiary magistrate in St. Ann until his death in 1859.

21. Paper . . . to warn him to court: a summons.

22. Stanley Rawlinson was appointed a stipendiary magistrate in 1834. As a result of the inquiry into the *Narrative* he was suspended in November 1837 and later dismissed. Although he was indicted for offenses revealed in the inquiry, the grand jury refused to pursue the case.

23. Knapdale estate adjoined Penshurst to the south. It was listed in the Jamaica Almanack of 1832 as having 275 resident slaves. The Jamaican Abolition Act did not specify that stipendiary magistrates could sentence apprentices to imprisonment in estate dungeons, but allowed that possibility by not forbidding it. Section 44 of the act stated that a magistrate could order punishment "as he shall think proper, not exceeding 50 lashes, nor three months' imprisonment to hard labour, nor 20 days' solitary confinement." According to Senior's letter to the *Jamaica Despatch* (p. 106), this sentence was imposed on 6 January 1835.

24. Rider's edition of the *Narrative* changes this phrase to "give we pint of water," referring to both Brown and Williams.

25. Cocoa or coco is a starchy root vegetable; it is not the same as coconut.

26. The *Falmouth Post,* Central Emancipation Committee, and Rider editions all change this to refer to both Brown and Williams, so that it reads: "he not done with we yet about the sheep."

27. William Dalling is identified in the 1817 slave registration documents as "Joe or William," belonging to Sarah Senior. In 1804, when he was a boy of about ten, he was sold, along with his mother Mary and brother Pompey, to Gilbert and Sarah Senior by Deborah Senior of Westmoreland (1RO Deeds 1 804 f 49). For his evidence to the inquiry, see pp. 51–55, and for the Seniors' affidavits identifying

him as the force behind all their problems on Penshurst, see pp. 109–12. Gilbert Senior's letter to the *Jamaica Despatch* (p. 106) locates this flogging as taking place on 4 April 1836.

28. Lancewood: tree of the genus *Oxandra,* recorded since the early eighteenth century as being used to whip slaves.

29. In much of the Caribbean, the time to start and stop work was indicated by the blowing of a conch shell, the equivalent of a factory's whistle or bell.

30. Bill: cutlass or machete. Bread-nut fruit: breadfruit. The breadfruit tree was deliberately imported to the Caribbean from its native South Pacific in the late eighteenth century to provide a cheap source of food for slaves.

31. According to the Jamaican Abolition Act nonpraedial apprentices were to be provided with food by their masters or mistresses.

32. The distance between Spanish Town and Browns Town is about fifty miles. According to Gilbert Senior, Williams left Penshurst on 12 May 1836. Both in attempting to present his case to a higher authority and in removing himself from his estate while remaining in the area Williams was following in a long tradition of Jamaican (and other American) slaves.

33. William Ramsay, a white Jamaican, was appointed a stipendiary magistrate in February 1834 and by December 1835 had additionally been made inspector general of the police. He was based in Spanish Town throughout apprenticeship. He was very close to Governor Sligo but was not trusted by Sligo's successor, Lionel Smith. In 1839 he became the custos of St. Catherine. He continued as a stipendiary magistrate until at least 1846. R. Emery was a stipendiary magistrate as well as a police inspector. He continued as a magistrate after the end of apprenticeship, returning to England in 1857 due to poor health.

34. A woman: Mary Jane Kidson of Southfield estate, belonging to Humphrey McLae. The *Falmouth Post* and Central Negro Emancipation Committee editions correctly alter Little-field to "Lilyfield." Lilyfield was also owned by McLae, who declared ownership of ninety-three slaves on the property in 1832. In her evidence to the inquiry Kidson stated that she was tried at Lilyfield (see pp.70–71). Southfield and Lilyfield were adjacent estates.

35. The Jamaican word for child is "pickney" (or "pikni" in Cassidy's orthography). At different points in different versions of the narrative and inquiry this and its plural are rendered as "piccaninny," "pickniny," "pickaninny," "pickaninys," "pickaninies."

36. According to John Pringle, who inspected the St. Ann's House of Correction in January 1838, the treadmill was 6 feet 9 inches in diameter. Those working on it had to step up 5½ inches with each step. "The motion," wrote Pringle, "is rather irregular; in sudden jirks [*sic*] from bad construction; the rate was from four and a half to five revolutions in a minute; there are straps for the prisoners wrists on the rail" (Report of Captain J. W. Pringle on Prisons in the West Indies. Part I Jamaica. British *Parliamentary Papers* 1837–1838 (596) XL, p. 52).

37. This "old woman," Mary James, gave evidence to the inquiry (p. 67). John Wallace was listed in the slave compensation records as one of four part owners of

Farm, an estate with 118 slaves. He gave evidence to the inquiry (not included in this volume), in which he stated that he had been the attorney at Farm for sixteen years.

38. Junior authorities in the houses of correction were known as both boatswains (a term drawing on naval terminology) and drivers (drawing on the terminology of the slave plantation). Many of them were enslaved (later apprenticed) convicts for life.

39. Shad: a small fish.

40. As the original note says, Samuel Drake was the supervisor of the St. Ann's Bay House of Correction. He had been in that position since at least 1828. In 1832 he was also the St. Ann's Bay town surveyor, clerk of the markets, and head constable, and owned nine slaves. He died in April 1837.

41. This practice would shock the pamphlet's readers both because the prisoners' labor was being used for the private benefit of the superintendent and because the prisoners were required to work on the sabbath.

42. It was illegal under the terms of apprenticeship for apprentice holders to imprison apprentices for more than twenty-four hours without the specific order of a stipendiary magistrate.

43. Dr. Edward Tucker gave evidence at the inquiry (not included in this volume). He was the regular doctor hired by the Seniors to attend their slaves and apprentices. As well as treating Williams he also treated Henry James. He was also a nonstipendiary magistrate for St. Ann; Sarah Senior swore an affidavit before him in October 1837, and Adam Brown and Mary Ann Bell, at the Seniors' prompting, swore affidavits before him in November 1837.

44. This period lasted from roughly August 1835 to November 1836.

45. November 1836.

46. The question of the "half Friday" led to much conflict between apprentices and apprentice holders in Jamaica. At issue was the distribution of the compulsory 40.5 hours of work through the week. Apprentices, in the main, wanted to work four days of nine hours, plus one of four and a half hours. Planters wanted to divide the week into four days of eight hours plus one of eight and a half hours. The dispute described here by Williams is slightly different from the frequent conflicts over the eight hours and nine hours system. At Penshurst, Senior had conceded that apprentices could work on the "nine hour system," but wanted them to take the ordinary breakfast break between 9 and 10 A.M. The apprentices wanted to work through this break, finishing at noon rather than at 1 P.M., thus enabling them to begin work on their provision grounds an hour earlier.

47. The Seniors' slave registration returns include a Joe, born in 1807, and a Joseph, born in 1820. Joseph Lawrence was more likely to be the former, as the latter would have been very young to be a constable in 1836. Several of the other Lawrences mentioned in the *Narrative* are not listed on the returns, making it difficult to confirm this identification.

48. In addition to William Dalling and William Grant, who are listed with last names as well as first names, there are two Williams in the Seniors' slave registra-

tion returns. The first was probably William Mills: he was listed as "negro" and "African" and was born in 1787; the other, listed as "mulatto" and "creole," was born in 1822. Mills gave evidence at the inquiry (pp. 59–60). The returns include a man named Ben, born 1787, who may be Benjamin Higgins.

49. Five pounds was the maximum that a stipendiary magistrate could fine an apprentice holder.

50. The Seniors' slave registration returns do not include Amelia Lawrence. The Amelia they do list, James Williams's sister, was born in 1824 and thus was too young to be Amelia Lawrence. Amelia Lawrence gave evidence at the inquiry (pp. 60–62).

51. Broke him from being constable: removed his authorization to act as a constable.

52. Enslaved children became free in 1834 if they were under six years old on 1 August of that year. If they were six years or older, they became apprentices. Thus, two of Amelia Lawrence's children were born before 1 August 1828, and two were born after that date.

53. Not a so so drop of water: not a single drop of water. See F. G. Cassidy and R. B. LePage, *Dictionary of Jamaican English* (Cambridge, England: Cambridge University Press, 1980 [1967]): So-so: "alone, by itself."

54. In 1832 Hiattsfield had 268 slaves and belonged to the estate of John Hiatt.

55. Mashed up: a common Jamaican expression for crushing or smashing.

56. Although Williams does not refer to them as such, the "life people" were almost certainly all apprentices themselves, as free people were almost never sentenced to life imprisonment.

57. Betty Williams testified at the inquiry to using almost identical words while on the treadmill.

58. To dead left them: to die and leave them.

59. Solomon Cohen, proprietor of Cool Shade, gave evidence to the inquiry (not included in this volume). In the 1832 Jamaica Almanack he is listed as having seventy-four slaves at Cool Shade.

60. James Thomas and "Robert Laing, alias Lyne" both gave evidence to the inquiry, where they were identified as, respectively, formerly a driver and formerly a convict in the House of Correction. Only Thomas's evidence is extracted in this volume (p. 83).

61. Supple jack: a whip made from switches of a Jamaican climbing shrub with very flexible knobby stems.

62. Penguin: the plant *Bromelia pinguin,* used to make hedges because of its prickly leaves; also known as "pinguin." Springfield belonged to Mary Robertson, with nine slaves. Robertson probably hired the penal gang to work for her because she had rights to so few apprentices of her own.

63. Since 1823 the Colonial Office had been trying to persuade colonial legislatures to pass legislation preventing field drivers from carrying whips. In Jamaica, this legislation was never enacted, but the onset of apprenticeship in 1834 made it illegal for apprentices to be whipped without the order of a stipendiary magistrate.

However, it continued to be arguably legal for drivers of prison gangs to carry and use whips: the argument could be made that the whip could be used on free prisoners as well. Apprentices, it was claimed, were being flogged because they were "criminals," not because they were apprentices. In fact, their offenses were primarily "status offenses": offenses that derived from their status as apprentices and could not, by definition, be committed by free people.

64. Williams refers to Mary Murray as "him." This is the only place where the *Narrative* employs the standard Jamaican Creole usage of "him" to refer to women as well as men.

65. Planters commonly argued that the law did not specify that apprentices should have time for child care, and that therefore women should not be allowed time to care for young children. The fact that young children were now free made this argument especially powerful from planters' point of view.

66. Probably James Lawrence Hilton, a St. Ann magistrate. Hilton was a cousin of Sarah and Gilbert Senior, the son of their mother Mary's sister Sarah Lawrence, who married John Preston Hilton. He was an assembly member from 1826 until his death in March 1836. Hilton was one of the founders of the Colonial Church Union, the organization that persecuted dissenting slaves and missionaries in the wake of the 1831 slave rebellion.

67. Byndloss was an estate in the parish of St. Thomas in the Vale, neighboring St. Ann.

68. A major market town in St. Thomas in the Vale.

69. Williams was incarcerated on this occasion as a runaway apprentice rather than sentenced by a magistrate. Runaways were held until their masters sent someone to fetch them and to pay the expenses for their imprisonment, rather than for a specified length of time. During slavery the St. Thomas in the Vale workhouse at Rodney Hall had a reputation as one of the most severe prisons in Jamaica.

70. Cardiff Hall was owned by John Blagrove, with 227 slaves. The Blagroves were a powerful landowning family in the area. Within St. Ann, John Blagrove or members of his family also owned Orange Valley, Unity Pen, and Bell Air estates in 1832, with a total of 917 slaves. Blagrove's forebears had purchased some of their land from the Seniors' maternal relatives, the Lawrences, in the early nineteenth century.

71. The *Falmouth Post* and Central Negro Emancipation Committee editions change this to "Elizabeth Watson from Mount Carmel." Eliza Watson gave evidence at the inquiry (not included in this volume). Mount Carmel belonged in 1832 to the estate of Thomas Thompson and had 112 slaves.

72. Margaret Jane Campbell gave evidence to the inquiry (pp. 71–72). David Chrystie reported owning five slaves in 1832. The Bay: St. Ann's Bay.

73. This woman was Elizabeth Bartley; she gave evidence to the inquiry (p. 78). Drax Hall, a large sugar estate, belonged in 1838 to the executors and trustees of John Pink and had 349 apprentices. Archaeological excavations were performed there between 1980 and 1983, the results of which were published in Douglas V. Armstrong, *The Old Village and the Great House: An Archeological and Historical Exami-*

nation of Drax Hall Plantation, St. Ann's Bay, Jamaica (Urbana: University of Illinois Press, 1990).

74. Give her belly: made her pregnant.

75. The same Mary Murray referred to earlier as chained to Sally from Cool Shade.

76. Seville was a sugar estate that belonged in 1832 to Samuel Heming, with 179 slaves.

77. Busha: overseer.

78. Major Light was a former British military officer who became a stipendiary magistrate. He was in St. Ann from November 1836 to February 1837. Governor Smith reported in February 1837 that he was removing him from the magistracy due to "insanity"; he died in April 1837.

79. New Ground was owned in 1832 by the estate of John Higgin, with 232 slaves. It had been made famous among readers of antislavery pamphlets when it featured as the sugar plantation of the title in Henry Whiteley's *Three Months in Jamaica in 1832: Comprising a Residence of Seven Weeks on a Sugar Plantation* (London: Hatchard, 1833). Whiteley's pamphlet sold 200,000 copies in the first weeks of its publication.

80. William H. Sowley, a white Jamaican, was appointed a stipendiary magistrate in December 1834. Smith suspended him in November 1836 for authorizing overly severe punishments, writing that "a love of torture pervades all his sentences" (Smith to Glenelg, 20 November 1836, P.R.O. CO 137/213). He was later dismissed as a magistrate.

81. Elizabeth (Bessy) Osborn, Jarvis Webb, and Nancy Webb gave evidence to the inquiry (not included in this volume). Nancy Webb testified that prior to apprenticeship she had not worked in the fields because she had seven children; after 1 August 1834, she was sent to work in the great gang, which performed the most physically demanding work on the estate. Her punishment arose because she believed she should not have to do field work, both because of the number of children she had had and because she was sick. She was accused of idling and sentenced to the workhouse.

82. John Clarke gave evidence to the inquiry, where he was identified as "formerly an Overseer on Knapdale estate" (p. 68).

83. From Clarke's evidence to the enquiry, as well as from this paragraph's placing immediately after the paragraph above, it is clear that the two women referred to here are Nancy Webb and Bessy Osborne. In his evidence to the inquiry, Clarke denied having said this.

84. Hackled: roughly treated.

85. The Seniors' slave registration returns include a Marianne, born in 1809 and identified as mulatto, who was almost certainly Mary Ann Bell. She was the daughter of Maria, who later became the partner of William Dalling, with whom Maria had five more children. Mary Ann Bell gave evidence to the inquiry and made an affidavit in favor of the Seniors in November 1837.

86. This woman was Janette Saunders, who later gave evidence about the inci-

dent to the inquiry. Under the terms of apprenticeship, free children under six could be apprenticed to work for planters with their mothers' permission. In Jamaica very few mothers agreed to have their children apprenticed. It was illegal to punish a woman for refusing to apprentice her free children.

87. Orange Valley, like Cardiff Hall, belonged to John Blagrove. He reported owning 416 slaves there in 1832.

88. I have found no evidence of a property named Hinton Hill, but the property immediately to the north of Penshurst was named Hilton Hill. In 1838 it belonged to Frances Gordon, but may well have originated in the Hilton family. John Preston Hilton married Sarah and Gilbert Senior's aunt. His son was the James Lawrence Hilton mentioned above. The Seniors' grandmother, Sarah Senior Lawrence, mentions Hilton Hill in her will (proved in 1805) as a property from which money may be owing to her.

89. This man did not give evidence to the inquiry. Joseph Sturge later asked the missionary John Clark to send him more information on the case so that abolitionists could publicize it (p. 104).

90. The Seniors' slave registration returns include a Nanny, born in 1816, who was undoubtedly Nanny Dalling. She gave evidence to the inquiry (not included here).

91. The Seniors' slave registration returns include three Johns, born in 1767, 1817, and 1828. The eldest died in 1825 and so could not be John Lawrence. His age makes it more likely that John Lawrence was the one born in 1817, the son of Judy. John Lawrence was presumably related to Edward, Joseph, Thomas Brown, Richard, and Amelia Lawrence, but because Edward and Amelia cannot be identified from the registration returns, and there are two potential Josephs, the precise relationships among them cannot be charted.

92. Tief: stole.

93. Magistrates did not have the power to sentence apprentices to pay fines. William Dalling claimed in his evidence to the inquiry that Williams proposed to pay this sum as a "settlement" (p. 54).

94. Williams never names his father, although this and other evidence, including references in Joseph Sturge's letters to John Clark, demonstrates that they had a significant relationship.

95. January 1837.

96. James Finlayson features prominently in George Henderson's account of the St. Ann's Baptist Church, as the founder of the Browns Town church and the man responsible for converting most of the original church members in the area. According to Henderson, he died in about 1865. In 1998 in St. Ann I was told the story of Finlayson, who was better remembered than James Williams. Finlayson is not listed in the Seniors' slave registration returns.

97. Maugre: thin, lean; by implication, underfed, half-starved.

98. Sturge's letter to John Clark of 30 May 1837 noted that Williams had "gained I should think near ⅓ in weight" (D/FEN 1/2, Angus Library, Regent's Park College, University of Oxford; reprinted this volume, p. 96).

99. There were two Baptist missionaries named John Clark(e) in Jamaica in this period, based respectively at Browns Town, St. Ann, and Jericho, St. Thomas, in the Vale. The *Narrative* refers to the Browns Town–based Clarke. In his publications his name is spelled "Clark."

100. Lalla and D'Costa note that this term has evolved into the contemporary Jamaican phrase "my endeavour-best," which they describe as "a heritage of missionary language." See Barbara Lalla and Jean D'Costa, eds., *Language in Exile: Three Hundred Years of Jamaican Creole* (Tuscaloosa: University of Alabama Press, 1990), 165.

101. Under the Jamaican Abolition Act apprentices were entitled to buy their freedom by paying their masters or mistresses a sum decided on by a panel of three magistrates: the stipendiary magistrate, whom the apprentice notified of his or her desire to be valued (in this case, Rawlinson); a regular magistrate nominated by the apprentice holder (Isaacs); and a third magistrate decided on by these two or appointed by the parish's senior magistrate if the first two magistrates could not agree. The assumption was that the sum agreed on should represent the financial loss to the apprentice holder by estimating the amount the apprentice could have earned for the apprentice holder if hired out for the remaining period of apprenticeship, and deducting one third for "contingencies": clothing, medical expenses, and so on. However, this formula was not specified in the law.

102. Joseph and Abraham Isaacs both gave evidence at the inquiry; part of Joseph's testimony is included in this volume.

103. In this period Jamaica and the other British Caribbean colonies used Spanish coins for most transactions. A bitt was a Spanish silver real; a dollar was a Spanish peso, equal to 8 reales or bitts; a doubloon was a Spanish gold coin. These coins also had equivalents to values in "Jamaican currency" reckoned in pounds, shillings, and pence, although there were no actual Jamaican coins. Jamaican currency was valued at less than sterling: £1.4 currency equaled £1 sterling; thus Williams's valuation of £46 4s 7d currency was equal to £33 0s 5d sterling. The editors were right in asserting that Williams's valuation was high. Valuation lists for the period August 1834 to June 1835 indicate that the median value placed on a nonpraedial apprentice then was £35 currency, at a time when there was still between three and four years of apprenticeship to run for nonpraedials calculated from enclosure 1 in Sligo to Glenelg, 22 June 1835 No. 149, British Parliamentary Papers 1836 (166) XLVIII, pp. 20–27.

104. This advertisement appears only in the Haddon first edition.

105. Fourteen issues of *Slavery in America* appeared between July 1836 and August 1837. They were collected in a volume entitled *Slavery in America, with Notices of the Present State of Slavery and the Slave Trade Throughout the World,* conducted by the Rev. Thomas Price, D.D. (London: G. Wightman, 1837), with a foreword stating that the publication was suspended due to "the necessity of directing our energies in future to the condition of the professedly emancipated slaves of our own colonies." Wightman was also the publisher of the Central Emancipation Committee's edition of the *Narrative.*

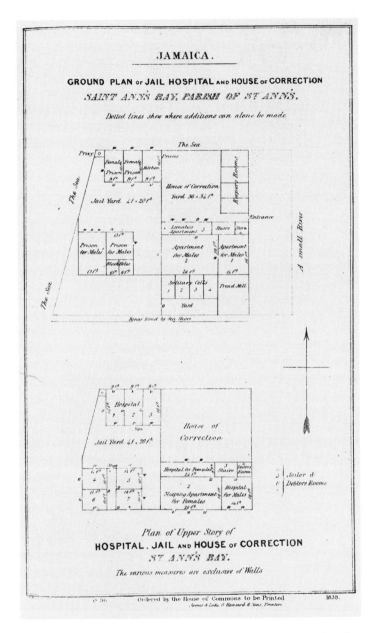

Plan of the St. Ann's Bay Jail and House of Correction, 1838. This plan of the workhouse in which James Williams and other apprentices were held was produced in response to British inquiries into the state of Jamaican prisons. Apprentices were held in the House of Correction, on the right-hand side of the building, rather than in the jail, on the left. Courtesy of the Public Record Office, CO 318/136.

(above) Portrait of Joseph Sturge. Courtesy of the National Library of Jamaica.

(right) Portrait of John Clark, Baptist missionary at Browns Town, St. Ann. Courtesy of the National Library of Jamaica.

NARRATIVE

OF THE

CRUEL TREATMENT

OF

JAMES WILLIAMS,

A NEGRO APPRENTICE IN JAMAICA,

FROM 1ST AUGUST, 1834, TILL THE PURCHASE OF HIS FREEDOM IN 1837, BY JOSEPH STURGE, ESQ., OF BIRMINGHAM, BY WHOM HE WAS BROUGHT TO ENGLAND.

GLASGOW:

PRINTED BY AIRD & RUSSELL, 75, ARGYLL STREET;
AND SOLD BY G. GALLIE, BUCHANAN STREET;
J. M'LEOD, ARGYLL STREET; D. ROBERTSON, TRONGATE;
AND WILLIAM SMEAL, GALLOWGATE.

MDCCCXXXVII.

[1837]

Title page of 1837 Glasgow edition of the *Narrative*.

A REPORT

OF

EVIDENCE TAKEN AT BROWN'S-TOWN

AND

ST. ANN'S BAY,

In the Parish of St. Ann's,

UNDER

A COMMISSION

FROM HIS EXCELLENCY SIR LIONEL SMITH,

GOVERNOR OF JAMAICA,

DIRECTED TO GEORGE GORDON, ESQUIRE, JUSTICE OF THE
PEACE FOR THE PARISH OF ST. JAMES,

AND

JOHN DAUGHTREY, ESQUIRE, SPECIAL MAGISTRATE,
ST. ELIZABETH.

———

TO WHICH IS PREFIXED,

A NARRATIVE OF EVENTS

SINCE THE 1st of AUGUST, 1834.

———o———

BY JAMES WILLIAMS,

Late an Apprenticed Labourer to G. W. SENIOR, Esquire.

———o———

Jamaica :

PRINTED AND PUBLISHED BY JOHN CASTELLO, PROPRIETOR OF
"THE FALMOUTH POST," TRELAWNY.

1837.

Title page of "Report of Evidence," 1837.

A

NARRATIVE OF EVENTS

SINCE THE 1ST OF AUGUST, 1834.

BY JAMES WILLIAMS,

TOGETHER WITH THE

EVIDENCE TAKEN UNDER A COMMISSION

APPOINTED BY

THE COLONIAL OFFICE

TO ASCERTAIN THE

TRUTH OF THE NARRATIVE;

AND THE

REPORT OF THE COMMISSIONERS THEREON:

THE WHOLE

EXHIBITING A CORRECT PICTURE OF A LARGE PROPORTION OF WEST INDIAN
SOCIETY; AND THE ATROCIOUS CRUELTIES PERPETRATED UNDER THE
APPRENTICESHIP SYSTEM.

LONDON:

PRINTED FOR THE CENTRAL EMANCIPATION COMMITTEE,

TOKEN-HOUSE YARD.

SOLD BY G. WIGHTMAN, 24, PATERNOSTER ROW.

Price Six Pence.

1838.

Title page of 1838 London edition of the *Narrative*.

AN INTERIOR VIEW OF A JAMAICA HOUSE OF CORRECTION.

THE WHIPPING OF FEMALES *you were informed by sad effiracly,* WAS IN PRACTICE, and I called upon you to make enactments to put an end to *conduct so repugnant to humanity, and so* CONTRARY TO LAW. So far from passing an Act to prevent the recurrence of such cruelty, *we have already over expressed your disapprobation of it.* I communicated to you my opinion, and that of the Secretary of State, of

"An Interior View of a Jamaican House of Correction." This engraving was produced by Sturge's allies at around the same time as the publication of James Williams's *Narrative.* In one edition of the *Narrative* it was included as a frontispiece. It depicts many of the criticisms made of the workhouse in the *Narrative* and elsewhere, including the flogging of women on the treadmill, the exposure of women's bodies while on the treadmill, the cutting of women's hair, and injuries to prisoners. The text at the bottom is from a message from Jamaican Governor Lionel Smith to the Jamaican House of Assembly. Courtesy of the National Library of Jamaica.

A REPORT OF EVIDENCE
TAKEN AT BROWN'S-TOWN
AND ST. ANN'S BAY IN THE PARISH
OF ST. ANN'S, UNDER A COMMISSION
FROM HIS EXCELLENCY SIR LIONEL
SMITH, GOVERNOR OF JAMAICA,

Directed to George Gordon, Esquire, Justice of the Peace
for the Parish of St. James, and John Daughtrey,
Esquire, Special Magistrate,
St. Elizabeth.

———

MINUTES OF PROCEEDINGS
AT BROWN'S-TOWN, ST. ANN'S

The Commissioners commenced their sittings at this place by directing that the Commission from which their authority is derived, and the
Letter of Instructions which accompanied it, should be read in open
Court; they, at the same time, announced that their proceedings would
be public.[1]

Copy of the Commission
JAMAICA, *SS.*

VICTORIA, by the grace of God, of the United Kingdom of Great
Britain and Ireland Queen, and of Jamaica Supreme Lady, Defender
of the Faith, &c. &c. &c.

To our Trusty and well-beloved subjects, JOHN DAUGHTREY, and
GEORGE GORDON, Esqrs., Greeting:[2]

WHEREAS we have thought it expedient, for divers good causes and
considerations We thereunto moving, that an Enquiry should forth-
with be made into the Administration of Justice under the Provision
of the Law for the Abolition of Slavery, and for promoting the Industry of the manumitted Slaves in this our Island,[3] but particularly
with respect to the administration of the said Law, in the Parish of St.
Ann's, touching the nature and truth of the Allegations contained in
the Pamphlet of James Williams, late an apprentice of G. W. SENIOR,
Esquire, with the Narrative of Events contained in the same Pamphlet,
as having taken place in the said Parish of Saint Ann's:

KNOW YE, That we, reposing great trust and confidence in your
fidelity, discretion, and integrity, have authorized and appointed, and
do and by these Presents authorize and appoint you, the said JOHN
DAUGHTREY and GEORGE GORDON, to make a diligent enquiry,

whether any and what part of the said Law have not been faithfully administered by the Justices who then held, and who now are holding Special Commissions in the said Parish, and to ascertain the truth of the Allegations contained in the said Pamphlet of James Williams, and for the better discovery of the truth in the premises, We do, by these presents give and grant to you, as Special Justice of the Peace, in and over the Island of Jamaica, and as a Local Magistrate, according to the authority of your Commissions respectively, full power and authority to call before you, or any one of you, all persons being apprenticed labourers or free persons as you may judge necessary, by whom you may be better informed of the truth in the premises, and to enquire of the premises and every part thereof, by oath, and all other lawful ways and means whatsoever, and you will certify to us your proceedings, when the same have been completed and perfected.

Witness his Excellency Sir Lionel Smith, Knight Commander of the Most Honourable Military Order of the Bath, Knight Grand Cross of the Royal Hanoverian Guelphic Order, a Lieutenant-General in Her Majesty's Land Forces, and Colonel of the 40th Regiment of Foot, Captain-General, Governor-in-Chief and Commander of the Forces in and over the Island of Jamaica and the Territories thereon depending in America, Chancellor, Ordinary, and Vice-Admiral of the same, at St. Jago de la Vega, the eighth day of September, and in the first year of the Reign of Our Most Gracious Sovereign Queen Victoria, Aunoque Domini 1837.

By His Excellency's Command,
(Signed) Lionel Smith[4]

Copy of the Letter of Instructions

The King's-House, Spanish-Town
9th September, 1837.

Gentlemen,

As you have kindly consented to be associated as joint Commissioners to investigate and report on certain abuses in the Administration of Justice towards the Apprenticed Labourers, represented in a Pamphlet stated to be "A Narrative of Events, since the 1st August, 1834, by James Williams, an Apprenticed Labourer in Jamaica," I now do myself the honor to enclose you a Copy of the Secretary of State's Despatch, calling for enquiry, together with the Pamphlet itself.

I have to request that, at your earliest convenience, you will proceed to the different places in which the abuses complained of are said
to have occurred, and there, by Depositions of Parties cognizant of
the different transactions, you will probably be able to substantiate or
refute the various allegations against either the public authorities or
accused individuals.

I need not impress upon two Gentlemen, distinguished in society
by upright principles, that it is no less due to the cause of Justice, than
to the credit of the Colony at large, that you should carefully search
for, and faithfully declare the whole Truth, and nothing but the Truth,
and it is a source of great pleasure to me to reflect that your honourable
characters will guarantee this object to the satisfaction of Her Majesty's
Government as well as to the people of Jamaica.

In examining into the different allegations stated in the Pamphlet,
you will probably find it convenient to number each case in the order in
which they occur and may require to be inquired into, and to aid your
enquiry, as regards the accusations against Mr. Special Justice Rawlinson, I transmit Copies of his Diary and the Entries of his notice of
"James Williams's" offences.[5]

I have the honor to be, Gentlemen,
Your most obedt. humble Servant,
(Signed) Lionel Smith
John Daughtrey, Esq., Special Justice
and
George Gordon, Esq., Genl. Magistrate
. . . .

THURSDAY, SEPTEMBER 21

EDWARD LAWRENCE, an apprentice to Penshurst, sworn. . . . Henry
James's flogging was very severe; his stomach was bruised by the cart
wheel to which he was tied to receive his punishment, and his back was
more cut up than that of James Williams; Henry James was old and
weakly; he had been a watchman, but was working in the field in the
great gang at the time he received the flogging; I never heard him complain of his stomach before he got the flogging: Henry James went to
the hospital after he was flogged, and complained that he could not
get any medicine: he then went to Captain Andrew Dillon at Brown's

town; I saw him on his way, and he had with him a small calabash con-taining what he said he had brought off his stomach; I looked at it and saw it all bloody. I saw his dead body on the place where he fell; some blood was oozing from the mouth; the calabash was empty, and the contents appeared to be spilt out on the ground where he dropped. . . . . . .

MARY ANN BELL, a mulatto,[6] non-praedial apprentice to Penshurst, sworn. I remember being sent to the workhouse and tread-mill by Mr. Rawlinson when I was quite heavy in the family way, nearly half of my time being gone; I was tried on the 26th August, and I gave birth to my child in the third week of January: Two or three weeks after I returned home I felt pains in my wrist; the pains were on that part which had been strapped to the Treadmill; I also felt pains in my knees; I do not feel the pains now at all times, I only feel them now and then; I have the perfect use of both my arms and hands, with the exception of the little finger on the left hand, which I cannot straighten owing to the effects of a sore, which was caused by the hoe at the time that I was in the penal gang and digging cane holes. The pains in my arms and knees left me soon after the birth of my present child: I was able to keep the step on the treadmill except once, when I hung for a short time by the strap; Mr. Drake then stopped the Mill and took me down; I never knocked my shins against the wheel so as to cause a sore; Mr. Drake knew me at Penshurst, and I believe he was more kind to me on that account; I only saw one woman (from Ballintey) flogged whilst on the Mill, because she could not keep the step; she was whipped about the legs and shoul-ders, and wherever they could strike her. I was never punished again after my return from the workhouse, but one day when I was in the kitchen and unable to go to my usual duty from the pains already de-scribed, Mr. Rawlinson was at the house, and the house people having been called up, I heard Miss Senior complain to Mr. Rawlinson about my not doing any work, when he said that if she would bring a charge against me, that he would send me back to the house of correction; this circumstance I believe took place about a month after I returned from the workhouse: mistress did not wish me to be sent back there, or Mr. Rawlinson would have done it. Before Mr. Rawlinson began to visit Penshurst, my mistress gave the house people Friday and Saturday one week, and Sunday the next; but Mr. Rawlinson told her that they were not entitled to half a day in each week, and advised her not to give it to them any more;[7] my mistress, however, has continued to give them more time than that, but not so much as they received before. I know that Henry James sent to Miss Senior for medicine when he was sick in the hot-house, and that she always gave it when he sent.

Mr. JOHN PATTERSON, a carpenter, and residing at Ridge settlement, in the parish of Saint Ann, sworn. . . . I lived at Penshurst up to November, 1836, and had the management of Mr. Senior's tradesmen: I knew Henry James as a sawyer in 1820, or 21, but of late he was a watchman; he was put to watch from inability to do other work; he used to complain of his stomach, and was a very old man, about sixty years of age. When I first knew him he was a true African. I mean by that, that he was a very good negroe, not like a Creole; he was always willing to do his work; . . . I knew James Williams; when I first knew him, in 1820, he was then a little boy, and would often come and play with me; but when I returned to Penshurst, in 1835, he was a wicked worthless boy, and was very impudent to his master and mistress; he was also a great thief, stealing every thing that he could lay his hands upon, indeed he was so bad, that at last I would not have him near me; he would not mind his master's cattle, and Mr. Rawlinson used to talk to him by way of intimidating him; I am not aware that he was flogged seven times; he did not work under my management, but I often saw him, and considered him a very unfaithful servant. I never preferred any charge against him for theft, although he used to rob my cupboard. He never stole any valuables from me, all that he took was something to eat and drink. He was always coming about me, and, whenever I came in on horseback, he would run to hold my horse and take my saddle and do any little thing for me; I only wonder he did not put me in the paper too. I believe that his motive in serving me this way was to get something for himself in return for his services, or to get opportunities to pilfer my cupboard. When James Williams was a child he was under my care, and used to call me father or daddy. . . . He always had plenty to eat, and did not steal from the want of food; he thought he could take the liberty with me, as he used to call me daddy, and therefore imagined that he could daddy me out of any thing. . . .

WILLIAM DALLING, constable on Penshurst, sworn. . . . Mr. Senior . . . and the Magistrate (Dr. Thompson) then came up and ordered the police to flog Adam Brown and Henry James. These two were very severely flogged. Henry James was very much cut up, and the next morning he went to the hospital. I saw him there the morning after he was flogged, when he complained of a great pain in his stomach, in consequence of having been lashed to the wheel like the rest. While they were flogging him he struggled a great deal. He was a short man, and when he stopped at each lick, the pit of his stomach came against the nave of the wheel. There was no doctor woman in the hot house.[8] Henry James remained there, and never left it till he went to Brown's-Town to complain to Captain Dillon; he died at Brown's-Town the same day that he went up. . . . He used to cough very badly in the hospital and spit blood; and the floor on which he used to spit always looked as if a pig had been stuck there.[9] He fell lower and lower, and, when he found himself getting very bad, he determined to go to Brown's-Town to the Magistrate. I saw the body after he died. I was at Brown's-Town, and saw it on my return home. It was on the road-side, and to prevent its being eaten by the hogs, I watched it from 6 o'clock in the evening until the next morning. I observed a great deal of blood all about the nostrils and the mouth, but I did not see any on the earth. I saw, close to the body, a little cocoa-nut cup with blood in it, which Henry James brought with him to shew Captain A. Dillon. Henry James was always a very weak and sickly man, but he did not cough and spit blood until after he received the flogging: he went to Brown's-Town to the magistrate, because he did not receive any attention in the hospital, and he wanted the magistrate to require my master and mistress, to give it. . . .

Sometime after the first flogging which James Williams received at Brown's-Town, Mr. Rawlinson came to Penshurst and slept there. On the next morning a complaint was made against James Williams, and Mr. Rawlinson ordered him to get twenty lashes. He could not receive it, as his back was not well, and my mistress, Miss Senior, ordered me to flog him with lancewood switches. The scabs were on the old wounds. They were not well yet, and, after I found they were so bad, I struck him lower down. He was not able to beg off, for as soon as the Magistrate gave his sentence, Williams was ordered off to receive it. When I first began to flog him with the switches, the scabs on the old wounds broke off, and the back began to bleed. It was then that I flogged him lower. I laid the flogging on lightly, as lightly as I could, and myself and some of the other apprentices bathed his back and rubbed it with grease. He went to work immediately to cut grass. Nothing stopped him from going—he did not seem to mind the flogging much, he was a very brave boy. . . .

I remember the Friday when the negroes were ordered to sit down and take breakfast, instead of working throughout the four and a half hours. I did not get any orders on the subject before that day, and when I went to tell them to take the usual breakfast time I saw the people in great confusion. When massa found that they would not obey his orders to take the breakfast time, he desired me to go and fetch up Joseph Lawrence, the other constable, and lock him up. Massa also ordered me to take up Thomas Brown, William Mills, and Benjamin Higgins. They were all put in confinement. Joseph Lawrence said that he could not help it, that the people would not obey. Master said that he would be obeyed. When I was going to the dungeon with Joseph Lawrence and the other people, I saw that master had secured James Williams and put him in the dungeon. Master ordered him to go in, and he went. I don't mean to say that Master put his hands on him. I did not hear James Williams make use of any expression as he was going in, but just as I locked the door, master told me that Williams had said, "God made the World, it wasn't man that made it, and man can't rule it." . . .

[Amelia Lawrence was sent to the workhouse with Joseph Lawrence and James Williams.] Amelia Lawrence is a married woman; she is the wife of Richard Lawrence. When she came back from the workhouse, she told me that the driver, James Thomas, was always persuading her to be unfaithful to her husband; that he used every means to deprive her of her virtue, and when he found, every evening, that he could not succeed, the next day he was sure to treat her ill at her work. She did not say that James Thomas had used any force, but told me that he kept following her every day until she was discharged, and the way he used her ill was by putting her to do two persons work, and giving her heavy weights to lift up. She said that her feelings were so much hurt at the way she was pursued by Thomas, that she was more than glad when she was discharged from the workhouse. She has four children; they are all by Richard Lawrence her husband. She further mentioned, that the same attempts made by Thomas to make her do wrong, were made on other women who were in the workhouse, and that with some of them he succeeded. . . .

I remember his [James Williams] being charged, on one occasion, with stealing pork out of a barrel in the cellar. James Williams and John Lawrence, at that time, always slept in the kitchen. Lawrence got a fork, which he tied with a piece of string to a stick, and lanced the meat in the barrel, which he drew near to the window. When I discovered that John Lawrence was concerned in the theft, Williams got ashamed of his share in it and ran away; he was absent for two days; I went after him and found him at Miss Smith's, at Runaway-Bay. On his way home he confessed to me that he had a share in eating the pork, but that he had no hand in stealing it. He was brought here to be tried by Mr. Rawlinson, when he said he should pay for it. He said he would pay 10s. The Magistrate then consented that he should pay 10s. as a settlement of the affair.[10] If James Williams had been encouraged he would have been a very good servant. I miss him now a great deal: he was trying to make a good ground, but he did not have his regular time, and his father, who is a watchman, also assisted him. I do not know that he was a bad thief; nor was he an upstart. He was always laughing and making fun, and I used to reprove him for it. I don't think he could, with justice, be called a dishonest man; he had never been brought before a Special Magistrate for theft, except in that one instance about the pork. He was never proved to have stolen any thing.

THE COURT. William Dalling, you have given your evidence in so correct and highly creditable a manner, that we cannot dismiss you without expressing ourselves extremely pleased with your conduct.

DALLING. Thank you, Gentlemen!

Mr. DAUGHTREY. You appear to have benefited much by the instruction of your Minister, the Rev. Mr. Clarke, and his predecessors (of the Baptist Mission). Observing many persons present, I cannot resist the inclination I feel to avow my perfect conviction that the labours of Ministers, Missionaries, not of the Established Church, have been of incalculable value to the Colony. In the district in which I have chiefly resided their efforts have always come in aid of the proceedings of the magistrate. Crime has been repressed and industry promoted by the influence they have exerted. For myself, indeed, I hesitate not to declare that, but for such auxiliaries, my own duties might have become so irksome and oppressive, that I should very likely have abandoned them.

Mr. SENIOR. Indeed, Sir! Then you have been a great deal more fortunate than we have been!

. . .

ADAM BROWN, apprentice to Penshurst, sworn.[11] . . . I was taken
to Knapdale dungeon and locked up with James Williams; it was very
damp, the ground was not floored; I could lay down at full length and
stand upright; the dungeon was very dark; there were no holes at the
top nor at the sides; there were small holes in the door which gave a little
air, but Mr. Patterson, the carpenter, came and peeped in, and when he
did that he stopped the holes. All the food that we got in the dungeon
was two plantains each, and sometimes three, with a pint of water for
a whole day's allowance. The last day that we were in the dungeon we
were pretty well fed; they gave us a good allowance of plantains and
cocoas. Our food was brought every day by William Atkinson,[12] the
head constable on Penshurst; since then he has bought himself free.
We were never let out of the dungeon for the necessities of nature; nor
did any body ever clean the dungeon out during the ten days; the filth
was allowed to remain in it the whole time in a bucket which was placed
for our use. I was very weak when I came out, but I went home the
same day, although I could scarcely walk; when I reached Penshurst,
before I could speak master cried out, *"You are not punished half enough
yet."* . . .

WILLIAM DALLING recalled. . . . I remember when Nanny Dalling
was locked up in the dungeon with her young child. Mr. Rawlinson
got into such a passion with her, that he would not allow her to say a
word. He was very violent; he laid his hands on Nanny Dalling, and
shoved her in the dungeon. She is my daughter. Mr. Rawlinson rode
away and returned some time after the same day; I did not go to hear
what orders he gave about her, as I was very much hurted. . . .

PETER WILLIAM ATKINSON, formerly an apprentice on Penshurst,
sworn.[13] I was at one time an apprentice to Mr. Senior, but I am now
a freeman. I purchased my freedom in February 1836. . . . I know the
cell at Penshurst, a short person like me could stand up in it, but a tall
man could not. One day Mr. Utten[14] went in to see it he was obliged
to stoop: he said to master, "this is very difficult." Master said, "it is
good enough to put them devils in." The dungeon at Knapdale is high
enough to stand up in, it is very damp however and swampy, and not
fit for a person to lay his body on; whenever there is rain, all the water
runs into the dungeon and any persons confined in it must lay down
in the wet unless a board is placed there for them; neither air nor light

can get in. James Williams and Adam Brown had two small tubs in the dungeon for the uses of nature which were never emptied until the last day that they came out; I used to let them out sometimes in the morning when I carried them their food; sometimes they would go out; at others they would not; I am certain that the tubs were never emptied until the last day. I know Mary Ann Bell; I can't exactly say who is the Father of her children; Mr. Drake the Supervisor of the House of Correction often visited Penshurst, but I don't know whether he had any improper intimacy with Mary Ann Bell. . . .

I remember that James Williams had to pay up a great number of days, by order of the Special Magistrate; I can't say how many, but it took him a long time to pay them; in consequence of that his ground was neglected; the stock used to get in and he became so short of provisions that I and others through charity were obliged to assist him with something to eat.

I was valued twelve months before I got the money to pay for my freedom; I was badly used and cheated of my time; I made a complaint to Mr. Rawlinson both for myself and the other people; . . . When Mr. Rawlinson went away Miss Senior came out and said "So Mr. Peter you went to complain about your time to the Magistrate, you ought to be well punished for it." Mr. Senior then came out of his room and said "I'll make you see the very devil before you get that freedom." He said this to all of us who were working before the house; he then began upon me; I was employed in sawing at the time; all that I could do would not please master; he came to me one day when I was at the sawing pit, and found great fault at my not having finished the piece of wood which I was sawing; it was a very hard piece of bullet-tree; he said "I'll see whether Mr. Rawlinson won't make you saw any more"; my general work was to saw fifty feet of Bullet-tree or ninety feet of Cedar per day. Master went away after saying what he did about Mr. Rawlinson; this happened on a Friday; on the Monday morning following it rained very heavily and I had to saw a stick in the yard where the pit was. George Henry Warren[15] and myself had to do it, the pit had a great deal of water in it, and the water reached as high as my breast . . . Mr. Patterson, the carpenter at that time was working near the gate with a brown man named William Grant;[16] Mr. Patterson brought William Grant to the pit and said, "William take over these two fellows to the Magistrate["]: I then came out of the pit, and said to myself, "it is hard for me to get a flogging when I am doing my work." I then run right off to endeavour and avoid it, Warren went away too. The police were sent after us but not being able to catch us they turned back; the place where we hid ourselves was a thicket so much covered with bush that nobody could see us, although we could see every thing that was going on in the great-house and negro-houses. I saw master and Mr. Patterson, the carpenter, go to the negro houses each of them with a stick in his hand; Mr. Rawlinson remained in the house; he was in the house but I did not see him; the first house they went to was George Henry Warren's; Mr. Patterson kicked at the door, but as it was very strongly secured it did not give way. . . .

My master took up a block and dashed the door open. After opening the door he went in as if to search for something: after that they went into my house the door of which they had kicked open, they turned my bed upside down as if they were searching, and then they came out and went away. I then went into my house, took up a bundle of clothes, and returned to the place where I was hiding. Mr. Patterson, the carpenter, returned soon after and began to sing—

"This is the house that these fellows preach in.
Hallelujah! Hallelujah! Hallelujah!"

He could not see me but I could see him and all that he did: I was accustomed to have family prayers in my house at night; While Mr. Patterson was in my house the people from the great-house came and took out all my chairs, tables, and benches and stools; they took out sixteen pieces altogether and carried them to the great-house yard. Mr. Rawlinson was in the great-house all the time; any body there must have seen the things when they were carried up to the yard; I thought to myself "if the Magistrate who is sent to protect the apprentices allows all this to be done, and sees that it is done, I must go to the Governor as I have no person else to go to and make my complaint." My furniture was lodged in a room where master keeps his saddles and corn in the great-house yard: Warren and myself went to the King's house and we saw Lord Sligo the Governor; we made our complaint to him and he told Mr. Ramsay to take down all that we said: after that he sent us by the police to Mr. Rawlinson at Brown's-Town, with a letter; when we got there Mr. Rawlinson read the letter and said "so you have been to the Governor with a heap of lies about your master, but you did not tell the Governor that you keep a Methodist Chapel."[17] Mr. Rawlinson then gave us a letter to master and sent us back to Penshurst; When I got to Penshurst I found that my house had been pulled down; on enquiry I was told that it had been cut down by four apprentices named Thomas Brown, William Mills, Joseph Lawrence, and Richard Lawrence, who were ordered to do so; I was also told that master was present at the time, and with a long stick assisted in breaking off the shingles. This information was given to me by the very people who were ordered by master to pull the house down; some time after Mr. Rawlinson came to the property and read to us a part of the Governor's letter;[18] he then desired us to go to work and saw fifty feet of wood per day: he desired Warren and myself to pay back six Saturdays for the time we had been absent from the property; from that time I was worked though all weather and at all times: by way of punishment we were given breadnut logs to cut through in their green state, even without stripping off the bark, so that it was impossible for us to get through our task; we were obliged to work even during our dinner time to endeavour to do so. At last, on the seventh Saturday, finding that I could stand it no longer, I then got the money and brought it to Mr. Rawlinson to purchase the remaining term of my apprenticeship. While we were working at the pit one day master came to us and said "you are not punished half enough by the Magistrate: I should like to get you in the Workhouse for six months as I am able enough to hire a pair of sawyers in your room"; he added "there is one good thing! the Governor did not hear your complaint."

My furniture was not returned until after I purchased my freedom, nor was any house given me to live in, in lieu of that which had been pulled down; I therefore was obliged to go to Knapdale to sleep at my wife's house; previously to mine being pulled down she used to come there occasionally and I would go to hers. After my house was pulled down, Thomas Brown Lawrence was desired by my master to dig up every one of my plantain suckers: he did so and they were planted in master's own ground.

I borrowed nearly the whole of my money to pay for my freedom;[19] when I was first valued I was valued for eleven doubloons, but when I got the money after a year and two months had passed I was valued for twelve doubloons;[20] I am still working to pay off the debt of my valuation; a few months after I bought myself I happened to meet Mr. Rawlinson at Beverley and applied to him about my things; a few days afterwards they were put out on the barbacue[21] and my friends took them and brought them to me. They did it of their own good will! All this has been done to me.

I consider that the treatment we all received from my master proceeded from his wish to do us all the injury he could; from the time that the 1st of August came he said he would do every thing to annoy us: he not only said this but he did it; he said that he would have a law of his own and that those English devils (the Magistrates) and those Baptist fellows should not do as they liked on his property; as to that boy James Williams, poor fellow! he was a boy with a good heart!

WILLIAM MILLS, an apprentice to Penshurst, sworn. I was one of the persons who master ordered to cut down Atkinson's house; there were four of us, we commenced knocking down the walls; those posts which we couldn't pull down, we were desired by master to cut away with our axes; master knock'd down a part of the Spanish wall,[22] with a long stick which he had in his hand; he said "I will have this house down and you must go somewhere else to preach; I won't have it for a prayer house." It was Atkinson's house and he used to live there; he kept every thing in it that he was worth; there were several tables and chairs in it which master made us take out and put into a room in the great house yard; the house was pulled down on the same day that Atkinson went away; he had a noble garden with plenty of plantain suckers in it; I don't know that they were dug up but master gave the garden to a girl named Mary Ann Bell and I afterwards saw the cows and hogs in it. We all of us, used to meet sometimes in Atkinson's house to join in prayer: I did not think it right in master to have the house destroyed, but as he gave orders we were obliged to obey. . . .

I knew James Williams, and remember his having had to pay a great number of days; it took him a great time to pay them back, and therefore he could not attend his grounds; the hogs would be one side and the cattle on the other eating it down. Sometimes he was poverty itself and would have starved if he had not got help from his brother apprentices. I hear that he was accused of stealing yams; it was not proved against him: it was at the time that he had to pay back so many days; he was very badly off for victuals. . . .

When master took Atkinson and Warren from the saw pit I was put to work there, but as I was a new hand I did not work well and master used me very badly for it: it was the first time I ever held a saw;

I was never given any regular task but I did all I could to give satisfaction. I was not sawing more than a week when master put me in the dungeon for not doing good work; he always threatened to bring me before Mr. Rawlinson: I was put to saw breadnut heart, which is the hardest of woods, with another young hand like myself; how then could I be expected to do well? . . .[23]

JOSEPH LAWRENCE, an apprentice to Penshurst, sworn. I was one of the people who was sent to pull down Atkinson's house. . . . I didn't hear him give any reasons for pulling down the house further than saying that the negroes were "playing the devil" by making it a meeting house; his words were, "it is here you all meet and play the devil in the negro houses; you shan't meet here again." . . .

We were used badly enough in the workhouse. Five persons used to be put on the Treadmill at a time and sometimes more than that. The first day I went on, the mill bruised my knee a great deal; the blood ran all down from my shins. When the people could not keep the step the driver flogged them, he did not flog me because I soon caught it. The women were flogged as well as the men; they were flogged on their legs, and some of them were flogged very badly; I have seen women hanging on the mill by their hands as they could not keep up; they were greatly bruised: I have seen many women on the mill who had young sucking children: the children were left in the yard when they were taken to dance the mill. The women were also put on the mill morning and evening and sometimes their pain would be so great that they would bawl loud enough to be heard a great way off. . . .

I remember that Amelia Lawrence complained to me of James Thomas, one of the drivers, for wanting her to consent to his improper wishes; my sister was persecuted a great deal by this man, and felt much hurt about it, as she was a married woman. The young women whom the drivers took a fancy to were put by them to light work. . . .

AMELIA LAWRENCE, an apprentice to Penshurst, sworn. I was tried once by Mr. Rawlinson in consequence of Master's disputing with me about work; Mr. Rawlinson sent me to the Workhouse, but did not mention to me how many days I was to be in the Workhouse; when I came back master told me that Mr. Rawlinson said I was to pay back ten days as an additional punishment. The next time that I was punished, I was sent to the dungeon at Penshurst, in consequence of a dispute about my working at the first row. The next morning I was brought up before Mr. Rawlinson and I begged him not to punish me. Master's complaint was that I worked at the first row, and that I took upon myself to do so because my brother was a driver; I was sent to the Workhouse for this. I am a married woman with a family of four children; I was put on the tread-mill morning and evening; there can be no harder work than tread-mill punishment; the mill bruised my legs and gave me great pain, but the greatest pain I felt was between my shoulders; I have never recovered up to the present moment from the punishment of the Treadmill; I have pains all over my body since then which I can't get over, particularly swelled even now. Some of the people used to feel very faint upon the mill, and when they could not keep up the boatswain would not take them off, but would whopp them well to make them go on. One day a man by the name of Jenkins[24] who was an under busha hit me a whopp, after I came off the mill and made use of very bad expressions to me; the expressions were so bad that I can't make use of them now. Jenkins had a spite against me, because I would not consent for him to have an improper connection with a girl named Catherine Bayley[25] who was in the Workhouse; I was obliged to say that Catherine Bayley was my daughter in order to protect her from Jenkins; James Thomas, one of the boatswains wanted me to consent to do what was wrong with him; he kept on following me for this purpose all the time I was in the workhouse; I couldn't get any rest for him. I saw a woman go one night to one of the drivers but I could not distinguish which of the drivers it was who called her. . . . The drivers always came before day to count them [the prisoners], and it was at that time they would endeavour to gain over the women for improper purposes; they frequently put questions of this sort to me, but I never consented; I know one woman however who was bad enough to do so. I never saw any Doctor come to the hothouse; to tell the truth if the people wanted medicine it was the boatswain who gave it. James Thomas was the driver who used to follow me and ask me to give myself up to him; I used to fret much and told James Williams about it; he said "never mind; they can't do you any thing." Mr. Drake often used to say, "You, Penshurst and Chester people[26] are always neglecting your master's business and minding preaching and I'll make you sick of coming here; I'll beat the methodist out of you."[27] Him and master were great friends; he used to visit master very frequently. When James Thomas found that I would not consent to his wishes he

used to treat me very badly; one day Mr. Drake gave Catherine Bayley a good beating saying she was Miss Senior's waiting maid and must
have been impudent to her or she would not have sent her to the Workhouse; the people were all shackled at night; when Catherine Bayley
and I were in the first time, we used to sleep in shackles and with big
chains about our neck every night; the last time I was in, they were not
so particular. The life people were fed with flour every day and the rest
were fed with corn; one shad was given between two persons. When
I came out of the Workhouse, some time after about Christmas I was
going to the hothouse, but was obliged to lay down on the ground
from exhaustion. Master passed and when he saw me, he laughed and
calling out to some of the apprentices said quite gladly "you see what
she is come to." He appeared quite glad at the way I was reduced and
made use of the most indecent expressions and oaths towards me; one
would not think that a gentleman could make use of such words. . . .

The negroes of Penshurst have no half Fridays now, and when we
complained about it to Mr. Rawlinson, he told us that the Governor
himself could not compel our master to give us the half Fridays.[28]

This witness after finishing her testimony informed the Court that her
master Mr. Senior is now in the constant habit of flogging her daughter, and that he does so every day without any cause whatever.

SATURDAY, SEPTEMBER 23

Mr. SENIOR appeared, and having been informed that Peter Atkinson
had charged him with pulling down his house, admitted having pulled
down a house *which had been considered as the house* of Atkinson, which he
afterwards claimed, as it was a nuisance. Mr. Senior said that he did
not consider the house as the dwelling place of Atkinson, as he did not
sleep in it, but went at night to his wife at Knapdale; Mr. Senior claimed
the right of pulling down the house as a nuisance, as it had been made
an improper use of; he admitted having done so during the tempo-
rary absence of Peter Atkinson. Mr. Senior then mentioned that Peter
Atkinson used to make excuses for turning out late, in consequence
of sleeping at Knapdale, alleging that he had no house at Penshurst:
this was previous to the destruction of the house; Mr. Senior said, that
there was a small bed-room attached to the house, which was not taken

down, and that Atkinson had no other house on the property than the one which was destroyed; he considered it a nuisance, in consequence of the great noise made there at nights by the strange people[29] who congregated there, for purposes which he does not know; he considered their meetings unlawful, and wished to prevent them;[30] he did not know where the nuisance was previously to the day when he went to see if Atkinson had gone from the house; there was a bed there which he did not trouble, but he took out some chairs and benches, which were delivered up afterwards; there was only one bed in the room, which was not pulled down; the house appeared to be appropriated entirely as a sort of chapel; there were one or two packages with clothes, which were taken away, but were given up afterwards on being claimed.

ELIZA FINLAYSON, an apprentice to Penshurst, apparently between twelve and thirteen years of age, sworn. I am the daughter of Amelia Lawrence; I was born before she was married; I have been switched since the 1st August, 1834; no longer than Monday last, master flogged me with his chaise-whip; I have been fummed often, and put into the dungeon.[31] On Monday last, master came up and hit me a lick, and I run off; he then came back and hit me two licks with the chaise-whip over my head; I was digging dung in the yard with a boy named Richard Brown;[32] some of the dung was left, and master called me to dig it up: as soon as I went to the place, he took his chaise-whip and struck me. Master has flogged me often enough before this time, particularly one day when we were working in the grass-piece; he came that day with his chaise-whip and flogged me and a boy named Davy;[33] he flogged me on my back; he never made the constable fum me, but often said that he would make him do so; he flogged me this day because, he said, that we were standing up, and not doing any work. Master not only fums me sometimes, but he fums the other boys and girls. . . .

Mr. SENIOR, on question from the Court, said that he had at times put parties in the dungeon, but had always mentioned his having done so to the Special Magistrate on his visit to the property, although he had not preferred a subsequent complaint against them, and that the Special Magistrate had given his sanction to him to act in this manner.[34] Mr. Senior then asked the Court, as they mentioned that such a proceeding was illegal, What was to be done with the small gang when they committed faults; he wished to know whether he had not authority to switch them?

The Court—No, decidedly not; you have no legal right to do so.

Mr. Senior—Dr. Thompson, a Special Magistrate, told me that I had a right.

Ann Campbell, an old weakly woman, apparently about sixty years of age, sworn. I was driver to the little gang,[35] and master told me when they behaved wrong, I must switch them; I said no! I could not do it, as the Law would not give me right if I switched any body; I told him that if he wanted the children to be switched, he must carry them to them mammies and let them switch them. . . . One day, after the *Mulgrave* Law[36] came in, I was in the field, and I said to driver, that I wanted to go aside for a particular purpose, but when master heard it, he cried out, "There was no law for that." This was Friday; I was obliged to go aside, and master took and locked me up in the evening, and let me out on Saturday. Master told constable that he locked me upon that account. . . . Master threatened me after I came out of dungeon, to send me down to Brown's Town to the Magistrate. He then told me, "You are driver for the piccaninny gang, and if you won't fum them when they do wrong, you must work!" he then turned me out to work in the small gang, and I am now working there. . . .

Mr. Senior assured the Court, that there is very little truth in the statements made by Ann Campbell and the other apprentices from Penshurst: On being asked by the Court, whether he wished to ask any questions, or bring forward any witnesses to refute what had already been given in evidence, he replied in the negative, saying, at the same time, that it was unnecessary for him to do so, as it was his intention to bring a number of them before the Quarter Sessions, on indictments for perjury, more especially the man named William Dalling.[37] Mr. Senior also remarked, that there was no occasion for *his* further attendance, as it was his intention to go to Spanish Town, where he would communicate with his Excellency the Governor, and report to him all that he had seen and heard.

Susan White, an apprentice to Dunbarton estate, sworn. I recollect being sent to the workhouse some time ago; I was chained to Amelia Lawrence of Penshurst, and I was then in the family way; I was five months advanced, and had a mischance at seven months;[38] my pregnancy was plain to be seen by my size. . . . [O]ne day she [Amelia Lawrence] said to me, "Partner, look here: look upon this ring on my finger: I am a married woman, and the driver, James Thomas, is always putting bad questions to me." I felt for her and cried; I said to myself, "After Amelia is a married woman, and the driver puts such questions to her, what must I expect who am not a married woman." No question of the sort, however, was put to me at that time; but when I went in the second time, a man by the name of Thomas White,[39] who was a driver and boatswain, tried to do what James Thomas tried with Amelia Lawrence: I told him No, that I was a married woman, and to make him believe it, when my sister came to see me, I took a ring off of her finger and put it on. The next time he asked me, I shewed the ring as proof, and he did not trouble me again. . . .

MARIA HENDERSON, an apprentice to New Hope plantation, the property of Mr. WILLIAM CODNOR, sworn.[40] I have been in the St. Ann's Bay house of correction. No driver ever endeavoured to have any improper intimacy with me. I was sent to the workhouse for two weeks by Mr. Rawlinson. I was chained and worked with the other people in the field. . . . I was always locked up at night with the other women, and the drivers opened the door in the morning to let us out, but I never saw them endeavour to have improper intimacies with any of the women. I was never on the tread-mill.

Mr. RAWLINSON. I know that I sentenced you to be worked on the tread-mill.

MARIA HENDERSON, in continuation. The tread-mill was not yet finished; they were just completing it when I went in.

The COURT. We are glad that Mr. Hamilton Brown,[41] a magistrate of the parish is present, because we have been informed by Mr. Codnor, the owner of New Hope, that Maria Henderson had boasted that she had not been put on the tread-mill, in consequence of the very improper intimacy which existed between her and one of the drivers: It is necessary that such conduct should be checked by the magistrates of the parish.

Mr. BROWN admitted that he had heard of such reports, and Mr. RAWLINSON said, that the fact was quite notorious with regard to the witness Maria Henderson, and another woman, who is an apprentice on Bertram's Bowers. He was decidedly of opinion that Maria Henderson preferred being sent to the workhouse to any other punishment.
. . .

JANE SHAW PENNOCK, an apprentice to Penshurst, sworn.[42] The child in my arm is about five months old. Since its birth I have been

picking pimento in the great gang. I am obliged to break the branches myself, and therefore leave my child with the field nurse. . . . [One evening] about six o'clock; I was put into the dungeon, and kept there until six o'clock next morning without any thing whatever to eat. When I came out in the morning, I went to the negro-house, and took up something to carry to the field for breakfast: When I got to the field I found that massa had taken away Ellen Dalling,[43] who used to mind the sucking children in the field; she was not removed because she was sick, but massa said that the children were born free, and he was not going to give them any nurse as they were born free and did not deserve any mercy: After keeping her away two days, he put her back to mind the children. . . . Master does not allow us to give our children suck in the field: when he comes into the field, if he finds any of us in the act of doing so, he makes us get up.
. . .

ALEXANDER MILLS, an apprentice on Penshurst, sworn. . . .[44] I remember the row which took place between James Williams and the rest about the half Friday; they were put into the dungeon; I don't remember the expression said to have been made by James Williams as I was not bye.[45] The house of Peter Atkinson, which was pulled down was his own house; it was his dwelling-house; he lived there and slept there; his wife used to come from Knapdale sometimes to stop there. . . . We used to meet there for worship on Monday, Wednesday, and Friday nights. . . . The meeting never exceeded eighteen or twenty persons; sometimes eight or nine were strangers. We used to offer up a short prayer and then sing a hymn. . . . The meetings used to be held in Atkinson's house before the 1st of August, 1834, and master knew very well, long before Atkinson went away, that they were held there; master used to quarrel with us all along about it. . . .

MONDAY, SEPTEMBER 25

JANETTE SAUNDERS, an apprentice on Orange-Valley, sworn.[46] I remember being sent to the workhouse, handcuffed, to a very old man. . . . On my way down, I remember seeing a young man in the pasture at Penshurst, who gave me five oranges; he spoke to the Police, and they allowed me to stop; he then took my bundle off my head, loosed it and tied up the oranges in it. . . . He asked me if I knew the place where I was going to. I said, no. He then said, "You must keep a bold heart, you will find plenty more there like yourself; I know what that workhouse is, for I have been there myself." . . . The first day I was on the mill I got a catting on my back, because I could not keep the step. My clothes were lashed off by the cat. I had on a body frock of Oznaburgh.[47] I was not catted very severely on the legs. The flogging was laid on by order of the Police Captain. I remember that one of my hands slipped out of the strap and I hung by the other while the mill went round and knocked against me. The Police Captain ordered the driver to pull the other hand out and let me fall, but the driver did not do it; he took my hand out and let me down. . . .

MARY JAMES, a Guinea negro,[48] apparently about 60 years of age, very weak and infirm, an apprentice to Mr. Wallace, of the Farm, sworn.[49] I remember being sent to the workhouse, and as I could not dance the mill, Mr. Drake flogged me himself. . . . They made me take off my upper clothes, so as to leave my back and shoulders quite bare. I danced the mill for six days, twice a day, and was catted every day. When I was put on the mill it was impossible for me to keep the step, and I hung by the straps, and my shins used to be so badly bruised that Mr. Drake would make me go to the sea-side to wash them. I was put to dig cane-holes with the gang, and was chained to another woman. James Bolt was the driver who always flogged me. Sometimes when I hung on the mill and could not keep step I would call out, "massa, me da go dead, oh! my stomach, oh!"[50] Then Mr. Drake would take me off. When he saw the fum-fum quite bad on the back, he gave me some oil to oil it. The flies took my back, and when I got home some of the negroes saw how it stood, and said, "Old woman, your back is fly blown!" . . .

I knew James Williams; he was in the workhouse at the same time with myself. When he saw how I was treated he would say, "Grandy, keep heart—keep heart!—poor thing!—you no go dead in the work-house, you will live to go home!" After I got home . . . I worked along with the pickaninny mothers and the weakly people. After I got home, turpentine was put to my back by Amelia Lawrence to take the maggots out, and she bathed my back with warm water. I continued working in the field until my back got quite well. I did not lay up on account of it. It was Captain A. Dillon who sentenced me to the workhouse and treadmill because I went away about three months.

A REPORT OF EVIDENCE

. . .

Mr. JOHN CLARKE, formerly an Overseer on Knapdale estate, sworn.[51] I knew James Williams and urged his valuation, considering that it ought to take place as the legal notice had been given. Instead of looking black and not speaking, I said, "Well, James Williams, I am very glad that you are a free man: I shall be saved a great deal of trouble, and I hope you will behave much better, as a free man, than you have done as an apprentice." I had frequently to carry him over to Mr. Senior during his apprenticeship to intercede for him when he got into any trouble, and many a time I saved him from deserved punishment; I had, however, frequent cause to complain of him as the horses under his care often trespassed on the Knapdale canes by means of his neglect. . . .

JAMES FINLAYSON, formerly an apprentice on Penshurst, but now free by purchase, sworn. (Examined on 26th September.) I knew Henry James; he was an old sawyer, and it was under him that I learnt the trade. We were going on very well until he got weak and could not manage the saw. . . . [Henry James was transferred to work as a watchman but could not prevent cattle from trespassing on the corn-piece because there was no fence.] . . . He was catted, and when I came home, as he was a great friend of mine, I went to see him. He told me that he had been shamefully treated, but he did not mind the flogging so much as the pain he felt in his stomach from it; he did not go to watch that night, and laid flat on his belly on a piece of board. Next day he went to his watch. Some weeks after he came and told me that every night, as he went to his bed he coughed a great deal, and that whenever he coughed, blood came from him. I said, "You had better go to the hot-house and get something to check it." He went to the carpenter's shop, which was also used as a hot-house, and I saw him there every day. I asked him what they did for him? He said "nothing." He told me that Doctor Tucker had ordered a blister, but in place of that his mistress, Miss Senior, had sent him some candle-grease plaster, saying that he must put that on his stomach.[52] I saw him again next day, and asked him how he was last night? He answered, "Oh, brother, I will never get better again." He then shewed me a cup which held about a pint; it was half-filled with blood, which he said he had brought up during the night. The next day I returned, and he shewed me as much more. In the course of that day master went into the carpenter's shop, and said to him, "What! ain't you dead yet?" Henry James told me that he wanted to go to Brown's-Town to see Captain Andrew Dillon; he told me this the same day that I was to be valued; he set off before day, taking with him the blood which he had passed the night before! When he arrived at Brown's-Town, he complained to Capt. Dillon. Master was present, and said that there was nothing the matter with him, and "that he had had all the doctor ordered—that Doctor Tucker was not here himself, but that would be present at the next Court." The Magistrate said, "Do you hear that old man? Go back, and come again next week." Henry James replied, "Ah, massa, I don't know whether I am going to live to come back again. He went out, and a little while after somebody ran back to tell us that he was dead, and that his body was laying by the Jack-fruit tree,[53] near the corner of the Church. I was very much alarmed, and ran out to see. The place on which the body was laying was coloured with a great deal of blood, which came from his nose and mouth; he was an African, and must have been upwards of sixty years of age. . . .

I knew Peter William Atkinson's house at Penshurst; it was his own house, his dwelling-house. He used to sleep in it; I helped him to raise it. We used to live together at one time. Atkinson used sometimes to have prayers in his house in the evening. . . . When we met for prayer, we were always over before master's bed-time. The girls from the house used to come up to Prayer, when master was at supper, and go down again to mind their business before the family went to bed. We never made any noise to disturb the family. Sometimes about twenty persons used to be present at prayer; at others not more than half of that number. One of the elder brethren used to commence with a little prayer; after that we sung a hymn, which was given out by one of the brethren. Then we had another prayer and another hymn, and the meeting ended with a prayer. Every body then went away to get their supper, and nobody remained to make a noise. These meetings worked great good in me—they taught me to be honest in my dealings; to speak truth at all times, and to do to others as I would wish them to do to me; they taught me also to be thankful for all things. I used at one time to take a good deal of my master's time, without thinking that I was doing any harm, and I used to do many other bad things. Religion told me that all this was wrong. I never knew any of our people who would turn their backs on others because they did not belong to the

same Church as ourselves. That would not be a Christian feeling. I am now working for myself and getting a comfortable livelihood, and I am always ready to help a fellow-creature who is in want of assistance. Since I purchased my freedom I lent Peter Atkinson £30 5s. to buy the balance of his apprenticeship, and I have also lent £12 to Francis Johnson. I have a large family to support: there is my wife, myself, five of my wife's children before marriage, and five of my own, which I got before marriage. Atkinson is now working for himself: he first worked with me to pay me off the sum I advanced for him, but he was so sickly that I was obliged to let him off; he will pay me when he can, and if he should not be able, I don't mind the money. I paid £73 6s. 8d. for my freedom. I have bought a little land since I was free, and I have a ground which I work, but still I am obliged to buy ground provisions, as I have so many mouths to feed. I have been free two years and a half. I think that the negroes are generally better off as apprentices than they used to be as slaves, for there is not the same interruption to the acquirement of gospel knowledge than there used to be, and they have better opportunities to get Justice now than they had then.
. . .

WEDNESDAY, SEPTEMBER 27

CATHERINE BAYLEY, apparently about 15 or 16 years of age, an apprentice to Penshurst.[54] I remember Amelia Lawrence and myself being in the workhouse about two years ago. I was in for seven days; the women were all locked up in one room at night with chains on our necks; our feet were put in shackles. A man by the name of Jenkins came into the room one night and put improper questions to me, but I would not listen to him; he stopped some time endeavouring to persuade me to do wrong. Amelia Lawrence heard him and bawled out. She told the boatswain that she would not allow him to follow me that way, because my mother had begged her to keep me safe. It was the second night after I went in that Jenkins came to put these questions to me. I heard him put the same questions to a girl belonging to Mr. Moncrieff;[55] it was the same night that he came to me. He asked her first, and as she would not consent he then came to me. . . .

MARY JANE KIDSON, an apprentice to Southfield, sworn. . . .[56] I was tried at Lily-field, and went down to the workhouse with James

Williams, of Penshurst: we were handcuffed together. I had a young sucking child, which I carried, tied to my back; I had on my head a basket, containing my baby's bed and clothes; when I was tired of carrying the child on my back, I begged the police to stop and slack my hand out of the handcuff, so that I might carry it in my arms; they refused, but allowed me to stop, and I then loosed the child, and rested it on my arm, and carried it in that manner all the way till I got to the workhouse; I never gave it suck on the road; I asked the police, but they would not allow me. . . .

THURSDAY, SEPTEMBER 28

Mr. JOSEPH ISAACS, merchant of Brown's Town, sworn. I was called upon to give evidence in the valuation of James Williams: . . . I said that I very much wanted a boy like him, and that I would give him two dollars per week if he would come to me: I am actually now paying that sum for a man servant, and a like sum for a woman servant: I cannot get a negro with a good character for a less amount. I did not hire James Williams when he applied to me after being valued, as I heard he was a bad character and was always carrying his master before the magistrate; I also heard that he was a thief, and as I had silver plate about my house, I told him that I did not want him; . . . My opinion of him was altered about two or three hours after his valuation: Somebody said, "Are you going to hire that boy?" I said "Yes." I was then advised not to hire him, as he was a thief. . . .

FRIDAY, SEPTEMBER 29

MARGARET JANE CAMPBELL, a sambo non-praedial apprentice to Miss Ford of Rio-Bueno about 18 years of age: sworn. . . .[57] I remember being sent to the House of Correction; . . . My shins were very badly bruised by the mill; after I came off the mill my stomach hurt me a great deal and it continued to hurt me for a long time afterward; my stomach never pained me before I was sent to the Treadmill; Mr. Drake often came to the Workhouse when we were on the mill, and quarrelled with the boatswain for not making it go fast; he told him to flog the people when they would not dance quick; I was sent to the Workhouse because Mr. Chrystie sent me to buy a bottle of castor oil; I bought the

oil and the bottle broke as I was going home; I went home and told
him of the accident but I did not carry the broken bottle to shew him;
Mr. Chrystie told me that I must go and bring the oil or the money,
and I then ran away for four days. . . .

[S]everal of the town's people used to come in the evening to see the
mill going; they used to stop outside and see the mill at work as the
door of the millhouse was kept open. The persons who used to come
were principally negroes; I never saw any of the gentlemen of the town
nor any of the Magistrates belonging to the parish come to the Workhouse; I never saw any of the drivers wishing to take improper liberties
with the women, nor did I ever hear any of them say so. James Williams
used to call after me and tell me to keep the step good, that I must
not put my feet too far in on the treads but just on the edge: he always
worked next to me on the mill: when I came off the first day he shewed
me himself how I was to put my feet on, so that they might not get
cut. . . .

ELIZA NATHAN, an apprentice to Mount Carmel, sworn. I remember being sent to St. Ann's Bay Workhouse; . . . Before I was taken to
Mr. Rawlinson at Brown's Town for trial I was put into a dungeon and
confined there for five nights. When I was going to Brown's Town I
was taken out of the dungeon and was not even allowed to go to my
hut to get a suit of clean clothes to bring with me: I came down here
quite dirty and my sister who was in the market went aside and took off
her own clean shift, which she gave to me to put on; I was taken to the
Workhouse . . . On Monday morning, they put me on the Treadmill; I
kept the step very well when I was first put on, but when the mill turned
hard I felt very faintish, and my knees got very weak, but still I kept
on; we were sent to work in the field after being put on the Treadmill
in the morning, and when we returned in the evening we were put on
again; the edge of the steps of the mill always cut my shins; whenever I
got tired on the mill and cried out, Mr. Jenkins used to flog me with the
whip but he did not hurt me a great deal; I was quite sick in the Workhouse in consequence of being in the family way and was put in the
hothouse for three days. . . . [After my release] I went to my work and
kept at it until the week before Christmas; I was then near to my time
and I went to the Busha to ask for a month to sit down; but he refused
to give me; my child was born on the new year's day; when I was near

my time and went to Busha to ask for a month to sit down I stated what I wanted to do; I wanted to pick oil nuts to make oil for burning after my delivery.[58] The busha then ordered me to be locked up in a dungeon and sent for the Magistrate. When the Magistrate Mr. Rawlinson came, he boxed me all about my jaws and head, and put me again in the dungeon; he boxed me with a paper book which he had in his hand. When Mr. Rawlinson and the busha go into the house together if the apprentice have ever so much right he is not allowed to speak. . . .

MONDAY, OCTOBER 2

. . .

Maria Henderson, recalled. I remember that some apprentices were passing by one Friday from Hylton Hill; they had the half Friday and stopped where we were working: we said to ourselves "every body's negroes have the half Friday except us;" master heard it and said "shut your mouths women; I have my eyes upon 2 or 3 of you." . . .

Mr. William Codnor, proprietor of New Hope Pen, sworn. . . . I have been working on the nine hours system but in consequence of the general bad conduct of my people, by way of punishment I adopted the eight hours system.[59] On Friday the 27th March 1835 I rode out to where the people were working on the road and while there about eleven o'clock the Mount Edgecombe negroes passed by. The New Hope men had just taken up a turn of stones, and the women were in the act of doing so, but when they saw the Mount Edgecombe people passing they called out "massa negroes you have the half Friday, it is we who are killed: it is we who are punished; we don't get any half Friday." They broke out in a very noisy and violent manner; Maria Henderson and Clemence Brodie were the most conspicuous: I threatened to make the constable lock them up unless they ceased and told them that I would send for Mr. Rawlinson: they then became more clamourous. . . .

. . .

TUESDAY, OCTOBER 3

Julian Morison, an apprentice to "Dornoch," sworn.[60] I was sent some time ago to the Workhouse and was put on the Treadmill: the field driver persuaded me to consent to his wishes, and I did so three times; I used on these occasions to go to his room and remained with him during the whole of the night; his name is Thomas Aikin; in consequence of my consenting to his wishes, he made a difference of my work in the field.

This witness on being asked why she consented to the desires of the driver said "I was afraid if I did not go that he would punish me." . . .

WEDNESDAY, OCTOBER 4

The Rev. JOHN CLARKE, Baptist Missionary, sworn. . . .[61] On many of the properties where there are individuals attending the Chapel of which I am minister, a class is formed consisting of those who lead moral lives and are desirous of obtaining religious instruction. To each of these persons a ticket is given, and his name is entered in a book kept for the purpose. A person is selected or recognised by me to conduct the meetings of the class, and from time to time to report on the conduct of those composing it. Whenever any persons are found to have been guilty of improper conduct or immorality, their names are erased from the book and they are requested to return their tickets.[62]

On some properties the Classes meet once a week, on others two or three times, in the largest or most convenient of the cottages which can be procured for the purpose.

The strictest injunctions are given that such meetings be conducted in a quiet orderly manner, that they be broken up at an early hour; that especial care be taken to avoid disturbing the inmates of the great-house, and these directions are carefully attended to. The meetings are solely for religious purposes; two or three Hymns are sung, the scriptures are read, prayers are offered, and enquiries are made as to the Christian consistency of the members of the class. . . .

In reference to a question put by the Court respecting James Williams, the Rev. Mr. Clarke said "Mr. Sturge saw James Williams here and had some conversation with him and requested me to purchase his freedom for him. James Williams came to me in consequence of a message having been sent to Penshurst by James Finlayson at my request, informing the people that two gentlemen were here who were desirous of knowing how the apprentices were treated. Mr. Sturge after receiving the statement of Williams requested me to purchase the remaining term of his apprenticeship. I asked him the several questions stated by him in the narrative, and he promised on my advancing the money to work hard and try to pay me back. . . . [A]fter the payment of the money I told Williams that he must go to Spanish-Town or Kingston to Mr. Sturge, as he wished to take him to England and would take good care of him. I previously enquired whether he would like to go to England, and he immediately assented and expressed a great deal of pleasure at the idea of going.

. . .

Before the Commissioners left the neighbourhood of Brown's Town, they made it their duty to ride over to Knapdale to inspect the dungeons there. These cells were found to be exactly 6 feet square and about 12 feet in height. Although not now observed to be damp, yet having been just completed at the time of the incarceration of James Williams and Adam Brown, and being from their situation totally excluded from the influence of the sun, it is impossible that considering the strong masonry with which they are built they could have been otherwise than damp.

. . . The Commissioners inspected also the dungeon of Penshurst which they found about seven feet in breadth and not deficient in ventilation. It is however so low that a person of ordinary size must be denied in it even the slightest but natural alleviation of an erect position.

. . .

ST. ANN'S-BAY, THURSDAY, OCTOBER 5TH, 1837

GEORGE GORDON, Esquire, General Magistrate, and JNO. DAUGHTREY, Esquire, Special ditto, removed their Court to this place, where the investigation was continued.

The Commission, and other documents having been published as before, the Commissioners repaired to the House of Correction, and made a minute observation of the state of that Institution, the result of which will be detailed at length in the report of the proceedings of the Commissioners in this town. The Commissioners were put in possession of the books and papers relative to the discipline of the House of

Correction, and were subsequently afforded every opportunity, at the office of the Clerk of the Peace, to obtain whatever information they required. . . .

FRIDAY, OCTOBER 6TH

JAMES BROWN, Head-Constable on Drax-Hall, sworn. . . . I was present on two occasions when Major Light tried the people; one of those occasions was after dinner, and he was so tipsy that he was obliged to hold his head over the paper. He then asked busha what to do, and busha told him what to write. Two of the bookkeepers were present. One day Major Light was so drunk that he fell off the step. . . .

SAMUEL PINK, Head-Carpenter and a Constable to Draxhall estate, sworn. . . . Another woman, named Lavinia Reynolds, got very much damaged on the shins; she has been in the hot-house for five months since her return from the workhouse, and is still there. She was tried for quitting the hot-house frequently; she was in it at that time with a sore toe. Her shin is very bad now, and at one time the wound was so bad on it that I saw the bone. The whole of the shin was in one sore, and I began to think that it would have been necessary to cut the leg off. . . . Major Light was the Special Magistrate who sent Lavinia Reynolds to the House of Correction. He was a man who was scarcely ever sober; he drank too much spirits, and used to commence very early in the morning. I have seen him at his business, between nine and ten o'clock in the morning, quite tipsy. I have seen him so bad that way, that he could not sit down in his own chaise: I have seen him at Draxhall going away, after he had done his duty, so tipsy that his servant was obliged to hold him in his chaise. He never allowed the apprentices to have much to say for themselves before he committed them. At the off-set, when the New Law first set in, the people were very ignorant and unruly; but within this year they have begun to behave a little better. This has been since the new Magistrate (Capt. Reynolds) came; he gives them much satisfaction. Mr. Sowley was the Magistrate before Major Light; he used to flog the people very hard.
. . .

LAVINIA REYNOLDS, an apprentice to Draxhall estate, after exhibiting her leg with a very bad sore, was sworn. I was in the hot-house with a sore toe. One Wednesday morning the doctor-man ordered me out to sweep the yard. I told him my breakfast was on the fire, and he ordered me directly into the dark-room. He complained of me to the busha, who sent off for Major Light. He came in the afternoon, and I was brought up and tried, and, on the evidence of the doctor-man, Jones McFarlane was convicted and sentenced to the house of correction. I was carried down on the Wednesday night, and put on the treadmill the next morning. When I went in the evening, I was locked up in a dark room. The room was very dark. When I was put on the treadmill my toe was still bad; and as I knocked my shins against the mill, Mr. Drake took a cat with his own hands and flogged me on the feet. On Tuesday evening I was taken ill with fever, and I told Mr. Drake, the next morning, that I had fever, but he did not take any notice of me, and still put me on the mill. They never flogged me after the first time. Every time I went on the mill, I knocked my shins. The day that Mr. Drake licked me with the cat, he licked me on the bruises, and that made the shins so bad. When he put me on the mill, he took a handkerchief off my head and tied my clothes up above my knees. I was kept the whole of the first week on the mill, as Mr. Drake would not believe that I was sick. Dr. Bailey did not see me at the workhouse, nor any other doctor while I was there. The second week I was very sick. I couldn't help myself; he said he did not care, and that I should go on the mill. He didn't care whether I broke my shins or not. He put me on the mill on that Monday, and I was so weak that I couldn't keep step, but hung on it. It was going very fast, and bruised the shin so much as to make it bleed. The next morning Mr. Drake said, he would not bother with me again, and locked me up in the dark room. I was kept in that dark room the whole of the two weeks that I was in the workhouse, except when they took me out to put me on the treadmill. I used to be let out a little in day-time to wash the sore. The morning that Mr. Drake was flogging me on the mill, he flogged all the other people who could not keep step, and tied all the other women's clothes the same way as mine. To the boatswain and others standing below, our persons must have been indecently exposed. From the time I have been out, I have been in the hot-house until now, nearly three months. Dr. Bailey, the doctor of Draxhall, has seen the foot, but never told me what to do with it. I don't know whether he gave any directions to the doctor-man. I have been washing the foot and putting leaves on it.

. . .

ELEANOR HOWELL, an apprentice to Draxhall estate, sworn. I re-member being sent to the workhouse and put on the treadmill. I was well mashed up; that is, my shins were mashed up. When the legs were mashed by the mill and I could not keep the step, particularly as I was troubled with a shortness of breath, Mr. Drake ordered the man who acted as boatswain to flog me with a cat. I was cut upon my back and my feet. I was put on the treadmill twice every day for three days—every God's send day, that I was put on the mill, it bruised my knees, and as I hung on it from inability to keep the step, it cut my shins dreadfully, when I called out for "Mercy." Mr. Drake said, "No mercy is here, you should have looked for mercy at Draxhall before you came here." . . .

ELIZABETH BARTLEY, an apprentice to Draxhall estate, sworn.[63] I was tried some time ago and sent to the treadmill. The first time I went on I did very well, but afterwards, as I was in the family way, I could not keep the step, and when I could not keep it from weakness, I begged Mr. Drake, and told him, "Massa, I can't keep up, I am in the family way." Instead of letting me off he ordered Thomas White to flog me with a cat. Thomas White flogged me on my shoulder, my feet, and on my rump; I told him often that I was in the family way, and he said, "if you had done good busha would not have sent you here." Before putting me on the mill my clothes were tied up very high, and any body standing up below could observe how I was exposed. . . . I was not in the gang, but placed in solitary confinement.[64] The other women went out on Sundays to fetch water and sweep Mr. Drake's yard. I remember calling out to Mr. Drake, "Massa, I a'nt able, I am in two flesh," but I do not remember hearing the answer of Mr. Drake, as the mill was going round, and the people crying out upon it.[65]
. . .

Mr. CHARLES BRAVO, Deputy Clerk of the Peace, at St. Ann's sworn. . . . I have had occasion to see many negroes in the House of Correction, and they invariably declared that they would prefer any other punishment to that of the tread-mill. When on, they always ex-claimed very piteously, crying out to be taken off; that their time was up, &c. &c., and uttering various cries which a person suffering great pain would be supposed to do. . . . With regard to the mill itself, I consider that the steps are two [sic] wide and deep, and that the hand-rail is very defective from its height and position. I also think that it is highly improper that it should be worked merely at the caprice of the officer who attends it, instead of being mechanically regulated. . . .

. . .

ROBERT STIRLING, a Convict in the House of Correction, sworn.[66] I have been in the workhouse 22 years. In Mr. Drake's time I have often seen the people flogged, both men and women: sometimes they were flogged on their backs, at others on their legs. I have often seen the steps covered with blood, and I saw a pregnant woman, named Susan White, of Dumbarton, put on the treadmill. I knew that she had belly, for I had eye enough to see that she was pregnant. . . . The drivers were all selected from the convicts. I have heard that Mr. Jenkins and James Thomas had illicit intercourse with the women in the workhouse, but I never saw it. I, however, know that a fellow servant of mine, named Polly Brown, had her face scratched out by Mr. Jenkins's kept mistress, because she was jealous of her. . . .

Mr. ALEXANDER LEVI, Supervisor of the House of Correction, sworn. I took charge of the workhouse on the 18th April, 1837, soon after the death of Mr. Drake. I still keep the people in the penal gang, at nights, with their chains and collars on, in consequence of the in-security of the workhouse. When the people are put on the treadmill now, the cat is never used, nor any other instrument of punishment; and, if I find any woman sent to the treadmill in a state of pregnancy, I take it on myself to relieve her from working on it. It is my practice also to relieve those women who have sucking children by not work-ing them to the extent of their sentence if I find them suffering, and the same care is taken of their children. . . . I know Mr. Jenkins, the late under superintendant of the workhouse; he was also the jailer; he was dismissed by the Magistrates and Vestry about two months after I took charge, in consequence of his gross neglect of a sick patient in the jail, who, it is said, died from his inattention. He is a man of the most violent character, addicted to liquor, and was very partial in the execution of his duty; he was a long time with Mr. Drake, not less than 12 months. . . . Since I have taken charge of the House of Correction, the boatswains have not been allowed to open, in the mornings, the doors of the room in which the women are confined. I keep the keys myself, in consequence of the reports that the boatswains, while they had the keys of the workhouse room in which females were confined, often urged them when opening the rooms early in the morning to re-sort to them for improper purposes. I have also received instructions from Mr. Parke, the Custos of the Parish,[67] to lean always to the side of mercy, and that whenever any of the prisoners in the House of Correction commit faults, instead of punishing them myself, to carry them up before the Stipendiary Magistrate, and prefer complaints to him for their improper conduct.

ANN BURKE, a free woman. I lived with Mr. Jenkins when he was in the Workhouse, and positively deny ever having had any quarrel with a woman named Ann Broom; I don't even know her.[68]

SATURDAY, OCTOBER 7

. . .

BETTY WILLIAMS, an apprentice to Hiattsfield, sworn.[69] I remember being sent to the workhouse near last Christmas: twenty-one of us were sent there. Several women who went in had sucking children: Felicia Smith, Cornelia Johnston and Dianah Johnston; there were several others, but I don't remember their names. I don't think that there were any pregnant women among them. When we were put on the mill and could not keep the step, Mr. Jenkins always flogged us with a cat on the legs. Mr. Drake told Jenkins to cat us well, if we did not keep the step, as busha sent us to be punished. One day, while I was dancing on the mill, I fainted on it, and dropped down. My hands dropped out of the straps and I fell down to the ground. I did not know any thing of it myself until next morning, when my friends told me that I had fainted, and that they were obliged to burn pennistone[70] and put to my nose to restore me: it was in the evening tread-mill punishment that I fainted. We had come from the field, and I had nothing to eat the whole day. I had not teeth to eat the boiled corn which they gave me, and I bought a bread when coming down; my sister also bought a bread, but Mr. Drake made us throw the bread away, and a man named Robert Stirling picked it up and took it for himself. . . . We were sent to the workhouse on a charge of taking a day without permission: we were brought up before Mr. Woolfrys, but he would not allow us to give any explanation: the whole of the great gang took the day.[71] The men were catted on the estate, and we were sent to the workhouse. . . .[72]

LEANTY THOMAS, an apprentice to Hiattsfield, sworn. I remember being sent to the workhouse from Hiattsfield. I was sent for five days, to dance the mill twice a-day. There were a great many of us sent down: twenty-one of us. Isabella Richards was pregnant, Isabella Taylor was pregnant also; and Phillis Hayden, Sibby Byfield, Camilla Johnston, Diana Johnston,[73] Felicia Smith, Eleanor Bailey, Maria Richards and Louisa Williams, had sucking children. When I went on the tread-mill my hands were strapped, and I could not keep the step: the mill cut my legs very bad, and Mr. Drake ordered Mr. Jenkins to cat me: he abused me by calling me all manner of indecent names, and said to the boatswain, Give it to her well—cat her away. My handkerchief that was on my head slipped down over my head, and covered my eyes; my coat was loose, and it tripped my foot, and I could not keep step good: I called to Mr. Drake, and I begged him quite hard to give time to catch up myself, and my daughter begged him quite hard, but all to no purpose: I called out, "Massa, I am dying"; but he took no notice of me, and would not take me off until the time was out. I hung on the mill, and it cut me quite bad. . . . The day I came out I could not walk, and Affy Brown and Sibby Byfield carried me to a house on the Bay and put me there, until my husband brought a beast down and took me home. When I got home, Philip Martin, one of my Christian brethren, took me on his back, and carried me to the hot-house yard. . . . When we went back to Hiattsfield, I saw Bella Richards in the field crying, and on asking her what she was crying for, she said that the rest of the people carried her name to her husband saying that one of the drivers Charles Rose had had improper intercourse with her. I used myself to see Charles Rose kind to her, carrying soup and water to her, and one day I saw her go into his room but I can't swear for what purpose she went into his room. I have heard from several people that this girl was kept in the Workhouse; when she first danced the mill, she complained of her belly as she was pregnant and she was sent to the Hothouse and it was then I saw the intimacy between her and Charles Rose. . . .

BELLA RICHARDS, an apprentice to Hiattsfield, sworn. I remember when the whole of the women were sent to the Workhouse, I was put on the Treadmill and I told Mr. Jenkins that I was pregnant and could not dance the mill; he said he could not help it; I hung on the mill and Mr. Jenkins took a cat and catted me on the legs; the cat did not cut my legs, it swelled them and the mill cut my shins. I was only able to dance twice and I was then sent into the hothouse: I was 3 months in the family way; I also told Mr. Woolfrys the Special Magistrate that I was breeding, I told him so after he sentenced me to the Treadmill but he said he could not help it; that the sentence was passed already! My back gave way when I was on the mill and kept on until after I went out of the Workhouse when I had a mischance. . . .

. . .

REBECCA SMITH, a prisoner in the House of Correction, from To-bolski estate, sworn. I was in the Workhouse in Mr. Drakes time; I have often seen Mr. James Hylton[74] then deputy clerk of the peace come to the Workhouse and desire Mr. Jenkins to take the weights off by which the mill was guided, so as to make it go round quick, and when the weights were taken off, the mill got away and we hung up by the straps, and then he would tell Mr. Jenkins to flog us till we got the step; some-times also he would come in the evening and stop in the mill-house, and send to Mr. Jenkins to tell him to bring the people out, that he might see them worked on the mill: Mr. Jenkins then called out to Martin Brown to bring us out: this was at our regular time of punishment. . . .

I was once flogged with a bamboo by a man named Robert Laing, who, first of all, chained two other women and myself together; he put two heavy chains on me, as I was the middle woman, and I then had a young sucking child in my arms: he first hit me across the stomach with a bamboo, and afterwards on the back; the bamboo cut my back, and the mark is still on it. When Mr. Jenkins came up, he quarrelled with Robert Laing, and told him that if I was a bad woman I might prosecute him when I went out. We always slept with either the chain or collar on at night. I have often heard that the drivers, James Thomas and James Bolt, used to have improper intimacies with the women, but I never saw it: a woman named Jane Gordon was mentioned as one of the women who James Bolt had an improper intimacy with.

JANE GORDON, a prisoner in the house of correction, from Home Castle, sworn. I was in the workhouse before this time, in Mr. Drake's time. James Thomas used to open the door in the morning: he called me to his room and asked me to have an improper intimacy with him; I consented from fear: for he had asked me once before, and when I refused to go to him, he beat me near the river and knocked me into it.

The Rev. JOHN WILLIAMS, Wesleyan Minister, sworn.[75] I have been a resident here one year and eleven months. . . . With regard to the working of the Abolition Law, a respectable man, an apprentice to

Mr. Hull, by the name of Jones,[76] informed me that he had been frequently disturbed in his family worship by the late Mr. Hull, the owner of the property to which he was attached. Mr. Hull frequently threatened him, if he continued to hold family worship, to pull his place down. I often inquired whether he disturbed his master; and the information afforded me was, that he was so near that his master could hear him singing psalms; but, at the same time, several of the other apprentices who would sing songs, were not complained against as disturbers. I have frequently inquired whether any thing like a public meeting was held: but I have been assured that, with the exception of one or two strange persons, the meeting was entirely confined to the family. . . .
. . .

RICHARD HEMMING, Esq., Magistrate of the parish of St. Ann's, sworn.[77] I have been in the habit of visiting the Workhouse frequently during the last four or five years, and more constantly since 1832. I have seen the tread-mill at work: I have seen the people when taken off, during the supervisorship of Mr. Drake, and never saw but one case where the shins of the party were materially injured: I have heard that others were injured. . . . Mr. Drake often assured me, that the reason why the knees of some of the persons were bruised is, their determination of not treading: One instance of this determination not to tread, I saw myself; the man however was not bruised: he was taken down immediately, to be put on again when a weaker gang was on; this, I believe, to have been Mr. Drake's general conduct. . . .

JAMES THOMAS, formerly a field-driver in the House of Correction, sworn. . . . I never carried a cat in the field: Mr. Drake told me not to do so; I carried guava-switches. . . . I never saw any driver in the field having improper intimacy with the women. I never had any improper intimacy with them myself; but when the women were mashed upon the treadmill and came in the field, I used to have consideration for them. . . . Sometimes, however, Mr. Jenkins would call me himself, and beg me to flog the people: some of them would not dance at all and then they hung. I never saw the women's clothes tied up beyond their knees. Mr. Jenkins gave orders to be very particular in not tying the clothes up in an indecent manner. . . .
. . .

ISRAEL LEMON, Esq., Magistrate of St. Ann's, and President of the House of Correction, sworn.[78] I was present once or twice during the Supervisorship of Mr. Drake, when the people were on the mill. I did not stop until they had finished. The people were stubborn, and hung, and the drivers touched them occasionally, to make them keep the step. I did not see any cruelty practiced. When they hung, I gave directions that the mill should be stopped, and Mr. Drake immediately complied, and I have even known him to take them off. It has never occurred in my presence, that lame persons, or pregnant women, or any debilitated person, has been put on the mill. . . . I do not think that Mr. Drake's conduct was harsh: I think he was rather indulgent to the negroes: the convicts were so indulged by him, that they will now scarcely do anything. They did not receive any greater proportion of food than the apprentices, but they had several indulgences: many of them were drivers, and consequently received more than the others. . . . I do not think it proper to employ convicts as drivers, but we cannot get persons to take those situations: it is, however, my intention to advertize for competent persons. . . .

MARTIN BROWN, late convict in the St. Ann's Bay House of Correction, sworn. . . . The same evening [when Betty Williams was put on the mill] a girl from Hiattsfield, named Effy Brown, begged me to give her a drink of water: she had not yet been put on the mill. I brought it, and Mr. Jenkins quarrelled with me for doing it; and as we got to words, he fell upon me and tore my shirt to pieces: we both of us went to Mr. Drake, and when Jenkins told him what was the matter, Mr. Drake told him to carry me down to the workhouse, and he would come down and see about it: when he came he ordered Mr. Jenkins to put me in the dark cell under the jailer's room, where they can put people who are condemned to be hung: The place is very dark, and no air can get in it at all. I was kept there for seven days, and never brought before a magissrate [*sic*]. There is no seeing at all in the cell when the door is closed. The girl, Effy Brown is a young girl: the reason why I was kind to her, is because it is in my nature to be kind. I never had any improper intercourse with any of the women myself, nor did I ever hear of Mr. Jenkins or any of the drivers doing so. . . .

EDWARD JONES, an apprentice to Chester plantation, the property of Mrs. Hull, sworn. I am an apprentice to Mrs. Hull. One Sunday morning at sunrise, I thought it my duty to give thanks to God, by prayer and hymn, in the morning. My wife and my five children, and a woman who is a sister-member, were the only persons present: after we had finished singing, my master sent down the constable, Thomas Wilson, to see who was there: when Wilson came down, he said for what he was sent, and I shewed him the people. A little after he called me up to master's house: master then told me, I have spoken to you about your preaching. I replied, "I was not preaching; I was merely praying with my family, I did not pretend to be a preacher"; he then told me he had often spoken to me about this praying, and on Monday he would take me to the magistrate, Mr. Sowley, to give an account of myself.[79] He charged me with holding meetings all about, and I told him, No, that it was only in my house with my family, and that on Tuesday evenings, I would have a few of my friends and neighbours, not exceeding eight or nine; we had nothing but prayer and hymn. He told me that my singing on the Sunday mornings disturbed him, and charged me with singing at nights. I replied, I never sung the hymns until after the rise of the sun in the morning, and that some of the people sung songs at nights, from Friday to Sunday, and I asked if that did not disturb him: he said No, and that I was impudent. On the Monday morning, I was brought before the magistrate under a charge of disturbing master by singing, and also for impudence: He explained my case to the Magistrate, who said that my master could not hinder me from praying, but that he would punish me for insolence; he then ordered me to be catted. I received twenty lashes; I never was flogged but then since the apprenticeship. I have continued to hold my meetings since then to the present day, as I consider it my duty to do so.

. . .

[As well as the investigation into cases arising out of James Williams's *Narrative,* the commissioners also investigated a further twenty-two cases of abuses not mentioned in the *Narrative,* the evidence regarding which was printed along with the evidence above.]

REPORT OF THE COMMISSIONERS

Falmouth, 21st October, 1837

To His Excellency Sir Lionel Smith, &c. &c. &c.

May it please your Excellency,

The Commissioners, in the prosecution of the inquiry which your Excellency was pleased to entrust to them, having taken the fullest evidence they could obtain upon the several subjects which the investigation was designed to embrace, have now the honor to transmit, for your Excellency's information, an authentic Copy of their entire Proceedings.

In reporting upon the general results of this extended inquiry, it has become the duty of the Commissioners to state, that the allegations of James Williams's narrative have received few and inconsiderable contradictions, whilst every material fact has been supported and corroborated by an almost unbroken chain of convincing testimony.

Such being the conclusion of the Commissioners with respect to the Narrative, it can scarcely be necessary for them to add, that the Abolition Law has not been properly administered in some parts of the Parish of St. Ann's—that the House of Correction of that Parish was, until recently, a place of licentiousness and cruelty—and that the treadmill has been, from the time of erection, and still is, an instrument rather of torture than of just and salutary punishment.

Upon these topics the Commissioners have thought it right to report specifically, but with reference to others, of no less interest, they leave the evidence to speak for itself; persuaded that the whole detail will be found important enough to command your Excellency's immediate attention.

Geo. Gordon, J.P. St. James'
J. Daughtrey, S.M.

(True Copy)

NOTES

1. This is an abridged version of the minutes of the inquiry. The full minutes are available in British *Parliamentary Papers* 1837–1838 (154) XLIX, pp. 146–263, and in the editions of the *Narrative* published by the *Falmouth Post* and the Central Negro Emancipation Committee. The *Falmouth Post* edition was used as the copy text. Elisions are marked ". . . ." I have also silently added some paragraph breaks, mostly after the elisions. For clarity, I have in a few places summarized the content of the elided material, indicated by enclosure in [ ]. Where ". . ." is positioned flush left, one or more individuals' entire testimony is omitted.

2. John Daughtrey arrived in Jamaica as a stipendiary magistrate in 1834. He served primarily in the parish of St. Elizabeth. He became general inspector of prisons for Jamaica in 1840, a position he held until his retirement in 1861. George Gordon came to Jamaica in 1808, where he became a slaveholder and attorney and eventually a regular magistrate. Joseph Sturge wrote that he was "esteemed one of

the most judicious and humane planters in the island" (Sturge and Harvey, *West Indies in 1837,* 257). He played a major role in the suppression of the slave rebellion of 1831.

3. The title of the imperial abolition act of 1833 was "An Act for the abolition of slavery throughout the British Colonies, for promoting the industry of the manumitted slaves, and for compensating the owners of such slaves."

4. Lionel Smith had been governor of Jamaica since September 1836. Prior to that he had served as the governor of Barbados.

5. Rawlinson's diary was not published with the inquiry minutes.

6. The inquiry minutes give color designations for all the apprenticed witnesses except those considered black.

7. The house people: the apprentices who worked in the great house. They were nonpraedial apprentices and as such their working hours were not restricted by law.

8. Doctor woman: the woman responsible for caring for sick slaves in the estate's hospital or hothouse. There were "doctor women" on most estates.

9. Stuck: slaughtered.

10. In the *Narrative* Williams says he was fined 10 s (p. 23). Dalling's version is more likely, as magistrates did not have the power to fine apprentices.

11. See Adam Brown's later affidavit, pp. 114–15.

12. William Atkinson gave evidence later in the inquiry, where he is referred to as Peter William Atkinson (pp. 55–59).

13. There is one Peter in the Seniors' slave registration documents, born in 1797. He was one of nine slaves, including his mother, June, and brother, Thomas, willed to Gilbert Senior by Sarah Senior Lawrence, Gilbert's grandmother, whose will was proved in 1805. According to Gilbert Senior's letter and Joseph Lawrence's testimony, Atkinson was married to a woman on Knapdale estate, with whom he had two children, Peter and Willy, who were presumably named for their father.

14. Three Mr. Uttens, John, James, and William, all received compensation for slaves in St. Ann.

15. There is one George in the Seniors' slave registration documents, the son of Myrtilla, born in 1799. He, Myrtilla, and three other slaves including his siblings Grace and Henry were willed to Sarah Senior in the will of her grandmother, Sarah Senior Lawrence. George Henry Warren was valued at £55 in 1834 or 1835 but did not purchase his freedom, presumably because he did not have the money to do so.

16. William Grant was listed in Gilbert Senior's slave registration documents as a mulatto, born in 1781. A slave named William, probably William Grant, was willed to Gilbert in Sarah Senior Lawrence's will, along with eight other slaves.

17. Atkinson was in fact a member of John Clark's Baptist church. Rawlinson's reference to Methodism is an example of the way opponents of the missionary project considered all forms of nonconformist Christianity interchangeable and oppositional. The term "Methodist" was derogatory.

18. The Governor's letter: This phrase may refer either to the governor's letter to Rawlinson, or to one of the many proclamations to apprentices made by Sligo.

19. James Finlayson's evidence reveals that Atkinson borrowed this money from Finlayson (p. 70).

20. The increase in Finlayson's valuation cost testifies to the unfairness of the procedure by which he was valued. According to the standard procedure (estimating the amount a planter could earn by hiring out the apprentice for the rest of his or her apprenticeship, then deducting one third for expenses), Finlayson's price should have decreased over time.

21. Barbacue (more commonly spelled barbecue): a rectangular platform used to dry pimento berries or coffee beans after picking.

22. Spanish wall: a wall made by filling the interstices in a wooden frame with small pieces of broken stone and clayey earth, then plastering and usually whitewashing the result.

23. Being moved from one task to another was a common cause of conflict between apprentices and estate managers.

24. Richard Jenkins gave evidence to the inquiry (not included in this volume). He was identified there as "formerly overseer in the House of Correction."

25. Catherine Bayley gave evidence to the inquiry, where she was identified as an apprentice to Penshurst.

26. Chester and Penshurst were connected through property ownership. Chester plantation was owned by members of the Hull family, Gilbert and Sarah Senior's half siblings. Gilbert and Sarah's mother Mary married William Hull after the death of her first husband, also Gilbert Senior. The other Hulls, Charles, Eliza, Mary Jane, and Helen, were Gilbert and Sarah's half-siblings, the children of Mary and William Hull. William left Chester to Mary Hull in his will, proved in 1799.

27. Like Stanley Rawlinson as quoted in Dalling's evidence, above, Drake here refers to the Penshurst apprentices as Methodists although they were in fact Baptists.

28. Rawlinson's assertion was legally accurate: after considerable discussion between the Colonial Office and legal officers in Jamaica it was decided that the apprentice holder had the legal right to allocate the 40.5-hour work week in any way he or she liked.

29. Strange people: people from estates other than Penshurst.

30. Under the slave codes meetings of slaves at night were unlawful and slave owners had a legal responsibility to prevent them; "preaching and teaching" by slaves was also illegal.

31. Chaise-whip: the whip carried ostensibly for use on horses pulling a chaise. Fummed: flogged.

32. The Seniors' slave registration returns include one Richard, born in 1819 to Maria, who may have been Richard Brown, although other evidence suggests he was known as Richard Dalling. However, one of Maria's other children, Adam, is almost certainly the Adam Brown who figures in the *Narrative*. Richard may have used both names.

33. The Seniors' slave registration returns include no slaves named Davy or David.

34. Planters' use of estate dungeons was a major source of conflict during apprenticeship. Many planters claimed, as Senior does here, that stipendiary magistrates had granted them power to put apprentices in plantation dungeons whenever they believed it necessary. However, the governor and Colonial Office argued that the law did not grant stipendiary magistrates the power to delegate their authority in this way.

35. Little gang: gang made up of children. Caribbean estates usually organized their slaves and apprentices into several gangs: the great gang, made up of the strongest workers, usually men and women age roughly sixteen to forty; the second gang, made up of weaker and elderly adult workers; and the little gang, pickney gang, or third gang, made up of children. It was standard practice for the driver of the little gang to be a woman. Drivers of the other gangs were almost always men.

36. Mulgrave law: apprenticeship. Lord Mulgrave was the governor of Jamaica when apprenticeship was announced. By the time the system began in August 1834 he had been replaced by the Marquis of Sligo.

37. There is no evidence that Senior brought prosecutions for perjury against any of his apprentices.

38. Mischance: miscarriage.

39. Thomas White was still the boatswain of the prison yard when he was interviewed in 1837 by John Pringle, who had been sent by the Colonial Office to investigate Caribbean prisons. He told Pringle that he was a convict for life who had been in the House of Correction since 1828.

40. William and Elizabeth Codner (*sic*) are listed as receiving compensation for a total of eighty-eight slaves on New Hope. William Codnor gave evidence to the enquiry.

41. Hamilton Brown appears several times in the slave registration documents as a guardian and trustee of others' property, as well as making claims in his own right. He was a founding member of the Colonial Church Union in 1832.

42. The Seniors' slave registration returns include one Jane, but she cannot have been Jane Shaw Pennock, as they reported her death in 1829.

43. The Seniors' slave registration returns include one Ellen, born in 1827 to Maria. In other sources Maria is identified as Maria Dalling and as the wife of William Dalling.

44. The Seniors' slave registration returns do not include anyone named Alexander.

45. I was not bye: I was not close by.

46. Saunders reports here the incident described by Williams in the *Narrative*. See p. 21. The *British Emancipator* reprinted her testimony in its issue of 9 May 1838.

47. Oznaburgh (or Osnaburgh or Osnaburg): a thick, coarse fabric out of which slaves' clothes were made.

48. Guinea negro: from Africa.

49. Williams refers to Mary James in the *Narrative* as an "old woman, with grey head" (p. 10).

50. Williams reports an almost identical phrase being used by women on the treadmill but does not attribute it to an individual. See p. 15.

51. Clarke is referred to in the *Narrative* as "the busha at Knapdale."

52. Blister: the application of material or suction designed to raise a blister on the patient's body. Candle-grease plaster: a poultice made of the melted grease from an animal-fat candle.

53. Jack-fruit tree: the tree *Artocarpus integrifolia;* it produces a large, edible, bulbous fruit.

54. The Seniors' slave registration returns do not include a Catherine, but do list a Kate, born 1822, the daughter of Judy, and a Kathrine, born 1825, the daughter of Gracey. Given the age identification, the former is more likely to have been Catherine Bayley. Bayley's father, Thomas Bayley, a Penshurst apprentice, also gave evidence, which is not included here. Thomas may have been Peter William Atkinson's brother, who, along with Peter and seven other slaves, was willed to Gilbert Senior by Sarah Senior Lawrence in 1805.

55. Benjamin Moncrieff (or Moncrieffe), a St. Ann magistrate, was one of the very few truly wealthy Jamaican free colored men. He claimed compensation for more than four hundred slaves on several estates and was also in possession of others as the mortgagee, executor, and trustee. He was a founding member of the Colonial Church Union in 1832.

56. Mary Jane Kidson is described in the *Narrative* as "a woman belonging to Little-field." See p. 9.

57. Campbell is described in the *Narrative* as Margaret, a "young mulatto girl" who "belong to Mr. Chrystie." Campbell's testimony reveals that she worked for Chrystie, although she did not belong to him. "Sambo" means having one black and one mulatto parent. The difference in Castello's and Williams's designations suggests the fluidity of these racial categories.

58. To sit down: not to work in the fields. This was a common expression in this period in Jamaica, used especially by women who asserted their rights to "sit down" either because they were heavily pregnant, because they had young children to look after, or because they had many children.

59. For explanation of the eight hours and nine hours systems, see n. 46 of the *Narrative.*

60. Julian was a common female name in nineteenth-century Jamaica. Julian Morison is not mentioned in the *Narrative.*

61. Rev. John Clark(e)—his name was usually spelled without an "e"—of Browns Town, not John Clarke of Jericho.

62. The "ticket system" that Clark describes here was used by the Baptist and Wesleyan missionaries in Jamaica. Clark does not specify here that slaves on the estates became leaders, and it was they who recommended to the missionaries whether to issue an individual with a ticket. The system facilitated the building

of very large congregations and had the consequence (unintended by the white missionaries) of giving members of those congregations additional scope for developing syncretic Afro-Christianity. The churches that used this system were attacked for it. Other missionaries, as well as planters, claimed that it meant their members were not "real" Christians.

63. Williams refers to Bartley in the *Narrative* as "another woman from Drax Hall." See p. 19.

64. John Pringle's report on the St. Ann House of Correction described the solitary cells as 6.5 feet by 4 feet, and 6 feet from floor to ceiling, with a 10-by-4-inch hole for ventilation. He said that they were recently built and not being used because of damp.

65. Williams quotes an almost identical phrase: "Massa, me no one flesh, me two flesh." See p. 19. The structure of this sentence ("I remember . . . but I do not remember") suggests that Bartley did not spontaneously testify to having used the phrase but rather was asked if she remembered using it and Drake's response, which, according to Williams, was to say that "he didn't care, it wasn't him that give her belly."

66. John Pringle interviewed Robert Stirling in 1837. He confirmed then that he had been in prison for twenty-two years. Pringle described him as having "lost his leg since he was a convict, by a bank falling upon him; has charge of the gate in the day; he was sold with the others 24th May last year; could not agree with his master, and was sent back here."

67. The Custos: the most senior magistrate of a parish.

68. Burke appears to be referring to the woman named in Robert Stirling's evidence as Polly Brown. The minutes do not explain why the different names are used.

69. Williams refers to Betty Williams in the *Narrative* as "one of the women from Hiattsfield" who "fainted on the mill." See p. 15.

70. According to the *Oxford English Dictionary,* pennistone (or penistone) was a kind of cloth made in Penistone, Yorkshire. However, Betty Williams may intend a different sense of the word.

71. Took the day: took the day for their own purposes; did not work for the plantation that day.

72. The Central Negro Emancipation Committee's newspaper, the *British Emancipator,* reprinted the evidence of Betty Williams and several other apprentices from Hiattsfield on 8 May 1838 and published an accompanying article highly critical of Woolfrys. The article culminated in the rhetorical question: "We put it to the common sense and common humanity of our readers, if the man who could thus sentence to excruciating torture twenty-one helpless females—eight of whom had infants in their arms, and two were in a state of pregnancy, and all this for the offence of 'taking a day without permission'—is such a man, we ask, fit to remain invested with such tremendous powers over the happiness and welfare of his fellow-creatures?" In response, Woolfrys wrote to the governor, giving his account of the case:

My attention having been called to the examinations taken by Messrs
Daughtrey and Gordon in their enquiries into the punishment in St Ann's
Bay house of correction, in which commitments by me of certain apprentices of Hiattsfield Estate in my district, in the month of November 1836,
have exposed me in a London paper to imputations of unjust severity, I
have found it necessary to offer the following explanation of the case for
the information of Her Majesty's secretary of state.

His Excellency the Governor will perceive by the date of the commit-
ment, 21 November 1836, that the examinants were punished by me at a
time, when a general resistance among the planters of the island, and of
the parish in particular, prevailed against the 9 hours system of labour,
by which an almost universal spirit of discontent was created among the
negroes, and to allay which his Excellency had issued his circular no 45 18
Sept 1836.

Hiattsfield is one of only four sugar estates in my district. I had succeeded immediately in enforcing his Excellency's circular to secure a clear
half day in the week for the cultivation of the people's provision grounds.
In consequence however of great neglect of the Hiattsfield grounds by the
people, I was constrained to concur in an order, under the provisions of
the 38th clause of the abolition act, for the appropriation of a day in every
other week for working them under the superintendence of the plantation
authorities. This was also necessary on some other estates. When the necessity for this order should cease I intended to have recourse to a general
arrangement of assigning the half Friday in each week, or alternate Fridays
to this purpose. These orders so equitable and so absolutely necessary for
the people's welfare were opposed, and assisted by a combination of the
plantation labourers.

My district comprises that part of Saint Ann's where similar combina-
tions had taken effect with great danger to the peace of the colony in the first
month of the apprenticeship; it became expedient therefore that I should
put this spirit of lawlessness down with promptitude. I was necessitated
to do then, what I never had done before, and what I have happily been
spared the necessity of doing since, of inflicting the most degrading penal-
ties on the males and females who were prominent actors, in this resistance
of a whole plantation to the orders of the magistrate. The punishments
particularized were accordingly inflicted — viz.

10 men corporal punishment
13 women treadwheel, twice a day, 5 days
8 ditto, solitary confinement 5 days.

No females however, ever put forward a plea of pregnancy to stay the
sentence of the treadmill, or solitary confinement, or an increase of hard
labour in the house of correction. I should have been too happy to have
been spared by any warranted general plea the infliction of a punishment
which though a violence of my feelings, my urgent public duty compelled

me to. I should willingly have listened to a proper reason for clemency. I appeal to the readiness with which I have inflicted the heaviest penalty of the law on persons in authority on plantations, who have subjected pregnant women to severe labour or oppressive restraint, for the absolute impossibility of my disregarding so. (Woolfrys to Darling 16 July 1838, enc. in Smith to Glenelg No. 146, 7 August 1838, P.R.O. CO 137/229)

73. In Betty Williams's evidence, immediately above that of Thomas, this name is written as Dianah Johnston.

74. Probably James Lawrence Hilton. See n. 66 of the *Narrative*.

75. John Williams was a missionary with the Wesleyan Methodist Missionary Society from 1835 to 1846. In 1837 he was based in St. Ann's Bay.

76. Mr. Hull was probably one of Gilbert and Sarah Senior's half-brothers, Henry Allen Hull, Charles John Hull, or William Weaver Hull. Edward Jones, the apprentice referred to here, gave evidence (pp. 84–85).

77. A Richard Hemmings is listed in the slave compensation records as the attorney of Seville estate.

78. Israel Lemon of St. Ann's Bay applied for compensation for six slaves.

79. The distinction between praying and preaching was significant because the slave laws had made it illegal for slaves to preach, but not for them to pray.

ADDITIONAL DOCUMENTS

LETTERS FROM JOSEPH STURGE

Sturge to the Rev. John Clark, Browns Town, 23 March 1837

My Dear Friend [1]

James Williams arrived here this evening. I will have the money for his purchase and the cost of his clothes with our mutual friend James Phillippo [2] to be handed to thee [3] the first opportunity. The valuation is no doubt a very unjust one but it will only the more strongly exemplify the abuses of the system I rather expected they would have insisted upon making him a praedial in which case they would no doubt have ran the sum up much higher. We saw a weakly woman valued at 63£ —d at Four Paths [4] on Saturday. I make the sum according to the window on the back of thy letter. Say as under

| Valuation | 8 doubloons 10 dollars & half and 2 bits |
| Clothes | 6   ″   & three quarters [5] |
| 9 doubloons 1 1/4 dollars and 2 bits |

if this is not correct I will make it so — & I shall of course hold myself responsible as I mentioned at Savannah La Mar to the extent of 10£ — for any relief you may think it right to give in very pressing cases such as the poor sick woman we saw when with you. With kind regards to thy wife very truly thy affectionate fr.

Jos Sturge

Spanish Town March 23, 1837

Sturge to Clark, 30 May 1837

My Dear Friend

We arrived here safe on the 15 Inst. [6] at Liverpool after a most favorable voyage both from Jamaica to New York & from thence to Liverpool. James Williams from his easy life & good living has gained I should think near ⅓rd in weight and he excites so much notice that I fear he will be injured by it. Dr Palmer has been writing his history & observations since the 1st of August 1834 and we are getting it through the press as fast as we can but I fear it will not be ready to send you any by this Packet. I have had a valuable opportunity to bring the state of things before the members of the Society of Friends now in London at which 1,500 to 2,000 were present from various parts of the Kingdom I occupied about 2 hours in reading cases &c and towards the close read your letter to us.[7] A lively interest was excited and a unanimous conclusion come to that we shld endeavour to tour the country to demand the abolition of the apprenticeship at the earliest possible period. Please excuse haste & brevity but I did not like to let the packet go without writing thee a line. With very kind regards to thy wife thy affectionate friend

Jos Sturge

London 5/30 1837[8]

31st. I have been examined today before the Committee[9] at considerable length & have already I believe so far excited the ire of Sir G. Grey[10] that that [sic] I expect to get nothing from the Colonial Office except through their [illegible].

[Sideways down the center of the paper] The acct of James Williams is likely to excite considerable sensation in the character of him as given by the members of thy church thou omitted to witness to the signature. Wilt thou please to send me another copy so attested with any further confirmatory evidence as to his character especially for veracity. I have no reason to alter my good opinion of him.

[On the back flap] James delivers his love. The minister & his wife, to his father & sister & two brothers and Wm Dalling & Thomas Brown & he wish all on the pen to be told he is well likes England rather better than Jamaica.[11] Ja is quite well and hopes soon to learn to write so as to be able to send a letter himself.

Sturge to Clark, 15 June 1837
My Dear Friend
   The papers which will accompany this packet will tell you what lately we are doing here. I am now before the Parliamentary Commit-

tee and though it is not with my wish yet I am not without hope it may be useful. I have stated distinctly to them that I would not be shackled as to any thing I might do in Public either by printing or at Public Meetings we are attempting a Public Meeting shortly in London. James Williams history is likely to be useful here and will I suppose produce quite a sensation in Jamaica if it is published there you will get the greater part of it as copied in the Patriot[12] which we send thee by this mail. The annexed is a plate of the proposed memorial to Lord Sligo. James is at the Borough Road School at present and I expect to see him and add a message to his friends in this letter shortly before I close it.[13] I shall I expect have to give up some names but what is going forward will I expect lead at least to the dismissal of Rawlinson. Please keep a sharp look out to see if any who gave us information at thy house are persecuted and immediately inform R Hill.[14] Dr Palmer seems confident that they will not however dare to do so. Excuse great haste & [four illegible words] & with kind regards to thy wife. Thy affectionate fd

Js Sturge

London 6/15, 1837

[On back] Tell James Williams friends he is attending at the School at the Borough Road. I have not seen him today.

Sturge to Clark, 15 August 1837

My Dear Friend

The comparatively idle life and luxurious living but probably above all the attention James Williams has attracted and his introduction to persons and situations so different to what he was accustomed has as I ought perhaps have certainly to have expected produced an unfavourable effect upon him & although he perhaps behaves as well as I ought to expect I find him going on so very far from satisfactorily that I believe it will be the kindest thing to him or at least by far the best chance for him to escape complete ruin to send him back as soon as I can; we are looking out for a vessel and suitable person to put him under his care. I shall if he goes direct him to proceed to thee I think on landing in Jamaica for he will no doubt not be satisfied without seeing his father & family and though I think there is some risk in there being an attempt made to punish him for the facts which have been made public from his statement yet I think he is more likely to settle down over there in steady employment than anywhere else and the dread of falling into the hands of those from whom he suffered so much may be a good check upon him. If he gets into the hands of our enemies I think it likely they may make him contradict his story by some means or another and of the two I think there is more danger in this country of mischief from that than in Jamaica as well as perhaps their making greater efforts to inveigle him away. If he act with good sense and properly on his return to Jamaica I think it may be concealed from the public there and his own friends and acquaintances will I trust be too fully aware of the mischief that may result to him from its being known to disclose it. In case of his going I of course mean to write this more fully. I think the only means of bringing him to a proper sense of situation is for him to be compelled to labour for his bread and though I will of course see that thou art at no loss in contributing to his absolute need I believe he is in danger of being quite unmanageable unless he thinks he must depend upon himself alone for support & this while he is here cannot be accomplished. The statements which I have published & put in evidence before the Committee of the House of Commons are I understand to be violently assailed and contradicted by the West Indians [15] & this is no more than I expected and I suppose they will stick at nothing to accomplish their purpose. I think it likely that I may write but some of the statements we wrote down when with you and forward them for the parties to verify them. We must look mainly to your efforts I mean the Baptist Missionaries & those few who act upon the bold and evident ground that you do to protect the rights of the Negroes, if you will continue to supply us with the facts showing the violations of the imperial act our publishing them from time to time here will be the most effectual check to abuses. Thou would have heard of the defeat of T F Buxton at Weymouth [16] and this I fear will be seen as a help to the Pro Slavery Party in the West Indies but his health was so indifferent that several of his own family did not want him to stand again. I hope there is an increasing interest excited upon the Anti Slavery Question especially amongst your body. I think the publication of your addresses both the one you gave to us at Savannah La Mar & the one that was sent to John Dyer [17] by one of your brethren in Sept last year have had a very useful effect but my reading the latter at the public meeting at Exeter Hall [18] & putting it in evidence before the Committee of the House of

Commons did not please all your Mission Board in London I expect. With very kind regards to thy wife

Very truly thy affectionate fd

Jos Sturge

Birmingham 8/15, 1837

[On back flap] I hope to [illegible word] to buy thee the postage at a convenient opportunity but if they are had here I believe they are sometimes charged on your side also.

Sturge to Clark, 13 September 1837

Birmingham 9th month 13th, 1837.

My Dear Friend

I am in rcpt of thy letter of the 24th of July & was truly sorry to hear of our mutual friend Wm Knibb's heavy domestic affliction.[19] I had a letter from him the packet before conveying the heart cheering intelligence that all the members of his & Burchell's churches who held apprentices wld liberate them on the 1st of August.[20] Dr Palmer & I have concluded that it would be safest for James Williams to remain at Kingston when he lands. I wrote to thee about him by a former Packet. Dr Palmer has taken the passage for J Williams by the "Porter" which is expected to sail from Liverpool this week and I sent these few lines by him. The cases thou hast furnished me with are very striking ones I mean to have them published if not sent to the Colonial Office. Please forward others as they come to light. It will be a little less expensive to send single sheets than two together when they are over an ounce the last cost 8/8 instead of 4/4 on that amt. I merely mention it for thy guidance in future. If there should be an alarm about it oppressions exercised upon the Negroes driving them to desperation till would probably convince our Colonial Office to join us in breaking up this infamous apprenticeship—and the probability of this has been hinted at from another part of the Island in a letter I got from last packet. Excuse haste & brevity & believe me very surely very kind regards to thy wife.

Thy affectionate f

Jos Sturge

[On back in another hand] Recd yesty. JW is not yet come up.

Sturge to Rev. F. Gardner, Kingston, 29 September 1837
My Dear Friend[21]

We have found it needful to send James Williams back to Jamaica (the boy I brought home with me) and he sailed from Liverpool last week. I have given him a letter to thee and Dr Palmer has written to Jordon about him.[22] We think it best he should not go back to Brown's Town at least at present and though I am very sorry to give thee any trouble about him & I think for his own sake he should be obliged to work for his bread yet I should feel much obliged to thee to have an eye to him and if he behaves at all to thy satisfaction I leave it to thy discretion to incur some expense on my acct to get him into a satisfactory situation. The indulgence & attention he has had has done him a great deal of harm but I hope will not permanently injure his character but Dr Palmer & I both agreed that it was needful he should leave England at once. We think he is less likely to attract notice in Kingston than in the country and if he can be kept out of harms way the next 6 or 8 months even if he should turn out an indifferent character afterwards the *cause* might not suffer by it; with this view it may be well to bear with a little indiscretion or indolence in him for a time than cast him off at once but as I said before if it is possible it will be much better for him to feel that he is obliged to work for his bread and I think his fears of falling into his old masters hands will keep him in Kingston. I cannot at all tell what turn the question of the abolition of the apprenticeship in 1838 will take. There is a growing & spreading feeling in the Country in favor of it but we have reason to fear ministers are opposed to it. A good deal will depend upon the accounts we receive of how things are going on with you I expect. Those I have from your brethren in the Country give a melancholy picture of the suffering of the Negroes. The ladies memorial to the Queen is signed by upwards of 420,000 for England alone.[23] Will thou be kind enough to send this on to Jn Clark of Brown's Town by the next post to whom I have addressed a few lines on the other side. Please remember me very kindly to thy wife and our fd Anderson[24] when thou sees them. I hope you receive good acts from Joshua Tinson in America.[25]

Very kindly
Thy affectionate fd
Jos. Sturge
Birmingham 9th month 29, 1837

Kind and put this package to what thou may pay on James Williams acct for me.

(To Jn Clark Brown's Town)
My Dear Friend
    I am obliged by thy letters one with striking cases of cruelty and the other with attestations to James Williams character and the confirmation of the truth of his narrative which is very valuable as I doubt not at the opening of Parliament the truth of it will be assailed if the Committee is appointed which I understand it is intended to do by Government. They will continue this Committee to the end of 1840 or longer if the question is not carried in some other way and we are in hopes of getting the floor divided upon the question of abolition of the apprenticeship on the 1st August 1838.[26] It is probable when it is known that T F Buxton is no longer in the House of Commons that the West Indians will think it a triumph and proceed with you with more recklessness in their cruelties. I shall be anxious to hear whether things are going on worse or better. With very kind regards to thy wife. Very truly. Thy affectionate fd.

Jos Sturge

Birmingham 9/29 1837
    Thou will see by the annexed what we have concluded to do with James Williams. I hope the indulgence he has had will not be found to have *permanently* injured him. It does not appear that Senior attempts to deny the facts as far as he is concerned. It would be very desirable if possible to get some of his workhouse accts confirmed.

Extract from the Letter to the Editor of the Birmingham Advertiser,
16 October 1837, Reprinted in the Falmouth Post, *20 December 1837*
[Sturge responds to a letter copied in the *Birmingham Advertiser* from the *Jamaica Despatch and New Courant*, bearing initials A.B., "a well known pro-slavery writer." He refutes various of A.B.'s charges; his attacks on Negro character are "calumnious and untrue."]
    A.B. observes on my report, "the climax of his tale of horror is told by James Williams, one of the most worthless hell-cats that ever cheated the gallows!" This is a ripe specimen of the Colonial practice of rebutting testimony by vilifying the witness, but the poison carries with it its own antidote.

The "Narrative" dictated by James Williams to a third party in England, is perfectly consistent with his statements to myself and my associate in Jamaica, and with those of his fellow-apprentices, who were themselves sufferers in some of the scenes he describes. One of the Missionaries residing near the property on which he lived, says in a recent letter to me, "I have carefully read the 'Narrative' as given in the *Patriot,* and though not an eye-witness of what he relates, I had heard *from others* most of the particulars, *none of which had he at all exaggerated or misrepresented.*" [27] My correspondent states also, that he read the Narrative to three fellow-apprentices of James Williams; "In these three men," he observes, "I have the most perfect confidence; they declare that 'James Williams's Narrative' is true. In reading it to them the *only* error they could discover was, that Thomas Brown Lawrence (called in the Narrative Thomas Brown) was not one of the three flogged by the police; he was flogged by the constable of the property."

The correspondence in my possession, and other important documentary evidence of the truth of the Narrative, I shall be happy to show to any one who may be disposed to see them. I would also observe that the "Narrative" has been republished in the Jamaica papers, and has excited abusive and angry comments, *but not one of its facts has been attempted to be disproved.* His master, G. W. Senior, has published a letter which confirms its truth, as he admits many of the details of the Narrative, and does not deny one of the statements. Like A.B. he contents himself with vilifying James Williams's character; the sum at which he was valued (about three times the ordinary value of a domestic apprentice) is a sufficient answer to these calumnies. It was the price not only of an industrious and capable, but of an honest and orderly apprentice, (for moral qualities have a money value in Jamaica) and his master has either calumniated him, or he is in possession of the proceeds of a fraudulent valuation.

If there be, then, as I conceive there is, incontrovertible evidence of the truth of James Williams's Narrative, can any reader of it persuade himself that the Negroes would have been liable to greater oppression, or have endured a greater amount of misery when they were slaves in name as well as in fact?

It only remains to ask, whether it was to secure such a system as this that the British nation paid twenty millions sterling? and if not, whether our representatives and Government are not bound to cancel the contract which has been thus shamefully and fraudulently violated by the planters.

Sturge to Clark, 1 December 1837

My Dear Friend.

I am anxiously waiting the arrival of the full particulars of Daughtrey, Lyon & Gordon's investigations.[28] I had not time to write thee by last packet being closely engaged in the labours connected with the Anti Slavery Delegation to London an acct of which thou would see in the Patriots which have been forwarded. I now annex the copy of a resolution passed by the new Negro Emancipation Committee formed in London.[29] If some petitions of this kind could be forwarded to be presented in the spring Session they would I think have a very good effect. Government will I fear oppose us & nothing will make them yield but a fear of the consequences. I have just discovered that I do not appear to have brought the resolution of the London Committee with me from London. The substance of it was, That it was the opinion of the Committee that the Negroes had a perfect right to petition for the redress of their grievances & for their perfect liberty but in doing so the Committee commended them strongly to pursue the same peaceable conduct as the people of this country did when petitioning. If any petitions from them are forwarded I think there shld be as little delay as circumstances will admit. I have been so incessantly engaged that I fear that the haste in which I write will make me omit some thing I wish to say I fear the Colonial Office is so much against us that we must I expect adopt a different course to what we yet have but I think the people of England will stand by us if you are enabled to stand your ground in the colony and I trust you will be strengthened by divine aid to do so. I hope I shall shortly receive all the particulars mentioned in thy letter of the 24th of Septr which is the last I have had from thee. Please remember me very kindly to thy wife also to B. Dexter J Stainsby.[30] Our work is just out & I hope shortly to send them a copy.[31] I am very anxious to hear how James Williams goes on for though the official investigation has established the truth of his narrative I should be very sorry that his journey to England should have been a permanent injury to him which it would I am persuaded had he remained longer here. He will I trust now be safe even if he returns to Brown's Town but I have written to F Gardner and rather recommended his putting him to a trade in Kingston if he goes on steadily and satisfactorily. We are likely to issue a publication once a fortnight in London[32] & I expect it will be stampt I hope that you will all get it by and by.

Very truly & respectfully

Thy affectionate fd

Jos Sturge

Birmingham 12/1, 1837

Sturge to Clark, 30 December 1837

My Dear Friend

I am favored of the 21st of Otr only by the last packet though it brings thou intelligence up to the 15th and had I not recd a most favourable acct from some of thy brethren I should have been quite anxious under a fear that thou must not recovered from thy severe illness. I hope & trust that the anxiety & suffering to which thou has been subjected in reference to the deeds of darkness disclosed in James Williams pamphlet will be abundantly rewarded both to thyself & the poor suffering negroes I have not yet recd the evidence & we are anxiously expecting it. The report of the Commissioners has reached us and a number of private letters besides them stating that far more than was stated in the narrative had come to light. When I go to London next I mean to read the letter to the Negro Emancipation Committee respecting remuneration to Castello[33] & though our funds are low and the demands upon them at present unusually heavy it shall not be my fault if *some* present is not sent him for his labours of course I shall not propose it till we are in possession of the Evidence. There was one case of an old man that had been shockingly mangled that James Williams mentions as meeting with on the road that Dr Palmer was very desirous should be fully investigated. I doubt not that we shall find that it is the case. Thou shall I trust get by the packet a copy of our new periodical the British Emancipator. You will I hope in future get one generally every packet as it is to be issued once a fortnight being stamped it goes free of expence. I have forwarded to the care of Joshua Tinson some copies of our new works for our friends of course it contains one for thee. I think I understand by the papers Rawlinson is suspended.[34] I greatly hope James Williams may again settle down comfortably in Jamaica. I was sorry to hear that it was supposed he had the small pox on board

the vessel in Kingston harbour when the last accts came away. I believe
I told thee in a former letter that I had recommended James Williams
stopping at Kingston but I leave his friends to judge of this. It was Dr
Palmers opinion but now his narrative is fully proved there is little danger of his injuring the cause if his conduct should not be satisfactory
to his fds which I hope it will not. Excuse extreme haste & with very
kind regards to thy wife believe me very truly thy affectionate fd

Jos Sturge

12/30, 1837
The papers sent from home to Tinson will inform thee of our Proceedings. We had a valuable meeting here on Thursday.

[On other side] Dont forget to charge postage to me. I am glad our
new publication will convey Anti Slavery information free of expense.
Kind regards to our fds Dexter & Stainsby I have enclosed each of them
a book in the box to J Tinson.

LETTERS AND AFFIDAVITS OF AND ENCLOSED BY
GILBERT WILLIAM AND SARAH JANE KEITH SENIOR

Gilbert Senior to the Editor of the Jamaica Despatch
and New Courant, *Published 11 August 1837*
Sir— In your last Saturday's Despatch you wish information respecting
the boy James, who was purchased by Sturge, and taken to England,
for the purpose of corroborating some of the Lies of the Quakers.

I know this boy James to be a great villain; James is the son of an
African woman, who was given to my sister by a relative; he was born
on this property; was brought up in the house, and treated with the
greatest kindness by his mistress; his evil propensities commenced
early, for he was such a thief that he was sent from the house to attend
sheep and other stock, but was still fed and clothed by his mistress.

Previous to the first of August, 1834, he went to Captain Connor, the
Special Magistrate, and got instructions from him to annoy us in every
possible way. He had so much influence with Connor as to prevent his
visiting the property on the 19th of December, 1834. Mr. Thompson,
a Special Magistrate, was ordered by the Governor to visit the property, and to enquire into the complaints I had found necessary to make
to him. This boy James was sentenced by him to receive 39 stripes for

repeated insolence to both master and mistress. As soon as Captain Dillon was appointed Special Magistrate of the District, he went to him and made his story good with him as he had done before with Connor, and I could not prevail on Dillon to visit the property but I was repeatedly summoned on the complaint of James, to attend his court at Brown's Town. Dillon at last found that James had been imposing on him, and on the 6th of January, 1835, sentenced him to be confined in a cell on the next estate, for ten days and nights. His conduct was still so bad, that I was compelled to bring him before Special Justice Rawlinson, who sentenced him to receive 20 stripes. On the 4th of April, he was again sentenced to receive 25 stripes. On the 12th of May, he was ordered to appear before Mr. Rawlinson, when he went away, and did not return till he was taken by a Constable, who was sent in search of him; he was then sentenced to the house of correction for 10 days.

In April, 1836, a barrel of Salt Pork had been opened, and only one or two pieces had been taken out on Wednesday the 6th, it was discovered that at least 6 or 8 pieces had been stolen, and James not to be found, a constable was sent to look for him, who brought him in, having found him on a property several miles distant; he confessed having stolen the pork, and was ordered by the magistrate to pay two or three dollars. On the 10th August he was again sentenced to receive 15 stripes for general neglect of work and insolence. On the 3rd September, having been detected by the watchman stealing yams from the garden, he absconded, and was absent 3 or 4 days when he returned with a note from a neighbour. On this occasion Mr. Rawlinson only admonished him, and advised him to behave better in future. On the 19th November he was so insolent that I ordered a constable to put him into the cell, when he said, in a threatening manner, "God never made the world for man to rule, and man shall not rule it." On the 23rd November I was compelled to complain again to the magistrate, who sentenced him to the house of correction for one month. On the 9th December, after neglecting his work, and being very insolent, he again absconded, and was taken in St. Thomas in the Vale, on his way to see the Governor (Lord Sligo); he was again flogged and sent to the house of correction.

This is a plain statement of facts, which cannot be contradicted. More could be proved on oath by respectable persons, if necessary. I have every right to believe that the said boy James stole my stock, as he had the charge of them; and I lost in August, 1834, upwards of 20 sheep, and several cows and calves.

If roguery and bad conduct is what Sturge sought for, he could not have been more successful in his mission; for a fitter subject for the gallows than Williams could not be found in the world.

I am, Sir, your obedient servant,

G. W. Senior

Penshurst, Dry-Harbour, August 1, 1837.

Gilbert Senior to the Editor of the Saint Jago de la Vega Gazette, *Published in Edition of 5–12 August 1837*

Sir.

Some kind friend in England having enclosed to me one of the narratives of James Williams, at the expense of 18s 9d postage, gives me an opportunity of refuting the lies therein stated as facts. That the apprentices get more punishment now than when they were slaves is certainly true, but was not this caused by their own insolence, and setting the authority of the master at defiance, as soon as they knew that they could only be punished by a special magistrate, who they were led to believe would rather punish the master than the apprentice. This boy James was brought up in the great house, and treated with the greatest kindness till he turned out to be a thief, and was sent to tend the sheep, but was still fed and clothed by his mistress, his mother being unable to assist him. As he grew up, he had charge of a few cows, as well as the sheep, and generally slept in the kitchen, and was in the habit of stealing corn and provisions from the stores for some time before he was detected, but, as he acknowledges, never was punished severely. On the first of August, 1834, he was extremely insolent, told me he had been with Captain Connor, who was now his master, and that he had told him the law, and that he would not be imposed upon. I was obliged to submit to his insolence and neglect of duty for some time, expecting Captain Connor would visit the property, as he was bound to do by law. I wrote repeatedly to Captain Connor, who I found was under the influence of this boy, and the rest of the negroes, that he would not come to the property to enquire into my complaints. The insolence of the people was such that I considered the lives of my sister and self to be in danger. One day he was more insolent than usual, and tried to provoke me to strike him, but I went into the house. As I went towards the front of the house I observed this rascal watching me, and as there were most of the negroes with him, and the whole of them had been also very insolent, I did not know but that they intended to attack me, I therefore took my gun, and thought it necessary to be prepared for them. — He then said I saw you load your gun, that does not look well, I will go to Captain Connor and tell him. I said you may go to Captain Connor and tell him that I have a brace of pistols also in capital order. He went off immediately to Connor, who lived about eighteen miles off. What he told him I do not know but he would not come here, though I sent my overseer the same day to let him know how I was situated.

On the 3d of November, 1834, he followed his mistress to the fowl house and dared her to strike him. The whole of the negroes, who seemed to be urged on by this villain, continued in such a state of insubordination that I considered we were not safe, and stated the facts to Lord Sligo, who ordered Dr. Palmer to investigate the matter. Palmer came and left us just as we were. He would not punish any, though he found them almost in a state of rebellion. He talked to them for some time, and persuaded me to withdraw my charges, on their promising to behave better in future.

About the first of August, 1834, I had eighteen young lambs, under the charge of this boy James, I lost the whole of them, as well as several cows and calves, and yet this boy, whose veracity has been attested by six members of a Christian church, (all no doubt as veracious as himself), says "he was flogged for foolish, trifling thing, just to please massa." It would be endless to repeat the hourly insults and injuries we suffered from this chosen witness of the Quaker Sturge — "*Noscitur a Sociis,*" was never so completely verified.[35]

This boy of such veracity acknowledges having been an accessary [*sic*] in stealing one piece of pork out of a barrel, but it was proved before the special magistrate that there were six or seven pieces taken out, which he did not deny, and yet he says he was not punished, though I had vowed vengeance against him, and told him he should be of no use to himself after the apprenticeship. If the *boy James* had stolen only one piece of pork out of Joseph Sturge's barrel what would have been his punishment?

As to his keeping watch at night, I would rather have dispensed with his company in the yard, and have repeatedly ordered him not to remain there at night, but he persisted in staying, that he might help himself to whatever was within his reach in the stores. Repeated complaints were made by the watchmen that James stole corn, yams, or any thing they had under their charge. He even robbed his own father. His charges against Mr. Rawlinson are all false, for, so far from punishing him without sufficient cause, Mr. Rawlinson has frequently tried by admonishing him to prevail on him to behave well.

Will Joseph Sturge be able to persuade his brother Quakers that any person, to gratify his malignant passions, (perhaps he may judge of others by himself) will sacrifice his interest in the services of a servant (who is bound to him for a short time only,) by repeated punishment and consequent loss of labour, which I have suffered in the case of this boy James, whose services would have been invaluable had he conducted himself properly. As he has behaved, I feel much pleasure in knowing that such a villain is not in this neighbourhood, as I have been in nightly expectation of my stores being plundered by him, particularly when I sleep from home.

I am,
Your obedient servant,
G. W. Senior.
Penshurst, 8th August, 1837.

Affidavits of 10 and 11 October 1837, Sent to the Commissioners of Enquiry, Printed at the End of the Commissioners' Report

AFFIDAVIT OF GILBERT SENIOR

Jamaica, SS.—St. Ann.

Personally appeared before me, Gilbert William Senior, who being duly sworn, states that he has known William Dalling for many years. That previous to the 1st day of August, 1834, he considered William Dalling to be a faithful and attached servant, and had no fault to find with him, except that he frequently, when he had an opportunity, got intoxicated, but he was always civil and obedient, to both master and mistress, who had the greatest confidence in him, and could always believe what he said. On the first day of August, 1834, he became insolent and discontented; and though he claimed to be classed as a domestic, he took all the time allowed to the praedials. He seemed, from the first of August, to be the director of all James Williams' movements, urging him on to be insolent and disobedient. It was part of William Dalling's duty to see that James Williams dressed the sheep, before they were turned out every morning, but from the first of August every thing was neglected, and the deponent lost the greater part of eighteen lambs, which were under the care of these two apprentices.

From the 1st August, 1834, deponent observed an entire change in William Dalling. He joined the sect called Baptists, who had so much power over him, as to break him of the habit of intoxication, but they taught him another habit, never to speak truth.

In his evidence before the Magistrates, when he said he never carried food to James Williams and Adam Brown when they were confined in the cells at Knapdale, he said what was false. A sufficient quantity of food, rather more than was ordered by Captain Dillon, was given to William Dalling to carry to Knapdale for James Williams and Adam Brown, with orders to clean out the cells. Peter Atkinson might some-times have carried them food, but he was a sawyer, and it is not likely that he would have been taken from his work every day, leaving his fellow-sawyer to be idle till he returned. His evidence respecting the nave of the cart-wheel having injured Henry James's stomach when he was flogged by orders of Dr. Thompson, is false, for it is impossible that his stomach could have touched the nave of a cart-wheel five feet in diameter. Henry James had for years complained of pain in his stom-ach, and for that reason was taken from the saw and placed as a watch-man. His evidence that James Williams did not assist John Lawrence in stealing the pork is false; James Williams himself acknowledges the fact, and William Dalling was quite aware that they were both con-cerned in the robbery.

William Dalling said that he did not know if the people got medi-cine when sick. Marianne Bell[36] stated that medicine was never refused. William Dalling, being always in the yard, must have know that it was so. Previous to the 1st of August, 1834, William Dalling always took the medicine from his mistress to give to the sick, but his behaviour was so bad afterwards that he was not entrusted with it.

William Dalling swore that he did not know James Williams to be a thief. Deponent has no hesitation in stating, that William Dalling knew that James Williams was a notorious thief. He knew that he robbed the provision-grounds, and that he was several times detected by the watchmen, that he stole provisions of all kinds out of the Stores,

and that, the last time he was sent to the House of Correction, he stole
the house-dog, which he must have sold, as the dog was never heard
of again.

(Signed) G. W. Senior

Sworn before me, this 10th day of October, 1837.

(Signed) Thos. Raffington, Jr.[37]

James Williams, an apprentice to Miss Senior, has been about the
yard and house since he was a baby, his mother was a domestic and very
indolent and sickly; he was almost supported by his master and mistress till within a few years. Becoming troublesome about the house
he was sent to attend the stock (which he seemed to have a taste for)
and carry grass and breadnuts for them, which kept him still a good
deal about the yard, where he always slept. Once in my brother's absence, who had taken the other servants with him, he came in to get
my tea; when that was over, I desired him to see about his other business, but he would not, and laid himself down on the floor, to give me
an account of my cattle, he said, that his master might not cheat me.
When I told him to go away, he shut the door, put his foot against it,
and kept thumping it with his back for some time. I said, James this is
not to be borne with, will you go about your business? From the noise
he made, I think he must have had an accomplice, and wished to prevent my hearing what was going forwards. After repeatedly speaking
to him, he said he would go if I would give him a piece of candle. To
get quit of him, I told him to take a piece that was on the table, though
his master had often told him he should not get a candle, as there was
no occasion for it. Before going to bed, I went to the store, and was as-
tonished to find a large frock[38] that I had made Marianne[39] (one of the
house-women) put on the barrel of sugar at dusk, in the middle of the
room. I called Marianne, and, shewing it to her, she said, "Hi! misses
been make me put that on the sugar barrel before tea, and how it come
down here?" The watchman, who was asleep in the kitchen, declared
it could be no one but James Williams. A good deal of the sugar was
gone, and the flour barrel next to it was also plundered. We were, after
that out of provisions and obliged to purchase; I put the yams in the
same store, and was surprised that they lasted so short a time. I spoke to
the person I bought them from; she said they did seem to go fast, but I

could not blame her as I saw them weighed. I could not find out where they went, 'till one day my brother went to the provision-grounds and got half a basket of cocoas; he had them brought in to me, and said, you must make the most of those till we can get some more; they were mostly fine large cocoas; at night I went to give some of them out for breakfast, when, to my astonishment, most of the best were gone, and only a few of the smaller ones left; the servants pretended to look for them, but returned and said they were no where to be found. This kind of pilfering had been going on so long, that I then said I will search myself. After looking in several places, I thought of the kitchen; on going there, I found a large calabash heaped up with the very cocoas, and James fast asleep on a board by the fire, after, no doubt, having made a good supper on some of them. I kept what I found, and the next morning James claimed them. I then called William Dalling, who looked at them, and said, they are master's cocoas. James has none like them. The little boy (Graham[40]) was then called, who brought them in and said they were the same that he brought in. I considered the said James Williams so friendless that he would bring his clothes to me to have made for him, and I always had them done. He never made a proper ground or attended to it, so that he could not support himself without stealing from others. William Dalling knew all this, and yet comes forward and takes his oath that James Williams is an industrious boy and a good character. As soon as the apprenticeship began he did every thing to annoy us, and for no cause, for often when William Dalling wished to impose on him I have prevented it.

(Signed) S. J. K. Senior
Sworn before me, this 10th day of October, 1837.
(Signed) Edwd. Tucker.

AFFIDAVIT OF SARAH SENIOR

William Dalling, apprentice to Miss Senior, has been in her family ever since a child of eighteen months old: first with her grandmother, and at her death to Miss S.,[41] on whom and her brother he was waited on ever since, and always considered by them, and all acquainted with them, as a valuable servant, remarkably civil and attentive, never disobeying an order, or dissatisfied when required to do any thing in his own time. Every confidence was placed in him, and they would have vouched for his truth and honesty; but, since joining the Baptists and the Apprenticeship system, he has entirely altered; he has shewn his ill will to his owners every way; he has sworn to the most abominable falsehoods; he says he saw nothing wrong in James Williams' conduct. The last time James Williams was punished, before the apprenticeship commenced, was by Wm. Dalling in his master's absence from home, he came to his mistress and said, I have cut some switches for James. She enquired for what fault. He replied, he took the donkeys to go for breadnut, tied them at the gate, and went about his business, and when I spoke to him about it, he took them out of sight and beat them severely; he is really a bad boy.

(Signed) S. J. K. Senior

Sworn before me, this 11th day of October, 1837.

(Signed) Edwd. Tucker.

Letter from Gilbert Senior to Warren, the Governor's Secretary, Printed in the Jamaica Despatch and New Courant, *22 November 1837, and Forwarded by Smith to the Colonial Office 24 November 1837*

Penshurst, Runaway Bay, Nov 14 1837 [42]

Sir—I will thank you to lay before the Governor the enclosed affidavit.

This Adam Brown was in the house till he was big enough to clean horse, and after cleaning them used to go for breadnut leaves or grass alternately with James Williams, and when I went out followed me as groom; he was the only servant who attended me all through the late martial law,[43] and always went with me to town. When we went any distance we generally put 4 horses to the carriage, and Adam Browns [*sic*] drove the leaders as postillion; he was remarkably civil and obedient, and I considered him much attached to us.

On the 1st of August, 1834, he joined James Williams in annoying us in every possible way and he was repeatedly punished. At last he begged to be allowed to change his class and go to the field, and agreement was entered into, and signed by Mr. Rawlinson, since which I have not had occasion to find fault with him.

We always suspected that William Dalling was the instigator of the bad conduct of these boys, which Adam Brown now proves in his affidavit to have been the fact, and which would never have been ascertained had this quarrel not taken place.

The evidence of Charles Trueman[44] and Mary Ann Bell, taken before the commissioners, is now corroborated by Adam Brown, and shews that the evidence of William Dalling, and those under his influence, is not worthy of belief, and fully bears me out in the statements I have made.

I think this affidavit will convince every unprejudiced person that there has been a combination to injure my character, of which I never had a doubt, and should be able to clear, if I was allowed that justice which every man has a right to—for "truth is mighty and will prevail."

I hope the affidavit will be transmitted to Lord Glenelg as soon as possible, who I am convinced is desirous of hearing the truth only.

I have the honor to be, &c.

G. W. Senior

To S. R. Warren, Esq.

Jamaica SS
St. Ann's

Personally appeared before me, one of her Majesty's Justices of the Peace of the aforesaid Parish, Adam Brown, a praedial apprenticed labourer, belonging to Penshurst, who maketh oath and saith, that last Friday[45] he was in the field at 12 o'clock, when the shell blew to draw off; Joseph Lawrence said, all we sensible people must go to Brown's Town; deponent asked him, what for? he said, about the Friday; deponent then asked him, what about the Friday? he said, we must go and complain that massa did not give the full half Friday; deponent told him, the way they were going on, both white and black would find fault with them; Marianne Lawrence said, they must take deponent to the constable, for he and massa had made bargain; they said, Henry Brown and deponent "must" go to Brown's Town;[46] deponent said he would not go, for he had no charge against his massa, and advised Henry Brown not to go; deponent told them, if they kept on so, he would tell massa; Wednesday (the 8th inst.) all the gang, excepting Joseph Lawrence and Alexander Mills, attacked him in the negro-houses, and William Mills licked him with a rope, and twice with his fist, by orders of his (deponent's) father, William Dalling, who was present, and saw it well done; William Mills attempted to knock deponent down with a stick, but his (deponent's) mother ran and caught the stick; they (William Mills and Henry McCook[47]) threw deponent down upon the ground, choked and beat him, and tore his clothes; when deponent raised up, he told them he knew what all this was for, because he would not join in telling lies against massa; that before time when he used to carry massa to Court, it was by their advice; deponent's father, William Dalling, and some of those who bought up their apprenticeship, used to advise him (deponent) to bother massa; deponent has every reason to believe, that the beating he has received, was in consequence of having said that if he went to Brown's Town Court, he would always speak the truth, and that he would always speak the truth when carried to Brown's Town against his master.

(Signed) Adam Brown

Sworn before me, this 10th day of November, 1837.

(Signed) Edw Tucker

Gilbert Senior to the Editor of the Jamaica Despatch and New Courant, *Published 2 December 1837*

Sir—In consequence of seeing in the Despatch Messrs. Gordon and Daughtrey's letter, respecting their Report on James Williams' Pamphlet, I thought it necessary to procure some affidavits in contradiction of some of the evidence which they received, and have no doubt, transmitted to the Executive as gospel. Having written twice to the Governor's Secretary, on the subject of the investigation at Brown's Town, and neither of my letters having been acknowledged, I think it best to enclose the affidavits to you; as through your paper they will attract the attention of some of the Members, who may be desirous of knowing the truth, and the whole truth; and will shew how little dependence can be placed on the evidence taken by the Commissioners. Many of the Penshurst people, and some who have purchased their apprenticeship, having been examined in my absence, I am quite ignorant of the nature of their evidence. Having kept no copy of these affidavits, I will thank you to return them to me, as I may find it necessary to send them to the Colonial Office.

I could only get two affidavits in time for this post, there are two more to be sworn to.

I am, sir, your obedient servant.

G. W. Senior

Penshurst, Runaway Bay, Nov. 28, 1837.

ADDITIONAL DOCUMENTS

Jamaica, SS. St. Ann

Personally appeared before me, one of her Majesty's Justices of the Peace for the parish of St. Ann, Marianne Bell, a domestic belonging to Penshurst, who being duly sworn, maketh oath and saith, that at the time when James Williams and Adam Brown were confined in the cells at Knapdale, by sentence of Captain Andrew Dillon, the subject matter of which was brought before the Commissioners at Brown's Town, when Wm. Dallin [sic] and others, on being called for their evidence, stated on oath, that the said prisoners were not supplied with a sufficiency of food; said deponent swears to the best of her knowledge and believe [sic]; that proper allowance of food was daily sent by her mistress for the said prisoners, as she saw the food delivered to the constable, Peter William Atkinson. Deponent further declares that one evening she was with her mistress in the pantry, when she was ordered to put a cover on a barrel of sugar; on her mistress going to bed, she called deponent to take out breakfast, when she found the cover on the floor, and a quantity of sugar had been taken out of the barrel, as well as some flour; and that Jane [sic] Williams and herself were the only persons about the house at the time.

Mary Ann Bell

Sworn before me, this 28th day of Nov. 1837

Edward Tucker

Jamaica, SS. St. Ann.

Personally appeared before me, Thos. Raffington, Jun. Esq., this 25th day of November, 1837, Richard R. Inglis, of the parish aforesaid, planter, who maketh oath and saith, that hearing that Dr. Thompson, Special Justice, as at Penshurst on the 19th day of December, 1834; deponent went there with one of the Thatchfield apprentices to be tried;[48] that he was present, and saw a negro named Henry James (an old man) flogged on that day; that the punishment was inflicted by the Penshurst constable, who struck the wheel of the cart with the cat, more than the man's back, and the punishment was extremely light.

Thos Raffington, Jun.

ARTICLES IN BRITISH AND JAMAICAN NEWSPAPERS

The Christian Advocate, *London, 5 June 1837*
In the midst of our report of the Yearly Meeting of the Society of
Friends will be found some account of Mr. Joseph Sturge's visit to the
West Indies. No one can read that speech without being convinced
that apprenticeship is worse than slavery was: this is still more evident, if possible, from the pamphlet with a copy of which we have
been favoured, entitled, "A Narrative of Events, since the 1st of August, 1834, by James Williams, an Apprenticed Labourer in Jamaica."
A more sickening detail of fiendish cruelty we never read. It surpasses
all our conceptions of the hardness of the human heart, even under
the petrifying influence of colonial misrule. [The article here quotes at
length from the end of the *Narrative*.] Williams is the apprentice whose
remaining time Mr. Sturge humanely purchased. We happen to know,
that a *ci-devant* American slave has examined his emancipated brother's
person, and ascertained his experience; and that he bears witness, that
the sufferings he must have endured are unparalleled by any thing he
ever knew inflicted upon any slave in the United States.[49] If, therefore,
we mean our remonstrances to produce any effect on the other side of
the Atlantic, we must put our shoulders to the wheel, and show ourselves resolved to get rid of slavery in our own colonies, where it exists
in more terrific forms than ever.

The Patriot, *London, 8 June 1837*
We give in another part of our columns, a specimen of the evidence
which awaits their searching inquiries;[50] taken from "A Narrative of
Events, by James Williams, an Apprenticed Labourer in Jamaica," re-
deemed by Mr. Sturge, and now in this country. We entreat our readers
to procure the pamphlet. Some of its revolting details are unfit for our
pages: they rival the disclosures made by Mr. Whitehouse.[51] Williams
states, that when he was a slave, he was never flogged, but since he
was apprenticed, he has been flogged seven times on the most trivial
pretexts. "I have heard my master say," he tells us in his negro lingo,
"Those English devils say we to be free, but if we is to be free, he
will pretty well weaken we, before the six and the four years done; we
shall be of no use to ourselves afterwards." In this artless statement we

have the key to the wanton barbarity which these disclosures exhibit. These petty tyrants are inspired with the more infernal passion against their innocent victims, because they are aware that their time is short. But what shall we say of the reported babarities of the Dr Thompson, Capt. Dillon, Major Light, and Mr. Rawlinson, who figure in these statements?[52] What was Greenacre's crime to the fiendish amusements attributed to these—"magistrates," we cannot call them?[53] "Some of them magistrate," says Williams, "don't care what them do to apprentice, as long as them can get good eating and drinking with the massa and busha, and sometimes *them set the massa on to do worse than them want.*" No doubt there are exceptions, but what treatment have those individuals met with who have attempted to protect the apprentices? Law and slavery cannot coexist; and the present half measures have proved worse than useless. *The apprentices must be set free.*

St. Jago de la Vega Gazette, *Spanish Town, 22–29 July 1837*
We have published, in our first sheet, a speech of Mr. Sturge's. . . .[54] It contains many gross misrepresentations . . . Mr. Sturge has also published a six-penny pamphlet, entitled "A narrative of events since the first of August, 1834, by James Williams, an apprenticed labourer in Jamaica." It appears that he purchased the freedom of this man, and carried him to England as a person well suited for his purposes, he having, from his own confession, been flogged seven times, and placed in houses of correction four times, by sentences of magistrates. The tissue, we suspect, of falsehoods which this fellow has related to him forms the bulk of the pamphlet, and, in support of the character of such a man, Mr. Sturge says he procured the signatures of "six members of the Christian church," but does not favour us with their names. We should like to know them. This man was the property of Mr. Senior of St. Ann's, of Penshurst, of whom and his family he speaks in very disrespectful terms, and we hope that gentleman will be able to furnish us with some account of a character who has been exhibited by Mr. Sturge as a specimen of the apprentices in Jamaica. It seems to us, however, that Mr. S. has only been able to make a noise among his own people, and the newspapers connected with them, for we do not observe any notice of him or his proceedings in any of the English papers which we have seen.

Jamaica Despatch and New Courant, *Kingston, 15 August 1837*

Since the publication of the narrative of the boy James, in our paper of the 11th instant, we have had opportunities of conversing with gentlemen of every political creed and hue—not one of whom but have expressed their surprise and their indignation!—Surprise, that a tissue of farsical [*sic*] falsehoods could find credence in Britain;—Indignation that such gross libellous untruths should be urged against the different classes of Jamaica society, and that they should remained unrefuted.

A Special Magistrate, a coloured gentleman of high respectability, broached the subject—asking what was the general opinion regarding this veritable narrative; and upon his views being asked in return of it, he replied, "that knowing the negro character as he did, it was self evident this boy James had been 'well tutored to tell his story'—that he held it to be impossible for a man, even of the brightest intellect, without having 'made notes by the way,' to have related such a long continuous tale, with any thing like correctness,—that he had not the slightest doubt this boy, in common with many of the negroes, possessed a vast deal of low cunning; but that he was fully confident that James William's was of a *decidedly* bad character;—that Dr. Thompson, whose name this boy used as having treated him and others with injustice and severity, was *a most humane and impartial Magistrate*—a gentleman whom it was impossible to suspect of being guilty of the slightest injustice; as indeed were the other of the Special Magistrates whose names were used, and with whom he was acquainted, and whom, he felt confident, had not been guilty of cruelty *or excessive severity*." Mention was then made of Mr. Sturge—upon which this gentleman said, "that Mr. Sturge was with him at his residence, and was invited to go round his district with him. Mr. Sturge, however, refused to visit the district—and why?—Because it was a coffee district, and it was the sugar ones which he (Sturge) desired to examine." *This was Mr. Sturge's answer,* but the *truth* was, that this district was perfectly quiet, and apprentices and employers were contented. Such a district, it was not Mr. Sturge's intention or wish to see—it was not peace and happiness that he desired to visit; but only those parts where men of his own kidney had influence sufficient, to render the apprentices discontented and unhappy.

Falmouth Post, *Falmouth, 30 August 1837*

We have this day concluded our re-publication of "a narrative of events since the 1st of august 1834 by James Williams, an apprenticed labourer in Jamaica."

This narrative was first copied in this Island by the Despatch newspaper, and it was the evident desire of the Editor of that scandalous and truth-hating diurnal,[55] to procure what evidence he could to contradict, and if possible, to nullify the astounding statements of the boy Williams, who was taken to England by Mr. Sturge. His scheme has entirely failed, and we are of opinion that those who read the narrative will think with us, that it possesses all the characteristics of truth and authenticity.

James Williams appears to have related a "plain unvarnished tale";[56] the revelation of "the secrets of his prison house" is more than sufficient to

"harrow up our soul
Freeze our warm blood, and make each particular hair
To stand on end."[57]

Not to mention his having been seven times unmercifully flogged since the commencement of the apprenticeship, and enduring a series of heartless and unmitigated mal-treatment from his master Mr. Senior, the narrative details other circumstances of the most atrocious nature. If it is true, as James Williams states that apprentices had been flogged without being permitted to speak in self defence, or calling witnesses on their behalf; that in the penal gang of the St. Ann's house of Correction, the young and the old, the strong and the feeble were chained together, while the latter were inhumanly flogged, because their want of strength prevented their keeping up with the former; that the Sabbath is no day of rest to these wretched people, except so far as the tread-mill is concerned; that the persons of females were indecently exposed, and the flesh stripped from their feet by the continuous cutting of the drivers; if it be indeed true (and our blood runs cold while we write) that the old man Henry James, had been flogged because he could not perform impossibilities; that from the effects of his severe punishment, he dropped down exhausted, in the streets of Brown's Town, vomiting blood and—expired! and this too almost immediately under the eyes of Captain Dillon and Mr. Rawlinson, Special Magistrates, then it is surely high time that his Excellency Sir Lionel Smith, should order a legal inquiry to be made, and that an immediate stop should be put to such unlawful practices, to such revolting barbarities!

The Special Justices who figure conspicuously in the "narrative of James Williams," are Doctor Thompson, Major Light, Captain Dillon and Mr. Rawlinson. The two first have been called to their last account,[58] the other two still live to administer—we were going to say JUSTICE to masters and apprentices.

In perusing this narrative we cannot preserve our gravity, when we notice the conduct of Special Justice Rawlinson, who derives a *pretext* for punishing the boy, and *even suggests* language to the complainant. "Oh" he says "you mean insolence by manner"; he then passes over the real offence of Williams by merely fining him for a petty theft, but with unrelenting cruelty orders him to be flogged before his old wounds were healed; and yet, notwithstanding all this; although he had been so frequently sent to the Workhouse for punishment, although he is described by his former master Mr. Senior as a thief, as a notorious villain, and in fact as a wantonly depraved character, subjecting the family to repeated insults and injuries and urging the rest of the negroes to acts of insubordination almost amounting to rebellion, Special Justice Rawlinson did not hesitate to value him at £46 4s 7d for the remaining term of his apprenticeship which for a non-praedial was only one year and five months.

An attempt has been made by Mr. Senior to invalidate the testimony of James Williams, but we think that his exaggerations rather confirm the statements of the boy than otherwise; we do not think that Mr. Senior will get any one in his senses to believe that a boy of 15 years of age could have made away with upwards of 20 sheep, and several calves, within "one little month" without detection; besides how does Mr. Senior get over the rest of the narrative? We would advise him to say as little about it as possible, for the more he stirs,—but he knows the rest of the proverb, so we need not finish it.[59]

At all events, the narrative of James Williams has created a considerable sensation in England.—The people of that country say "If such are the horrors of apprenticeship (and Williams's case is not an isolated one) let us with one voice instruct our representatives to demand

peremptorily the instant, the unconditional, and the everlasting annihilation of the accursed system."

For our parts, we think that a full inquiry should be made into the
conduct of the Special Magistrates who are stated to have conducted
themselves so improperly. — If they have been wrongly calumniated,
their innocence should be publicly proclaimed; but if they have been
really guilty of the acts attributed to them we do most sincerely hope,
for the sake of humanity and for the honor of the Government of Jamaica that they will be punished for their deeds of wickedness. As we
said in a former number, strong measures *must* now be adopted to preserve the peace of the country. We therefore hope that every individual
concerned in the prosperity of our sunny Isle, will with a willing heart
give his aid to save Jamaica from those disastrous consequences which
must result from a system of persevering oppression.

Falmouth Post, *Falmouth, 11 October 1837*
St Anns Commission of Inquiry!

Messrs. Gordon & Daughtrey closed their Court at Brown's Town
on Wednesday evening last, and proceeded on the following morning
to Saint Ann's Bay, where they arrived at half past seven o'clock. . . .
The prisoners [in the house of correction] were all called up and examined, and they declared that they are now treated with the greatest
humanity; that the treadmill is not worked at present in such a manner
as to make it an instrument rather of torture than punishment, and, in
fact, that they have no fault whatever to find with the present superintendant, Mr. Alex. Levy. . . .⁶⁰ Proceedings were entirely closed on
Saturday evening; we believe the report will be sent to his excellency by
the next post. It would be both indelicate and dishonest in us to publish
any portion of the evidence which was taken both at Brown's-Town and
St. Ann's Bay, until the Commissioners have officially communicated
to the Executive the result of their inquiries.

The narrative of "James Williams" has been most strikingly corroborated, not only in substance but in every minute particular. We
regret being compelled to state, that the gross and wanton violation of
the Laws of the Country are not confined to Mr. Senior of Penshurst;
there are others, in the parish of Saint Ann's, who will shortly be shewn
up in their true colours! Nothing but religion could have restrained the

apprentices of that parish from rebellion against the Tyrants who have so long oppressed them!

Jamaica Despatch and New Courant, *Kingston, 10 November 1837*
Our readers will doubtless be surprised to learn that the boy James Williams, who was taken at the advice of the Baptist parsons, by Quaker Sturge,[61] to England, has returned to Jamaica per the brig Porter, (now lying at quarantine) from Liverpool. Strange too, to relate, he is infected with the small pox, which made its appearance two days after the brig had sailed—so that it would almost seem providence had destined this fellow to be a curse to Jamaica; for he has not only served as the tool of others who have defamed and reviled us, but now on his return to our shores he brings with him a foul pestilence, from the bare mention of which we recoil with dismay.

Is it not, however, rather singular that Friend Sturge, with his boasted philanthropy, should have so soon become tired of his *protégé*. Has Sturge discovered this boy Williams to be almost his own equal at exaggeration and mis-statement? Has he found out that his character is of the basest description,—that the fellow is all that Mr. Senior has stated him to be? We dare presume Sturge has; and now having attained his base desires, namely, to excite the feelings of our fellow-subjects in Britain against us, through the false statements of this boy, he sends the fellow back to Jamaica; for what purpose, or what end, we cannot imagine, except as we have before said, we suppose Sturge had become sickened of his darling, and having no further use for him, returns him to his friends, the Baptist Parsons.[62]

NOTES

1. This and all the other letters from Sturge to Clark and to Gardner reproduced here are held in the Angus Library, Regents Park College, University of Oxford, ref D/FEN 1/1–8. Reproduced with permission of the Angus Library.

2. James Mursell Phillippo was a Baptist missionary based in Spanish Town. He arrived in Jamaica in 1823 and remained there until his death in 1879. In 1843 he published an account of Jamaica's history entitled *Jamaica, Its Past and Present State*. Later in the 1840s he came into conflict with many members of his congregation when they shifted their allegiance to a different minister, arguing that Phillippo was hostile to black Jamaicans.

3. Sturge uses "thee" and "thou" rather than "you" because he is a Quaker. These forms had been the informal mode of address, in contrast to the more formal "you," but were archaic by the nineteenth century. The informal terms were always used by Quakers to emphasize equality among speakers, and were maintained by them after they were no longer commonly employed by others.

4. Four Paths was a settlement in the Jamaican parish of Vere, now part of Clarendon.

5. Three quarters: of a dollar. See n. 103 of the *Narrative* for explanation of these coins.

6. 15 inst: 15th of this month, i.e., the 15th of May.

7. Sturge spoke at a meeting of Quakers at the Friends Meeting House in London on 29 May 1837. The meeting took place on an evening during the week when the Friends' Yearly Meeting was being held. According to a report published in the evangelical newspaper the *Patriot,* 1 June 1837, and reprinted in the *Jamaica Despatch* of 1 August 1837 and the *St. Jago de la Vega Gazette* of 22–29 July 1837, "the large meeting-house was crowded to overflowing, and more than half filled by females." Sturge ended his speech by calling for a campaign to end apprenticeship in 1838. James Williams attended, but did not address, this meeting; Sturge referred in his speech to "the negro present" whose freedom he had purchased.

8. Sturge rarely uses the names of the months, but rather writes them numerically or as "fifth month," etc. As with the use of "thou" and "thee," this was characteristic of Quakers, who avoided the names of the months because they considered them to have pagan connotations.

9. The Committee: the Parliamentary Select Committee on Negro Apprenticeship, appointed by the House of Commons on 19 May 1837 "to inquire into the working of the Apprenticeship System in the Colonies; the Condition of the Apprentices and the Emancipated Negroes, and the Laws and Regulations affecting them; and also the State of Education of the Negroes in the Colonies." This was the second parliamentary committee to inquire into apprenticeship; the first had reported in August 1836. As well as giving evidence before it, Sturge sent each committee member a copy of James Williams's *Narrative.* The 1837 committee heard several witnesses, but did not publish a full report or the witnesses' evidence because the parliamentary session terminated before it was able to do so. However, the committee's brief report made special reference to Jamaican prisons. "There is, however," the committee members declared, "one subject to which they consider it to be their duty specially to advert: the state of the Workhouses and of the Prison Discipline is so intimately connected with the working of the Apprenticeship system, that it has engaged the anxious attention of Your Committee, particularly as it exists in the Island of Jamaica, to which their inquiries have been principally directed; and it appears to them to be indispensable that there should be instituted, without delay, a strict and searching examination into the state of the Workhouses in the West Indian Colonies, and especially into the construction and use of the Treadmills which are employed in them, and the nature of the coercion adopted to ensure labour among the prisoners." Sturge's evidence was probably significant

ADDITIONAL DOCUMENTS

in leading the committee to this conclusion. See British *Parliamentary Papers* 1837 (510) VII.

10. Sir George Grey, a Whig member of Parliament, was the undersecretary of state for War and the Colonies from 1834 to 1839 (with the exception of a few months in 1834). He was a member of both select committees on apprenticeship.

11. The Seniors' slave registration returns list two other children of James's mother, Mira, both female. I have not identified his two brothers. "The pen" refers to Penshurst.

12. The *Patriot:* a London-based weekly newspaper that, according to its inaugural issue of 22 February 1832, was "devoted to the maintenance of the great principles cherished by Evangelical Nonconformists . . . we shall be ever found, the firm friends of knowledge and education; and the consistent advocates of civil and religious freedom." It reported extensively on events in the Caribbean and on the antiapprenticeship campaign, including the controversy resulting from the publication of Williams's *Narrative.*

13. The Borough Road School, in Southwark, London, was founded by Joseph Lancaster, a Quaker, in 1801. Lancaster developed a system of education that became known as the "Lancasterian system." The system used older pupils, known as monitors, to teach and discipline the younger students, allowing for the schooling of large numbers of children at relatively little cost.

14. Richard Hill, a prominent Jamaican brown (mixed-race) man, had been made a stipendiary magistrate at the beginning of apprenticeship but resigned in October 1834 because he felt that his authority was not backed up by the governor in conflicts with planters. Sligo accepted his resignation, but soon after appointed him secretary to the special magistrate's department of the governor's office. As such he was responsible for analyzing the reports of the stipendiary magistrates. He remained active in Jamaican politics until the 1860s.

15. The West Indians: short for the West India Committee of Planters and Merchants, formed in the late eighteenth century to represent in Parliament the interests of those with property in the West Indies.

16. Thomas Fowell Buxton was the leader of the antislavery faction in the House of Commons, successfully pressuring the newly elected Whig government into undertaking emancipation in 1833. He had been a member of Parliament since 1818 and lost his seat in the election of July 1837. Sturge was critical of his moderation and reliance on parliamentary tactics rather than mass agitation.

17. John Dyer was the full-time secretary of the Baptist Missionary Society from 1818 to 1841. As such he was responsible for receiving letters from missionaries all over the world, the contents of some of which were made public through the Missionary Society's publications, or reported to the Colonial Office for investigation.

18. The major antislavery meetings were held at Exeter Hall in London. Sturge refers here to the meeting called by the Anti-Slavery Society, held on 11 July 1837, in the run-up to the general election held that month. Seven thousand people were in attendance. In his speech to the meeting Sturge attacked the abuses taking place

in the St. Ann's Bay House of Correction, among other things. He also read a letter from six Baptist missionaries to John Dyer, dated September 1836, in which they stated: "we feel it our paramount duty to denounce it [the apprenticeship system] as a most iniquitous and accursed one, oppressive, harassing, and unjust to the apprentice, liable to innumerable abuses, with but little positive and actual protection; that instead of assuming a more lenient aspect, it is become increasingly oppressive and vexatious; that the change is more in name than the reality. That the apprentices feel—yes deeply feel the disappointment of all their fondest hopes—and that the most fearful consequences are to be dreaded, unless the British Parliament is induced to proclaim full liberty to the predial as well as nonpredial [sic] apprentice in the year 1838" (report of Anti-Slavery Meeting in the Christian Advocate, 17 July 1837).

19. William Knibb was one of the most prominent Baptist missionaries based in Jamaica. He arrived there in 1825 and remained in Jamaica for most of the rest of his life. His station was near Falmouth, in the parish of Trelawny. He died in 1845. The "domestic affliction" referred to by Sturge was the death of Knibb's eldest son, William, who died at age twelve in July 1837. Another son had died the previous year, age two.

20. John Hinton, in his biography of William Knibb, quotes a letter from Knibb to Sturge dated 11 July 1837 in which Knibb stated that the members of his church who held apprentices had agreed to free them on 1 August 1838. Hinton does not refer to Thomas Burchell, who was also a Baptist missionary in Jamaica. Burchell was based at Montego Bay, St. James, from 1824 until his death in 1846. Samuel Sharpe, the leader of the 1831 slave rebellion, had been a deacon in his church.

21. Francis Gardner, a Baptist missionary, arrived in Jamaica in the midst of the 1831 slave rebellion and was one of three Baptist missionaries arrested in its wake. After his acquittal in 1832 he became the minister of the East Queen Street Baptist Church in Kingston. He died in May 1838.

22. Edward Jordon was the editor of the Kingston-based newspaper the *Watchman* which campaigned against slavery and for civil rights for free people of color. He was tried for treason in 1832, after the slave rebellion, and acquitted. In 1834 he was elected to the Jamaican Assembly and remained a member, with a short break, until 1864, in addition serving as a member of the Executive Committee, which advised the governor, in 1854. His career is extensively discussed in Heuman, *Between Black and White,* and Holt, *Problem of Freedom.*

23. Sturge refers to a memorial to the newly crowned Queen Victoria from the women of Great Britain and Ireland, calling for full freedom for the apprentices. The memorial was launched at the Anti-Slavery Society public meeting on 11 July 1837. As well as the 449,540 signatories to the English and Welsh petition, 135,083 women signed a Scottish and 77,000 an Irish petition.

24. Anderson: probably William Wemyss Anderson, a white Kingston magistrate and liberal, whom Sturge and Harvey met while in Jamaica.

25. Joshua Tinson arrived in Jamaica in 1822 and was a Baptist missionary there

ADDITIONAL DOCUMENTS

until his death in 1850. He worked at churches in Kingston, Yallahs (St. David), and Trelawny, and was a founder of Calabar College, which trained Jamaicans to become missionaries. In 1837 he visited the United States.

26. Sturge feared that the government would appoint a third parliamentary committee to investigate apprenticeship as a delaying tactic. This did not in fact take place.

27. Sturge is almost certainly quoting from a letter from John Clark.

28. Lyon: Edmund Lyon, a colored stipendiary magistrate. It is not clear why Sturge refers to him here, as he was not officially involved in the investigation.

29. Sturge and others launched the Central Negro Emancipation Committee in London in November 1837 to campaign for the immediate end of apprenticeship. Archibald Palmer, the amanuensis of Williams's *Narrative,* became its secretary. The committee's founders believed that the existing Anti-Slavery Society was both moribund and too moderate in its tactics. The CNEC became the leading antiapprenticeship organization in Britain.

30. Benjamin Bull Dexter was a Baptist missionary from 1834 until 1863. The Rev. John Stainsby was an Anglican clergyman based at Lucea, Hanover. Sturge and Harvey described him as "one of those who has ever manifested sympathy with the oppressed" and claimed that as a result planters considered him "worse than a Baptist" (*The West Indies in 1837,* 236).

31. Our work: Sturge and Harvey, *The West Indies in 1837.*

32. The publication was the *British Emancipator,* the first issue of which was published in December 1838.

33. John Castello, the editor of the *Falmouth Post,* who transcribed and published the evidence to the inquiry.

34. Rawlinson was suspended as a stipendiary magistrate in November 1837 and was later dismissed.

35. Noscitur a scoiis: A slightly garbled version of the Latin phrase, *"noscitur ex sociis, qui non cognoscitur ex se"* ("he who cannot be known by himself may be recognized by his associates").

36. In the *Narrative* and inquiry Marianne Bell is called Mary Ann Bell. However, in the Seniors' slave registration returns there is a Marianne but no Mary Ann.

37. Thomas Raffington was a St. Ann magistrate as well as a slaveholder.

38. Frock: a fabric covering.

39. Mary Ann Bell.

40. The Seniors' slave registration returns do not include a Graham.

41. This testimony is contradicted by a deed in the Island Record Office, which shows that Sarah and Gilbert Senior purchased Dalling (then known as Joe) and his mother, Mary, and brother Pompey from Deborah Senior in 1804, when Dalling would have been ten years old.

42. Enclosure in Smith to Glenelg No. 54, 24 November 1837, British *Parliamentary Papers* 1837–1838 (154) XLIX.

43. The late martial law: In response to the slave rebellion of December 1831

martial law was declared in Jamaica on 31 December 1831 and ended on 5 February 1832.

44. Not included in this volume. The Seniors' slave registration returns include a Trueman, an African reported to be fifty years old in 1817.

45. "Last Friday" would have been early November; thus, this testimony refers to incidents that took place after the inquiry had closed.

46. Neither Marianne Lawrence nor Henry Brown are mentioned in either the *Narrative* or the inquiry, although it is possible that Marianne Lawrence was the same person as Mary Ann/Marianne Bell.

47. On William Mills, see n. 48 of the *Narrative*. The Seniors' slave registration returns include two men named Henry, but neither of them seems likely to have been Henry McCook.

48. Thatchfield was a plantation close to Penshurst, to the southeast.

49. *Ci-devant:* former. This is the only reference I have come across to a former American slave being involved with Williams.

50. Their searching inquiries: refers to the newly appointed parliamentary select committee on apprenticeship.

51. The extracts reprinted in the *Patriot* do not include any of the references to sexual abuse of women; presumably these are the "revolting details" considered "unfit" for reprinting. Mr. Whitehouse: Isaac Whitehouse, a Wesleyan missionary based in St. Ann who exposed a case of severe abuse of a Christian slave, Henry Williams, in 1829.

52. All of these individuals were stipendiary magistrates.

53. I have not been able to trace the reference to Greenacre: presumably he or she was a briefly infamous British criminal.

54. The front page includes the text of a speech given by Sturge to the Quaker meeting in London on 29 May 1837, which the *St. Jago de la Vega Gazette* reprinted from the *Patriot*. This was the same meeting referred to by Sturge in his letter to John Clark of 30 May 1837.

55. Diurnal: daily.

56. The phrase "plain unvarnished tale" was commonly used to describe slave narratives. It derives from a speech in which Othello asks permission to explain how he won Desdemona's love: "Yet, by your gracious patience,/ I will a round unvarnished tale deliver/ Of my whole course of love, what drugs, what charms,/ What conjuration and what mighty magic —/ For such proceeding I am charged withal —/ I won his daughter." The "tale" he goes on to tell includes his experience "Of being taken by the insolent foe/ And sold to slavery, of my redemption thence" (*Othello* 1.3.89–93, 136–37).

57. Refers to *Hamlet* 1.5.13–20: Ghost: "But that I am forbid/ To tell the secrets of my prison-house/ I could a tale unfold whose lightest word/ Would harrow up thy soul, freeze thy young blood,/ Make thy two eyes like stars start from their spheres,/ Thy knotty and combined locks to part,/ And each particular hair to stand on end/ Like quills upon the fretful porcupine."

58. Called to their last account: died.

59. I have not located this proverb in any dictionary of British or Jamaican proverbs, but the meaning is clear from the context: the writer suggests that Senior's attempts to defend himself only incriminate him more.

60. See pp. 79–80 for Alexander Levi's evidence to the inquiry.

61. "Quaker Sturge" is intended to be derogatory, as is the designation "Friend Sturge" later on in the article. The term "Quaker" was not used self-ascriptively.

62. Like "Quaker Sturge" and "Friend Sturge," "Parsons" is also a derogatory term.

BIBLIOGRAPHY

ARCHIVAL SOURCES

Jamaica

ISLAND RECORD OFFICE, CENTRAL VILLAGE

Wills

Liber 45 folio 137, 1778. William Lawrence.
Liber 47 folio 150, 1782. William Lawrence.
Liber 66 folio 29, 1779. William Hull.
Liber 74 folio 208, 1804. Sarah Lawrence.
Liber 76 folio 187, 1806. Christopher Senior.
Liber 112 folio 29, 1831. Ann Senior.

Deeds

Liber 526 folio 33, 1803. William Whitehorne Lawrence.
Liber 535 folio 183, 1805. Christopher Senior Lawrence.
Liber 575 folio 200, 1808. Deborah Senior.
Liber 734 folio 95, 1825. Gilbert William Senior.
Liber 799 folio 147, 1835. Gilbert William Senior.

JAMAICA ARCHIVES, SPANISH TOWN

Index to Land Patents, Vol 1., Inventories

Liber 61 folio 138, 1780. Gilbert Senior.
Liber 66 folio 112, 1783. William Lawrence.
Liber 120 folio 119, 1812. Christopher Senior Lawrence.
Liber 157 folio 146, 1848. Sarah Jane Keith Senior.

NATIONAL LIBRARY OF JAMAICA, KINGSTON

Map collection, St. Ann.
Photograph collection.

Britain

PUBLIC RECORD OFFICE, LONDON

CO 137. Colonial Office: Original correspondence, Jamaica. 1837–1838.
T 71/ 43–51, 693–5. Treasury Records: Slave registration documents.

BIBLIOGRAPHY

SCHOOL OF ORIENTAL AND AFRICAN STUDIES, UNIVERSITY OF LONDON
London Missionary Society Papers.

REGENT'S PARK COLLEGE, ANGUS LIBRARY, UNIVERSITY OF OXFORD
Baptist Missionary Society Papers.
The Fenn Collection of Original Material from Jamaica, D/FEN.

NEWSPAPERS AND PERIODICALS

The Falmouth Post (Falmouth, Jamaica).
The Jamaica Despatch and New Courant (Kingston, Jamaica).
The St. Jago de la Vega Gazette (Spanish Town, Jamaica).
The British Emancipator (London, England).
The Patriot (London, England).
The Philanthropist (Birmingham, England).
The Christian Advocate (London, England).
Slavery in America (London, England).

OFFICIAL DOCUMENTS

Parliamentary Papers

1836 (560) XV. Report from the Select Committee appointed to inquire into the working of the Apprenticeship System in the Colonies.
1837 (510) VII. Select Committee on Negro Apprenticeship.
1837–38 (154) XLIX. Papers presented to Parliament, by His Majesty's Command, in explanation of the measures adopted by His Majesty's Government, for giving effect to the act for the Abolition of Slavery Throughout the British Colonies.
1836 (166) XLVIII. Papers presented in explanation of the measures for giving effect to the act for the Abolition of Slavery Throughout the British Colonies.
1837–38 (596) XL. Report of Captain J. W. Pringle on Prisons in the West Indies. Part I Jamaica.

Other Official Documents
Hansard, 14 May 1833.

BOOKS, ARTICLES, AND DISSERTATIONS

Alleyne, Mervyn. *Roots of Jamaican Culture*. London: Pluto Press, 1988.
Andrews, William L. *To Tell a Free Story: The First Century of Afro-American Autobiography, 1760–1865*. Urbana: University of Illinois Press, 1986.
Armstrong, Douglas V. *The Old Village and the Great House: An Archeological and Historical Examination of Drax Hall Plantation, St. Ann's Bay, Jamaica*. Urbana: University of Illinois Press, 1990.
Berlin, Ira, and Philip D. Morgan, eds. *Cultivation and Culture: Labor and the Shaping of Slave Life in the Americas*. Charlottesville: University Press of Virginia, 1993.

BIBLIOGRAPHY

————. *The Slaves' Economy: Independent Production by Slaves in the Americas*. London: Frank Cass, 1991.

Blackburn, Robin. *The Overthrow of Colonial Slavery, 1776–1848*. London: Verso, 1988.

Bolland, O. Nigel. "The Politics of Freedom in the British Caribbean." In *The Meaning of Freedom: Economics, Politics, and Culture after Slavery*, ed. Frank McGlynn and Seymour Drescher. Pittsburgh: University of Pittsburgh Press, 1992. 113–46.

Brereton, Bridget. "The White Elite of Trinidad, 1838–1950." In *The White Minority in the Caribbean*, ed. Howard Johnson and Karl Watson. Kingston, Jamaica: Ian Randle Publishers, 1998. 32–70.

Burn, W. L. *Emancipation and Apprenticeship in the British West Indies*. London: Jonathan Cape, 1937.

Burnard, Trevor. "A Failed Settler Society: Marriage and Demographic Failure in Early Jamaica." *Journal of Social History* 28, no. 1 (1994): 63–82.

————. "Family Continuity and Female Independence in Jamaica, 1665–1734." *Continuity and Change* 7, no. 2 (1992): 181–98.

————. "Inheritance and Independence: Women's Status in Early Colonial Jamaica." *William and Mary Quarterly* 3d series, 48, no. 1 (1991): 93–114.

Burton, Richard D. E. *Afro-Creole: Power, Opposition, and Play in the Caribbean*. Ithaca, NY: Cornell University Press, 1997.

Cardoso, Ciro Flamarion S. "The Peasant Breach in the Slave System: New Developments in Brazil." *Luso-Brazilian Review* 25 (1988): 49–57.

Cassidy, Frederic G. *Jamaica Talk: Three Hundred Years of the English Language in Jamaica*. London: Macmillan, 1960.

Cassidy, F. G., and R. B. LePage. *Dictionary of Jamaican English*. Cambridge, England: Cambridge University Press, 1980 [1967].

Clarke, John. *Memorials of Baptist Missionaries in Jamaica, including a sketch of the labours of early religious instructors in Jamaica*. London: Yates and Alexander, 1869.

Cooper, Carolyn. *Noises in the Blood: Orality, Gender and the "Vulgar" Body of Jamaican Popular Culture*. London: Macmillan Caribbean, 1993.

D'Costa, Jean, and Barbara Lalla, eds. *Voices in Exile: Jamaican Texts of the 18th and 19th Centuries*. Tuscaloosa: University of Alabama Press, 1989.

Davidoff, Leonore, and Catherine Hall. *Family Fortunes: Men and Women of the English Middle Class, 1780–1850*. Chicago: University of Chicago Press, 1987.

Deck, Alice A. "Whose Book Is This? Authorial versus Editorial Control of Harriet Brent Jacobs' *Incidents in the Life of a Slave Girl: Written by Herself*." *Women's Studies International Forum* 10, no. 1 (1987): 33–40.

Donnell, Alison, and Sarah Lawson Welsh, eds. *The Routledge Reader in Caribbean Literature*. London: Routledge, 1996.

Douglass, Frederick. *My Bondage and My Freedom*. New York: Arno Press, 1968 [1855].

————. *Narrative of the Life of Frederick Douglass, an American Slave, Written by Himself*. Ed. Houston A. Baker. New York: Penguin, 1972 [1845].

Drescher, Seymour. "Cart Whip and Billy Roller: Antislavery and Reform Symbolism in Industrializing Britain." *Journal of Social History* 15 (1981): 3–24.

Duncan, Rev. Peter. *A Narrative of the Wesleyan Mission to Jamaica; with Occasional Remarks on the State of Society in that Colony.* London: Partridge and Oakey, 1849.

Dunn, Richard S. *Sugar and Slaves: The Rise of the Planter Class in the English West Indies, 1624–1713.* New York: Norton, 1973.

Eltis, David, and Stanley L. Engerman. "Fluctuations in Sex and Age Ratios in the Transatlantic Slave Trade, 1663–1864." *Economic History Review* 46, no. 2 (1993): 308–23.

Equiano, Olaudah. *The Interesting Narrative and Other Writings.* Ed. Vincent Caretta. New York: Penguin, 1995 [1789].

Ferguson, Moira. *Subject to Others: British Women Writers and Colonial Slavery, 1670–1834.* New York: Routledge, 1992.

Garfield, Deborah M., and Rafia Zafar, eds. *Harriet Jacobs and Incidents in the Life of a Slave Girl.* Cambridge, England: Cambridge University Press, 1996.

Gates, Henry Louis, Jr., and William L. Andrews. *Pioneers of the Black Atlantic: Five Slave Narratives from the Enlightenment, 1772–1815.* Washington, DC: Civitas, 1998.

Gayle, Clement. *George Liele: Pioneer Missionary to Jamaica.* Kingston, Jamaica: Jamaica Baptist Union, 1982.

Glissant, Edouard. *Caribbean Discourse: Selected Essays.* Trans. J. Michael Dash. Charlottesville: University Press of Virginia, 1989.

Goldman, Anne E. *Take My Word: Autobiographical Innovations of Ethnic American Working Women.* Berkeley: University of California Press, 1996.

Gordon, Shirley C. *God Almighty Make Me Free: Christianity in Preemancipation Jamaica.* Bloomington: Indiana University Press, 1996.

Green, William A. *British Slave Emancipation: The Sugar Colonies and the Great Experiment, 1830–1865.* Oxford: Clarendon Press, 1976.

Hall, Catherine. "White Visions, Black Lives: The Free Villages of Jamaica." *History Workshop Journal* 36 (1993): 100–132.

Hall, Douglas. *Free Jamaica 1838–1865: An Economic History.* New Haven: Yale University Press, 1959.

Henderson, George E. *Goodness and Mercy: A Tale of a Hundred Years.* Kingston, Jamaica: Gleaner Co., 1931.

Heuman, Gad. *Between Black and White: Race, Politics, and the Free Coloreds in Jamaica, 1792–1865.* Westport, CT: Greenwood Press, 1981.

Higman, Barry. *Slave Population and Economy in Jamaica, 1807–1834.* Kingston, Jamaica: The Press of the University of the West Indies, 1995 [1976].

Hobhouse, Stephen. *Joseph Sturge: His Life and Work.* London: J. M. Dent, 1919.

Holt, Thomas C. *The Problem of Freedom: Race, Labor, and Politics in Jamaica and Britain, 1832–1938.* Baltimore: Johns Hopkins University Press, 1992.

Jacobs, Harriet A. *Incidents in the Life of a Slave Girl, Written by Herself.* Ed. Jean Fagan Yellin. Cambridge, MA: Harvard University Press, 1987 [1861].

Lalla, Barbara, and Jean D'Costa, eds. *Language in Exile: Three Hundred Years of Jamaican Creole.* Tuscaloosa: University of Alabama Press, 1990.

BIBLIOGRAPHY

Levy, Andrew. "Dialect and Convention: Harriet A. Jacobs's *Incidents in the Life of a Slave Girl.*" *Nineteenth-Century Literature* 45, no. 2 (1990): 206–19.

Long, Edward. *The History of Jamaica, or General Survey of the Antient and Modern State of that Island: With reflections on its situations, settlements, inhabitants, climate, products, commerce, laws, and government.* London: Frank Cass, 1970 [1774].

Lott, Eric. *Love and Theft: Blackface Minstrelsy and the American Working Class.* New York: Oxford University Press, 1993.

Manderson-Jones, Marlene. "Richard Hill of Jamaica: His Life and Times, 1795–1872." Ph.D. diss., University of the West Indies, 1973.

Marcus, Laura. *Auto/biographical Discourses: Criticism, Theory, Practice.* Manchester, England: Manchester University Press, 1994.

Marshall, W. K. "Apprenticeship and Labour Relations in Four Windward Islands." In *Abolition and Its Aftermath: The Historical Context, 1790–1916,* ed. David Richardson. London: Frank Cass, 1985. 203–24.

Martinez-Alier, Verena. *Marriage, Class, and Colour in Nineteenth-Century Cuba: A Study of Racial Attitudes and Sexual Values in a Slave Society.* Ann Arbor: University of Michigan Press, 1989 [1974].

Mathiesen, William Law. *British Slave Emancipation 1838–1849.* London: Longmans, Green, 1932.

————. *British Slavery and Its Abolition, 1823–1838.* London: Longmans, Green, 1926.

McDonald, Roderick A. *The Economy and Material Culture of Slaves: Goods and Chattels on the Sugar Plantations of Jamaica and Louisiana.* Baton Rouge: Louisiana State University Press, 1993.

Midgley, Clare. *Women against Slavery: The British Campaigns, 1780–1870.* London: Routledge, 1992.

Mintz, Sidney W. *Caribbean Transformations.* New York: Columbia University Press, 1974.

Olney, James. "'I Was Born': Slave Narratives, Their Status as Autobiography and as Literature." In *The Slave's Narrative,* ed. Charles Davis and Henry Louis Gates. Oxford: Oxford University Press, 1985. 148–75.

Olwig, Karen Fog, ed. *Small Islands, Large Questions: Society, Culture and Resistance in the Post-Emancipation Caribbean.* London: Frank Cass, 1995.

Paquet, Sandra Pouchet. "The Heartbeat of a West Indian Slave: *The History of Mary Prince.*" *African American Review* 26, no. 1 (1992): 131–46.

Paton, Diana. "No Bond but the Law: Punishment and Justice in Jamaica's Age of Emancipation, 1780–1870." Ph.D. diss., Yale University, 1999.

Payne, Ernest A. *The Baptist Union: A Short History.* London: Carey Kingsgate Press, 1959.

————. *Freedom in Jamaica: Some Chapters in the Story of the Baptist Missionary Society.* London: Carey Press, 1933.

Prince, Mary. *The History of Mary Prince, A West Indian Slave, Related by Herself.* Ed. Moira Ferguson. London: Pandora Press, 1987 [1831].

Ragatz, Lowell Joseph. *The Fall of the Planter Class in the British Caribbean, 1763–1833: A Study in Social and Economic History.* New York: Century, 1928.

BIBLIOGRAPHY

Richard, Henry. *Memoirs of Joseph Sturge*. London: S. W. Partridge, 1864.

Roberts, Peter A. *From Oral to Literate Culture: Colonial Experience in the English West Indies*. Mona, Jamaica: University of the West Indies Press, 1997.

Robertson, Glory. "Members of the Assembly of Jamaica from the General Election of 1830 to the Final Session January 1866." Typescript held in the University of the West Indies library, n.d.

Roediger, David R. *The Wages of Whiteness: Race and the Making of the American Working Class*. London: Verso, 1991.

Sekora, John. "Black Message/White Envelope: Genre, Authenticity, and Authority in the Antebellum Slave Narrative." *Callaloo* 34 (1987): 482–515.

Shelton, Robert S. "A Modified Crime: The Apprenticeship System in St. Kitts." *Slavery and Abolition* 16, no. 3 (1995): 331–45.

Shepherd, Verene. "Alternative Husbandry: Slaves and Free Labourers on Livestock Farms in Jamaica in the Eighteenth and Nineteenth Centuries." *Slavery and Abolition* 14, no. 1 (1993): 41–66.

Sistren, with Honor Ford Smith. *Lionheart Gal: Life Stories of Jamaican Women*. London: Women's Press, 1986.

Smith, Sidonie, and Julia Watson. "Introduction: Situating Subjectivity in Women's Autobiographical Practices." In *Women, Autobiography, Theory: A Reader*, ed. Smith and Watson. Madison: University of Wisconsin Press, 1998. 3–52.

Smith, Valerie. *Self-Discovery and Authority in Afro-American Narrative*. Cambridge, MA: Harvard University Press, 1987.

Sommer, Doris. "No Secrets." In *The Real Thing: Testimonial Discourse and Latin America*, ed. George Gugelberger. Durham, NC: Duke University Press, 1996. 130–57.

———. "Resisting the Heat: Menchú, Morrison, and Incompetent Readers." In *Cultures of United States Imperialism*, ed. Donald Pease and Amy Kaplan. Durham, NC: Duke University Press, 1994. 407–32.

Stanley, Brian. *The History of the Baptist Missionary Society, 1792–1992*. Edinburgh: T and T Clark, 1992.

Stepto, Robert. *From Behind the Veil: A Study of Afro-American Literary History*. Urbana: University of Illinois Press, 1979.

———. "Narration, Authentication, and Authorial Control in Frederick Douglass' Narrative of 1845." In *Afro-American Literature: The Reconstruction of Instruction*, ed. Dexter Fisher and Robert B. Stepto. New York: Modern Language Association, 1979. 178–211.

Stewart, Robert J. *Religion and Society in Post-Emancipation Jamaica*. Knoxville: University of Tennessee Press, 1992.

Stoler, Ann. "Carnal Knowledge and Imperial Power: Gender, Race, and Morality in Colonial Asia." In *Gender at the Crossroads of Knowledge: Feminist Anthropology in the Postmodern Era*, ed. Micaela di Leonardo. Berkeley: University of California Press, 1991. 51–101.

Strickland, S. *Negro Slavery Described by a Negro: being the narrative of Ashton Warner, a native of St. Vincents. With an Appendix, containing the Testimony of Four Christian*

BIBLIOGRAPHY

Ministers, Recently Returned from the Colonies, on the System of Slavery as it now Exists. London, 1831.

Sturge, Joseph. *Horrors of the Negro Apprenticeship System in the British Colonies: As Detailed at the Public Breakfast given by the Citizens of Birmingham, to Mr Joseph Sturge, on Returning from his Benevolent Mission to the West Indies, June 6, 1837.* Edinburgh, 1837.

Sturge, Joseph, and Thomas Harvey. *The West Indies in 1837; being the journal of a visit to Antigua, Montserrat, Dominica, St. Lucia, Barbados, and Jamaica; undertaken for the purpose of ascertaining the actual condition of the negro population of those islands.* London: Hamilton, Adams, 1838.

Sundquist, Eric J., ed. *Frederick Douglass: New Literary and Historical Essays.* Cambridge, England: Cambridge University Press, 1990.

Taylor, Yuval, ed. *I Was Born a Slave: An Anthology of Classic Slave Narratives.* Chicago: Lawrence Hill Books, 1999.

Temperley, Howard. *British Antislavery 1833–1870.* London: Longman, 1972.

Trumbach, Randolph. *The Rise of the Egalitarian Family: Aristocratic Kinship and Domestic Relations in Eighteenth-Century England.* New York: Academic Press, 1978.

Turley, David. *The Culture of English Antislavery, 1780–1860.* London: Routledge, 1991.

Turner, Mary. *Slaves and Missionaries: The Disintegration of Jamaican Slave Society, 1787–1834.* Urbana: University of Illinois Press, 1982.

Tyrrell, Alex. *Joseph Sturge and the Moral Radical Party in Early Victorian Britain.* London: Christopher Helm, 1987.

Vickery, Amanda. *The Gentleman's Daughter: Women's Lives in Georgian England.* New Haven: Yale University Press, 1998.

Viotti da Costa, Emilia. *Crowns of Glory, Tears of Blood: The Demerara Slave Rebellion of 1823.* New York: Oxford University Press, 1994.

Wedderburn, Robert. *The Horrors of Slavery and Other Writings by Robert Wedderburn.* Ed. Iain McCalman. Princeton, NJ: Markus Wiener Publishers, 1991.

Whiteley, Henry. *Three Months in Jamaica in 1832: Comprising a Residence of Seven Weeks on a Sugar Plantation.* London: Hatchard, 1833.

Wilmot, Swithin. "Not 'Full Free': The Ex-Slaves and the Apprenticeship System in Jamaica, 1834–1838." *Jamaica Journal* 17 (1984): 2–10.

———. "Sugar and the Gospel: Baptist Perspectives on the Plantation in the Early Period of Freedom." *Jamaican Historical Society Bulletin* 8 (1983): 211–15.

Yellin, Jean Fagan. Introduction to *Incidents in the Life of a Slave Girl, Written by Herself,* by Harriet A. Jacobs. Cambridge, MA: Harvard University Press, 1987. xiii–xxxiv.

INDEX

Numbers given in bold refer to testimony, letters, or depositions of that person. Numbers given in italics refer to the family trees on pages xxxiv–xxviii.

Diana Paton is a Lecturer in the Department of History
at the University of Newcastle.

Library of Congress Cataloging-in-Publication Data
Williams, James, b. 1818.
A narrative of events since the first of August, 1834 /
by James Williams, an Apprenticed Labourer in Jamaica ;
edited by Diana Paton.
p. cm.
Includes bibliographical references and index.
ISBN 0–8223–2658–2 (cloth : alk. paper) —
ISBN 0–8223–2647–7 (pbk. : alk. paper)
1. Slaves—Jamaica—Social conditions—19th century.
2. Jamaica—History—19th century.   3. Apprenticeship
programs—Government policy—Jamaica.   4. Jamaica—
Race relations.   I. Paton, Diana   II. Title.
F1886. W56 2001
972.92′04—dc21   00–047691